# What People are S… Conscious Br…



**My lung function has increase… 1% to almost 50%**

"I have been diagnosed with COPD. After regularly using the Relaxator for 18 months my lung function has increased from 21% to almost 50%! I've got my appetite for life back and can be both husband, father and grandpa in my family again, which is absolutely fantastic. I hope my positive experience can inspire others to also improve their breathing!"

*–Axel, 87*

**Breathing Retraining has helped me lose weight and gain more energy!**

"I have been bodybuilding for the past 20 years, working out about three times a week. Since I started practicing the Conscious Breathing Method I have lost about 5 kg of fat and gained about 3-4 kg of muscle mass, so I've been able to transform my fat into muscle. I have more energy and endurance and nowadays when I go to the gym I can add more weights and do more reps."

*–Stefan Jonsson, 51*

**15 years of terrible anxiety vanished with Conscious Breathing**

"For 15 years I have experienced terrible anxiety, nervousness, and internal stress. I tried everything to get rid of it, even anti-depressive medication and mindfulness. Then I read your book, and started to follow your advice and examples, and breathe through my nose. The anxiety, internal stress and nervousness all vanished as if they had never existed. It had never crossed my mind that breathing could have such a profound effect on my mental well-being. Mindfulness doesn't work without breathing properly.

*–Pär Rosenqvist, 30*

**Lower jaw in place and no braces needed thanks to taped mouth**

"My daughter Lisa, 13, used to have an overbite. We declined braces and instead Lisa started to tape her mouth at night. After a few months we had a new appointment with the dentist. Lisa told him that sometimes during this time she had experienced problems opening her mouth and that the jaw had cracked. 'This is because your lower jaw has developed significantly, and there is no need for braces anymore!' the dentist replied."

*–Therese Karlsson, 38*

**Life returns by leaps and bounds after many years of illness**

"It has been 20 years since I was diagnosed with fibromyalgia. During all these years I have been plagued with heavy inner stress, low energy, a lot of pain, tense muscles, sleeping difficulties, and stomach problems. Since I began to practice nasal breathing, taping my mouth at night and using the Relaxator every day, I've become so much better that it feels like a miracle! My inner stress has disappeared and my life is now filled with harmony and extra energy. It's like I've moved into my body again!"

*–Ulla Knape, 66*

**My back pain and lumbago has NEVER vanished so quickly!**

"Every few years I suffer from lumbago, and it really HURTS. I decided to try the Relaxator and Conscious Breathing Method as a way to lessen the pain and get better as quickly as possible. My lumbago and pain has NEVER vanished this quickly. I was feeling much better after only two or three days. Normally, it takes up to one or two weeks for me to feel better. ABSOLUTELY INCREDIBLE!"

*–Charlotte Blivik, 42*

**Sleep Tape has given me a new life!**

"I used to constantly sleep with my mouth open and wake up between 5-10 times per night. I was constantly tired. For a few weeks now I've taped my mouth at night and during these weeks I have slept more nights without waking up than I've done in the past 30 years in total. Your Sleep Tape has given me a new life!"

*–Catarina Johannisson, 50*

**My sex life is better than ever**

"I'm 78 years of age and my sexual potency is really something. My sex life is better than ever, almost like when I was a teenager! This has been the case for the last few years and I'm certain that taping my mouth at night for the last five years is the biggest reason for this."

*–Carl, 78*

**No asthma medication for two months - amazing!**

"Thank you for a brilliant course and especially for a revolutionary discovery/treatment. Before your course I would use an inhaler between two and five times a day, as well as about two puffs of the cortisone spray Pulmicort. As soon as I finished your course I started employing my new found knowledge and immediately felt an incredible improvement. I will always be grateful! In a way, you have saved my life."

*–Mattias Andersson, 37*

**The Relaxator has helped my racing heart**

"I have what is called a racing heart, which means I sometimes have to take medication—i.e., beta-blockers—to lower my heart rate, when my life becomes too stressful and demanding. Since I started using the Relaxator I haven't had a racing heart at all!"

*–Agneta Sjödin, 44*

**Breathing Retraining has improved my singing voice**

"Apart from deeper sleep, a better sex life and weight loss I have also noticed that my singing voice has improved. I sing in a barber shop quintet and thanks to the diaphragm exercises I do with the Relaxator, I'm able to maintain purer and longer notes."

*–Göran Bergling, 71*

**I feel incredible harmony after training with nasal breathing**

"I've been a professional triathlete for almost 15 years and the harmony I feel after training with my mouth closed is absolutely incredible."

*–Clas Björling, 35*

# Conscious Breathing

The Secret Key to Reshaping

- Your Looks
- Your Body
- Your Health and
- Your Weight

Anders Olsson

Text, setting: Anders Olsson
Translation from Swedish to English: Jessica Maria, Anders Olsson
Project leader, text processing: Ulrica Otterling
Text processing: Helene Sandström
Project leader, text processing, English version: Sandra Sedgbeer
Text processing, English version: Elisabeth Agar, Carol Holaday
Facts review: Cecilia Salmi, M.D. Pharmacology
Cover: Babar Zaman
Photo: Patric Stjernström, Perfect Shot, pages 68, 122-129
Photo: Karla Blum Fagerström, page 109
Illustrations: Kari C. Toverud, MS CMI (certified medical illustrator), pages 43, 45, 136, 149, 151, 182, 228, 229, 232
Illustrations: Katarina Kaino, pages 30-32, 246
Illustrations and photo: Anders Olsson, pages 77, 90, 91, 107, 137
Illustrations and photo: Shutterstock, pages v, 11, 39, 48, 49, 85, 131, 136, 145, 165, 196, 219, 230
Graphic layout: Lillemor Johansson, Monodesign
Printing: Tallinna Raamatutrükikoda, Estonia 2014

First edition, first printing, April 2014
ISBN: 978-91-976151-5-0

# Contents


Thanks ... xi

Seven Great Opportunities this Book has to Offer You ... xiii

Introduction ... 1

PART I - BREATHING IS THE ESSENCE OF LIFE

Chapter 1 – How Poor Breathing Impacts Your Health ... 13

Chapter 2 – How Breathing Works ... 25

PART II - IMPROVE YOUR BREATHING NOW

Chapter 3 – Five Simple Principles for Better Breathing ... 41

Chapter 4 – Retrain Your Breathing ... 61

Chapter 5 – Conscious Breathing for Stress Reduction ... 81

Chapter 6 – Conscious Breathing for Sports and Exercise ... 99

Chapter 7 – Working with the Relaxator to Improve Your Breathing ... 121

PART III - BREATHING RETRAINING FOR SPECIFIC HEALTH ISSUES

Chapter 8 – How Your Breathing Can Affect Your Teeth and Facial Development ... 133

Chapter 9 – Breathe Well, Sleep Well ... 147

Chapter 10 – Improving Your Breathing Protects Your Heart and Circulatory System ... 163

Chapter 11 – **Breathing Better to Reduce Asthma, Allergy and COPD** ..... 181

Chapter 12 – **Aches, Pains and Fatigue: How Breathing Right Can Help** ..... 199

Chapter 13 – **Fat or Fit: Why Breathing Affects Your Digestion, Metabolism and Weight** ..... 215

Chapter 14 – **The Science of Breathing** ..... 227

Chapter 15 – **How Conscious Breathing Changed My Life** ..... 243

References ..... 247

Index ..... 255

# Thanks

This book is dedicated, with deep gratitude, to my parents and my two wonderful sons—my father, with his immense power and warm heart, who has taught me to be curious about life and to never give up; my mother, with her good spirit and common sense, who has taught me about cooperation and generosity; my son Oscar, who has taught me about honesty and courage; and my son Eric, who has taught me about creativity and patience.

Many people have contributed to this book. I would especially like to thank all my breathing instructors and students for so generously sharing their experiences of how improved breathing has affected them and others around them, and for posing ever more challenging questions. I have been very inspired by the knowledge and insights they have shared. Special thanks to breathing instructors Kina and Sven Enqvist, Anette Jonasson, Ove Jadehov, Stefan Jonsson, Kristin Husa, Håkan Wester, Lina Alexanderson, all whom have inspired me a lot.

I would also like to extend my gratitude to Ulrica Otterling and Sandra Sedgbeer for their commitment as project managers for the Swedish and English versions respectively, helping me to structure my thoughts and making the text readable; Helene Sandström for great linguistic skills and knowledge of how the body works; and Cecilia Salmi, for her wise observations and feedback helping me develop the Conscious Breathing Method, and for putting up with all my crazy ideas and thoughts. Furthermore, many thanks to Jessica Maria, Elisabet Agar, Carol Holaday, and Catherine Boland for their great work in translating and editing the text.

Finally, I would like to thank Patrick McKeown, for inspiring me in such a humble way and for sharing all his knowledge of breathing in general, and the Buteyko Breathing Method in particular, and Dr. Johannes Lindh, who freely shared his long experience of working with patients suffering from breathing problems.

# Seven Great Opportunities this Book has to Offer You

1. To have a healthier life, a fitter body, more energy and better sleep.
2. To inspire you to do physical activity with your mouth closed, which promotes health, increses fat burning and endurance, reduces stress levels and makes your body feel good.
3. To face your daily life with more curiosity and humility and without critical judgment.
4. To increase your sense of faith, freedom, thankfulness, harmony, happiness and confidence.
5. To reduce feelings of concern, fear, anxiety, panic and despair.
6. To improve your communication skills, relationships and your ability to cope with criticism, avoid arguments and have better contact with your partner, children, friends, colleagues and people in general.
7. To stand up for yourself, to DARE to fail and be whom you are and follow your dreams.

If you're wondering what breathing has to do with standing up for yourself, living in harmony, improving your relationships, and increasing your overall happiness and confidence, you're not alone. Many people have no idea how something as simple as breathing can affect every single aspect of their lives. I used to be one of those people until I discovered the power inherent in my breath, and now I can testify that breathing has everything to do with feeling healthy, happy and whole. My purpose in writing this book is to help you see how you and your life also can be made better just by the simple act of changing how you breathe.

# Introduction

*As long as I can remember I've had a "hurricane of thoughts" bouncing back and forth in my head. However, I have been fortunate to come across tools that have helped me relax and find my inner calm. The most powerful of these tools has undoubtedly been to improve my breathing habits. In this book, I'd like to share with you the knowledge I have acquired in this area. I hope that this book will help you improve your breathing habits as well and that you will be able to apply the effective day-to-day breathing techniques that you will learn in any situation, anywhere.*

## WHY I WROTE THIS BOOK

The flow of information in our society today is enormous. We are awash with information via blogs, Facebook, television, newspapers and books. So why am I foolish enough to spend a lot of time and energy writing another book to add further to the flow? Especially when hundreds of books on the subject of breathing are available already? And now that I have written the book, why should you spend your precious time reading it? Both questions are legitimate and I will attempt to answer them.

What is it that makes us feel good or bad? Why are so many of us stressed out, angry and depressed, or suffering from various diseases that deprive us of the possibility of living a rich and fulfilled life? We try and try but may perhaps only experience brief, fleeting moments of health, harmony, love, happiness and satisfaction. Why is that so? Is life mostly a struggle and then we die? Is it possible to achieve wellbeing and harmony more often and more permanently?

The answer is that there is a fantastic tool, which can provide increased harmony, wellbeing and personal growth. Often, however, this most primitive of functions is completely forgotten, namely, breathing.

The basics of breathing that I teach participants in my Conscious Breathing courses are obvious for most. Yet, often when they start practicing improved breathing it seems quite revolutionary. Why?

It is because how we breathe is often overlooked. Many people take breathing for granted and pay it very little attention. We can manage without food for weeks, without water for days, but only for a few minutes without air. The fact that in a single day we inhale as much as 10–20 kilos of air, in comparison to the 1–2 kilos of food we eat, makes it apparent why good breathing habits are so important to our health.

The downside is that the worse our breathing habits are, the closer we are to our own death. The good news is that we can easily improve the way we breathe and reverse a negative health trend at any age.

## KONSTANTIN BUTEYKO

The Russian Medical Doctor and Professor, Konstantin Buteyko spent hundreds of hours during his medical training studying the respiration of people on their deathbed. He noted that the closer to death patients were, the worse their respiration. How they were breathing was a direct reflection of the status of their health, and the more they deteriorated, the faster, shallower and more labored their breathing became.

Professor Buteyko had experienced health problems himself, but thanks to a discovery in 1952, which was as brilliant as it was simple, he cured himself of high blood pressure. Only 29 years old, he suffered a galloping high blood pressure of 220/120. Once, when he attended to a patient with high blood pressure, who also had signs of labored breathing, an insight struck him like lightning. Professor Buteyko realized that his respiration, just like his patient's, was very poor. When the patient had been discharged, he immediately began to work on improving his own breathing habits. By taking control of his fast, heavy breathing, forcing himself to breathe slower and smaller, he was able to suppress his symptoms. Within minutes he managed to alleviate his symptoms altogether, but when he returned to his previous breathing pattern, the symptoms came back again.

Professor Buteyko was as enthusiastic as a child on Christmas Eve about his discovery. He didn't sleep a single wink that night. Instead, he ran around the hospital where he was working and more or less forced those seriously ill patients whose breathing patterns also were often fast and heavy to slow down their breathing. The positive results did not take long to appear. When the patients breathed slower and took smaller breaths, the rapid improvement in their health validated Professor Buteyko's own experience.

Professor Buteyko conducted research on thousands of patients with a variety of health problems, which confirmed the link between poor breathing habits and poor health. Professor Buteyko, who died in 2003, and his colleagues have helped tens of thousands of people improve their breathing habits and they were "miraculously" cured of asthma, cancer and heart disease. Today the Buteyko Method has spread all over the world.

## SIMPLE TIPS AND TOOLS

In today's busy world, the knowledge of a) what is a good breathing habit and b) how to achieve it, is more important than ever since all the stimuli we are exposed to affect our breathing patterns negatively. The problem is that we are often not aware of the fact that we have an impaired breathing habit or indeed, how to improve it. We may even have started to improve the way we breathe but haven't fully realized the great importance proper breathing has for our health and wellbeing.

After going through much of the available breathing literature, I have found that there is no really good summary of:

- The reasons for our breathing patterns becoming impaired.
- The connection between the way we breathe and various symptoms and diseases.

- How to recognize good, and less beneficial breathing habits.
- Simple tools and exercises to improve your day-to-day breathing habits.

The goal of this book is to fill the gap, and to help you—and others—understand the role that breathing can play in helping you achieve better health, greater happiness, more energy and improved athletic performance.

#### Conscious Breathing connects the dots

This book presents the Conscious Breathing Method that has evolved out of my personal experience, books and research I have found on relaxation techniques, yoga, qigong, the Buteyko Method, mental training and body awareness, as well as feedback from students, athletes, skilled doctors, therapists, and many other wise people.

It wasn't only Professor Buteyko who realized the importance of good breathing habits—this is common knowledge in many different areas:

- In Eastern traditions like yoga, qigong and Ayurveda, the importance of breathing has been known for several thousand years.
- Mindfulness, meditation, and other relaxation techniques have great focus on breathing.
- It is well known that good breathing is important in martial arts for achieving maximum balance and strength.
- Breathing plays a central role within tantric sex and other methods for increased sexual enjoyment and endurance.
- During childbirth women are often advised on how to breathe in order to increase endurance and reduce pain.
- A person seeking medical advice for panic attacks may be given a bag to breathe in and out of upon entering the hospital. Breathing through a bag rapidly increases the levels of carbon dioxide, which in turn allows more oxygen to be delivered to the brain, causing the person to relax.
- Breathing retraining to promote circulation and oxygenation is common after heart and lung operations.

- In an accident, the first priority is always to make sure that the person is breathing and that the airways are open.

Through Conscious Breathing we connect the dots from these vastly different areas to a greater wholeness of health through a simple method for effective day-to-day breathing, which is the foundation for our health, energy and harmony.

### An open mind

There are many scientific studies that I've been inspired by for this book. Regardless of how much we wish for it to be true, however, research seldom offers us any clear answer of a definite yes or no regarding proof of effectiveness of any technique or medication. Scientific "truths" are fluid, and what is true today may be obsolete tomorrow. Either the research is performed in a test tube, which is a very artificial environment, or comprises a group of individuals whose physical and emotional state at the time of the experiment plays a major role that can't be measured by instruments and analyses. We are extremely complex creatures, and our thoughts and feelings matter; wheter we are in the middle of a divorce, just started a new job, just ate, or trained hard the day before, may have a significant influence on the test results.

So if the information presented in this book challenges your established truths, I would like to ask you to step back and ask yourself if the information might be reasonable. An open mind and common sense can make it easier to evaluate information objectively.

## WHO IS RESPONSIBLE FOR YOUR HEALTH?

The developments within health care are impressive. There is an abundance of experience and expertise in many areas, such as emergency services, complex surgery, and treatment with insulin and penicillin, for instance. However, acknowledgement of the bigger picture, of mankind, seems to have been forgotten, as medical practice has become more and more like engineering, and where advanced equipment, operations and medication are the hard currency.

In the American National Heart, Lung and Blood Institute's (NHLBI) 2007 report on guidelines for the treatment of asthma, it was established that "*The Expert Panel concludes there is insufficient evidence to suggest that breathing techniques provide clinical benefit to patients who have asthma.*" This conclusion seems slightly absurd when most of us realize that there ought to be a very clear link between asthma and how we breathe, since this disease affects our respiratory organs.

Numerous studies show the link between impaired respiration and disease.[1,2] In a 29-year study at the University at Buffalo, comprising 1,195 individuals, a clear link was found between lung function and longevity. The worse the lung function the greater the risk of dying prematurely. The authors concluded "*It is surprising that this simple method has not gained more popularity as a way of measuring the general health status.*"[1]

When the link between poor lung function and poor health is already well established, it would seem natural to study whether improved respiration can have a positive health effect. Unfortunately, these types of studies are relatively scarce, which to some extent explains the conclusion of the NHLBI asthma report, and we end up in a catch-22 situation, which leads to decreased credibility of health institutions.

When I studied respiration physiology at university, I was struck by the incredible knowledge available in the field of health care. Lots of interesting and necessary information about blood gases, air flow, lung structures and diseases was presented logically and educationally. Even though I was saturated with knowledge, I felt empty inside due to the fact that focus was predominantly directed toward "hard facts" and somewhat mechanical thinking. The vast technical knowledge a trainee doctor is taught about the human body during his or her long training also comes with the risk that the basics, for example, paying attention to how a patient breathes, is lost in technology. In my Conscious Breathing courses I regularly hear comments like, "*I've had asthma for 30 years, but nobody has ever talked to me about my breathing habits.*"

My purpose is not to mock healthcare, which fills a very important function, but to point out the consequences that the mechanical way of thinking about disease can lead to if it is not balanced by an understanding of what good health entails.

If your doctor is dismissive of the Conscious Breathing Method, I suggest you show him or her this book and explain that the knowledge and exercises outlined herein are gaining wider acceptance.

It is wise to listen to knowledgeable people around you, such as physicians and other medical staff, but at the end of the day you are ultimately responsible for your own health and body. Do not abdicate this responsibility to anyone else. When you take full responsibility for your life and your health, you will probably find quick fixes like symptom-relieving medication less attractive. Instead, your curiosity to find the keys to improved health and wellbeing will increase.

## BREATHING—THE MOST POWERFUL TOOL TO LOWER INNER STRESS

The stopwatch has been my friend since I was little. When I was young, I timed eating breakfast, going to the bathroom, etc. The bicycle path to school was just over a mile long, and on this short journey I had five split times. My goal was always to set a new record, and if I didn't set a new record on the entire journey, I tried to set a record between, for example, split time 2 and 4. When I was 13 years old, I tried to enter the Guinness Book of World Records. My sister was my witness, and after much training, I did 50 push-ups in 35 seconds and 300 sit-ups in 250 seconds.

I've always had a strong driving force and have been running my own company since I was 19. The problem used to be that the fuel powering my engine was, to a large extent, fear and anxiety. The motivation behind my hard work was largely based on the fear of not being loved for who I am, but for what I do. According to my belief system at the time, hard work was the key to being loved, and as a consequence I filled my days to the brim with activities, hoping to be worthy of love.

As you will find out later in this book, there is a close link between stressful breathing patterns, hypoxia (lack of oxygen), and a brain that produces thoughts and feelings of anxiety, fear and anguish.

During the last few years, I've been lucky to come across tools that have helped me relax and find my inner calm. As I mentioned earlier, the most powerful of these tools has undoubtedly been to improve my breathing. Repetitive, meaningless thoughts, flashing back and forth at the speed of light, like an endless mental ping-pong game, have been replaced by greater joy and harmony. I feel very fortunate to have found the on/off switch and can now decide for myself when it's time to push the turbo button, or move along at a slower pace.

## DARE TO FOLLOW YOUR INNER VOICE

Do the improved breathing habits that have helped me find greater inner peace mean that I live like an ascetic, sitting cross-legged, meditating all day and nibbling on lettuce leaves? No, the truth is far from it. I still work a lot, eat what I want, get sick sometimes (although less and less often), lose my temper and end up in conflicts, workout several times a week, etc.

When I fancy sweets, ice cream, unhealthy junk food, or drink alcohol, I do it because I want to. I don't succumb because other people tempt me or because an invisible force takes control of my willpower in the shop and "forces" me to slip chocolate bars into the shopping trolley (I can assure you that has happened many times). When I exercise I do it because I enjoy both the workout and the harmonious feeling afterwards. The feeling of harmony comes from within, and the more often I experience that feeling, the more natural it becomes to make choices that are good for my body and my soul.

Previously, my body was just a simple tool in pursuit of the goal my brain chose. Reaching the goals was far more important than my body's wellbeing. Today my body is my best friend, and "we" only do things that we think are fun and make us feel good!

I hope that this book will assist you in your search for better breathing habits, which in turn will help you make wiser decisions in everyday life, and inspire you to be BRAVE enough to follow your gut feeling and your heart more often.

## HOW TO USE THIS BOOK

In Part I, we look at how breathing works and what happens in our bodies when we do not breathe optimally.

In Part II, we discuss five simple principles for good breathing. By answering a series of questions you will learn about the quality of your current breathing habits, and you will be given advice for improving your everyday breathing patterns for exercise, personal growth and stress reduction. The exercises in Chapter 7 are intended to help you create airways that are open and functioning well.

In Part III, we look at the connection between breathing and different health problems such as high blood pressure, insomnia, asthma, obesity, dental problems, poor digestion, low energy and sexual dysfunction.

## PRACTICAL SELF-HELP

Conscious Breathing is a simple and practical self-help book written for those of you who wish to improve your health, boost your energy and ability to enjoy life, and at the same time help you grow as a person.

The purpose of this book is to communicate simple knowledge of good breathing techniques that you can apply anytime, anywhere.

Okay, that sounds great—but what's the catch? There is no catch. The only potential obstacle is whether or not you are prepared to do what's necessary to improve your breathing habits. This book gives you the tools, but it is up to you to use them.

# PART I

# BREATHING IS THE ESSENCE OF LIFE

# Chapter 1 – How Poor Breathing Impacts Your Health

We spend an enormous amount of money on the quest for improving our health, our looks, our weight, our fitness, our sleep, our energy and our sex lives. But the fact is that we already have the secret key to better health, better looks, better sleep, more energy, reduced stress, a fitter body, and amazing sex—namely our breathing. And the good news is that it's absolutely free, we have it with us 24/7, and the results are a happier, healthier, longer, younger and more satisfying life.

When we repeat an action often enough, it soon becomes a habit. Once we have established incorrect breathing patterns, we risk them becoming permanent, which can cause us added stress, lack of oxygen and energy shortage. Over time, poor breathing habits deteriorate further causing even more stress and less energy.

## IMPAIRED BREATHING HABITS AFFECT OUR WHOLE BODY NEGATIVELY

Impaired breathing habits may produce many seemingly unrelated negative consequences for our health and wellbeing. Where the problem will arise in our body depends on what our individual weaknesses are.

Incorrect respiration reduces our ability to utilize the oxygen we inhale effectively. We compensate by increasing the respiratory rate and replace quality with quantity, much like an inefficient car consuming excessive amounts of fuel and oil. Our breathing habits may also be controlled by our thoughts and emotions, making breathing irregular and chaotic, and as a comparison, the car ride becomes bumpy and uneven, full of starts and stops.

Not only does inefficient breathing cause oxygen depletion and reduction in the cells' ability to produce energy, it will also result in us using more muscle power and effort to move the air in and out of our lungs.

## WHAT HAPPENS IN OUR BODY WHEN WE BREATHE INEFFECTIVELY

There are nine major negative effects of impaired respiration that prevent vital oxygen from reaching our working muscles and organs.

### 1. The oxygen is not released to the tissues

Poor breathing reduces the body's ability to deliver oxygen to the tissues. The oxygen is transferred to the blood in the lungs where it is picked up by hemoglobin in the blood for transport around the body. The mechanisms for releasing oxygen from the hemoglobin are to a large extent controlled by carbon dioxide. Carbon dioxide is produced in our body, and we get rid of it when we exhale. However, we need a certain amount of $CO_2$ in our body. When we over-breathe or have an irregular breathing pattern, we tend to lose too much carbon dioxide on exhalation. As a result, the pH level in the blood is elevated. This creates a problem as the blood pH has to decrease in order for the oxygen to be released from the hemoglobin. The oxygen is not released and delivered to the tissues. Instead, it remains in the blood, tightly bound to hemoglobin until we exhale it. So, our blood may be fully saturated with oxygen at 97-98 percent, but due to the lowered levels of carbon dioxide, not enough oxygen is released into the cells, which leads to oxygen depletion.

Another reason why high levels of $CO_2$ are important for oxygen delivery is that some of the carbon dioxide replaces oxygen in the hemoglobin. The ability of carbon dioxide to replace oxygen is the reason why $CO_2$ is used in fire extinguishers. When $CO_2$ is put on the fire it forces the oxygen away, and since a fire cannot last without oxygen it dies off.

**2. Energy deficiency**

Our ability to deliver oxygen to the cells is reduced when our breathing pattern is impaired. Still, our need for energy is huge, so when our cells receive less oxygen they lose the ability to produce sufficient energy to perform work at a normal level. The cells then become stressed and are forced to prioritize survival over development and growth.

It is much more efficient to produce energy with the aid of oxygen than without it, since this process provides up to 19 times more energy. It's the mitochondria of the cells that produce almost all our energy (ATP) through combustion of nutrients and oxygen, and the mitochondria cannot function without oxygen.

A typical cell usually contains a few hundred mitochondria, and the organs demanding a lot of energy have cells that can contain several thousand mitochondria. Therefore, the organs requiring a lot of energy suffer the most from impaired breathing, which of course leads to organ oxygen depletion. Some of our most labor-intensive organs are our heart, our brain and our muscles. A fertilized egg contains as much as a hundred thousand mitochondria.

When the available oxygen is reduced, the mitochondria become unemployed and gradually decrease. If the number of mitochondria decreases to a certain level the whole cell will die, which follows the principle "if you don't use it, you lose it."

Nearly half of our body weight is made up of muscles. When we move around quickly, for example, during a 100-meters race, we become tired more easily than when we walk as oxygen is consumed faster than it can be delivered to the muscles which results in increased lactic acid production. If our everyday respiration is poor, resulting in lack of oxygen, we possess less endurance power since our muscles become stiffer, tense, and tire more easily.

Furthermore, fat can only be burnt in the mitochondria. When the mitochondria don't work well or not at all because of oxygen deficiency, the ability to burn fat decreases. In conclusion, poor breathing may lead to being overweight.

### 3. Our nervous system gets out of whack

Our nervous system can be divided into two groups a) the central nervous system, or our conscious mind, controlled by our brain and willpower and b) the autonomic nervous system, or our subconscious mind, which we cannot control by our willpower.

Although our brain and nervous system only represent two percent of our body weight, they use a full 20 percent of the oxygen we consume. When our breathing is dysfunctional oxygen supply is limited, and the conscious mind will work a little slower and perceive incoming stimuli as slightly more stressful and threatening.

The subconscious or involuntary part of our nervous system is very powerful and controls automatic functions such as heartbeat, respiration and digestion. When our breathing is impaired, these functions suffer. Our nervous system is divided into a sympathetic, activating part (the gas pedal), and a parasympathetic, calming part (the brake), which work together and are always striving to meet our changing needs and maintain homeostasis—a body in balance. Sympathetic activity increases when we do physical activities, concentrate and focus, while parasympathetic activity increases during digestion, at rest and during recovery.

Breathing is crucial for keeping our bodies in balance because every breath has a direct impact on our nervous system. Inhaling is an active process in which our respiratory muscles are actively working to expand our chest so that air can enter. When we inhale our heart beats faster (the pulse is raised) and the sympathetic part of the autonomic nervous system is activated. Expiration is usually passive, where our diaphragm returns to its original position, and our thorax and lungs sink down without any muscle effort. On expiration, the soothing part of the autonomic nervous response, the parasympathetic nervous system is more active, which allows the heart to rest and recover, and the pulse drops.

Impaired breathing, such as short and forced exhalation, makes the sympathetic part more active, resulting in shallow breathing, a tense body, increased stress, and fight or flight behavior.

**4. Our heart has to work harder**

Our heart is constantly active and beats about 100,000 times in a single day at a pulse of 70 beats/minute. Our heart is a major consumer of oxygen, and a reduced oxygen supply means that the heart is not able to pump our blood as effectively as it should.

Impaired breathing also affects our 60,000 miles (100,000 km) of blood vessels in a negative way. Apart from the heart muscle, we have two additional types of muscles in our body: skeletal muscles and smooth muscles. Skeletal muscles are found in our limbs, neck, etc., and we can control them at will, unlike the smooth muscles found in the stomach, intestines, blood vessels, bronchus, bladder, uterus, etc. We are not in direct control of the smooth muscles, but they are controlled indirectly through our breathing. One of the main features of carbon dioxide is that it dilates our smooth muscles and thereby expands our blood vessels. When we have lowered the carbon dioxide levels in our blood, because of over-breathing and/or physical inactivity, it affects the ability to open and dilate the blood vessels effectively. Consequently, our blood pressure may increase, forcing our heart to work harder. Circulation is affected negatively, which may result in us getting cold hands and feet or skin problems like eczema. The constricted blood vessels may lead to angina pectoris and stroke.

***Test the effects of carbon dioxide:***

It is easy to test the vasodilatory effect of carbon dioxide, i.e., the blood vessels' ability to dilate, by taking a foot bath with baking soda ($HCO_3^-$), also called sodium bicarbonate, since it contains large amounts of carbon dioxide ($CO_2$). To make a foot bath, add about five quarts of warm water to a large bowl. Put your feet into the bowl first and then pour in a tablespoon of baking soda. When adding the baking soda, the feet become even warmer due to the dilatory effect carbon dioxide has on the blood vessels, hence more blood can reach that area. A 10-minute baking soda foot bath is very beneficial for increasing circulation in the feet, since carbon dioxide is absorbed through the skin. To increase the production of carbon dioxide and enhance the effect further, add a tablespoon of citric acid. Add the citric acid in small portions every two minutes, during the ten-minute bath. Adding the citric acid every two minutes will prevent too much carbon dioxide from being formed, and thus keeps it from escaping from the water as gas.

### 5. Our teeth and face are affected

Our tongue is one of the most powerful muscles we have in our body. Cheeks and lips are also powerful muscles. The muscles in the tongue, cheeks and lips determine the position of our teeth in both the upper and lower jaws. Braces work according to the same principle by exerting slight pressure over an extended period of time to move a tooth.

When we breathe through the mouth, the tongue doesn't rest in the roof of the mouth the way it should do. Instead, the tongue moves downward towards the center or the floor of the mouth, in order for the air to pass in and out, which has a negative impact on the development of the maxilla. Ultimately, the palate becomes V-shaped rather than U-shaped, and the mouth becomes overcrowded.

The maxilla (upper jaw) is a large bone situated in the middle of the face. It extends from the upper teeth to the eyes, and facial structure is, to a high degree, determined by the development of the maxilla. A common consequence of breathing through the mouth is that the upper jaw extends down and back instead of growing forward and wider, the way it should do, which leads to a narrower upper jaw and face. Furthermore, it makes the nasal passages narrower since they are to a large extent created and supported by the maxilla.

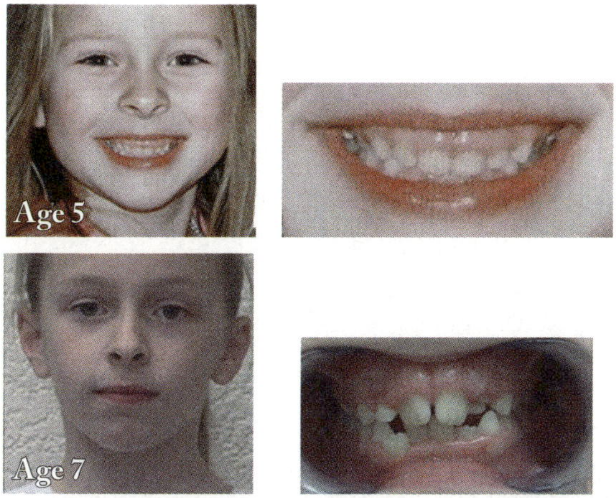


In only two years the girl to the left developed crooked teeth because of mouth breathing.

The boy below switched from nasal breathing to mouth breathing at the age of 14 because of allergies, which affected the growth of his face in a negative way.

*These pictures are published with the permission of professor John Mew.*

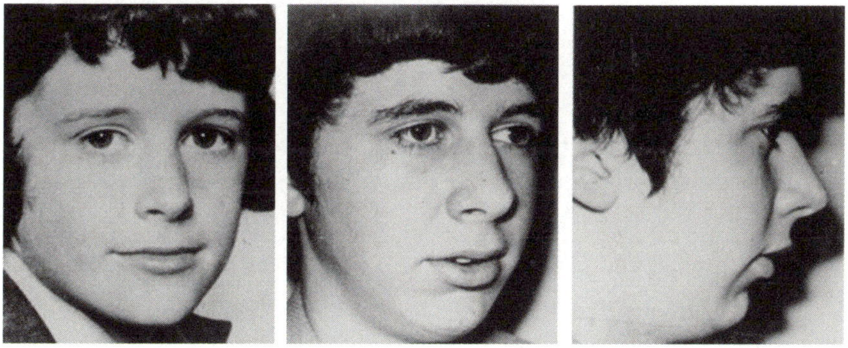

**6. Airways become narrower**

It is more difficult to pass air into and out from the lungs through narrow air passages. We then use more force and effort to move the air in and out, and breathe faster in order to compensate. It's like driving a car with the parking brake slightly engaged. You apply more pressure on the gas-pedal in an attempt to drive faster. This is a very inefficient way of solving the problem; instead the focus should be to unlock the parking brake and widen the airways. There are several problems associated with narrow airways:

a. Air resistance increases by as much as 16 times if the diameter of the airway is reduced by half. Narrow airways may occur in allergy sufferers, during asthma attacks, and with physical activity. Consequently, significantly more effort is needed to move the air in and out.[1]
b. Tight airways make us breathe faster to meet our body's needs and results in faster air-flow, which increases the mechanical abrasion in the airways narrowing them even further.
c. Not breathing optimally may cause carbon dioxide shortage, which among other things, can make the smooth muscles in the bronchial tubes contract and produce asthma-like symptoms.
d. Large quantities of nitric oxide (NO) are produced in the sinuses and are mixed with the inhaled air during nasal breathing. Just as carbon dioxide does, this gas dilates the bronchial circumference. When we inhale through the mouth, we are unable to benefit from the nitric oxide's dilating effect on the bronchi.[2]
e. Breathing through the mouth, allowing cold, dry, unfiltered air to pass through our throat, is a major contributing factor to narrowing of the bronchial tubes. Spending extended periods of time in a dry environment, and often needing to remove particles from the cilia in the throat, may increase mucus production, which can permanently enlarge the mucus glands. Both the mucus in itself and the enlarged mucus glands contribute to narrower airways.
f. Inflammation of the throat is another cause of narrow airways. Producing inflammation is a part of the immune defense mechanism, which protects our body. The stress hormone, cortisol, is a counterweight that suppresses inflammation. If we suffer from chronic stress, perhaps due to impaired breathing, the adrenal glands, which produce cortisol, become exhausted, and the production of cortisol may decrease after some time. When cortisol production is reduced, the counterweight to inflammation is reduced and we may become overly sensitive to dust, pollen, cold air, airborne chemicals, or the food we eat, because of the inflammation they give rise to.

g. The space in the nose and upper throat may be narrow because of allergies, increased mucus production, sinus infections, deviated septum, an underdeveloped upper and/or lower jaw, polyps, or enlarged tonsils and adenoids. A narrow space in the nose and upper throat makes it harder for air to pass through. Subsequently we begin to breathe through the mouth, as it is easier for us.

**7. The gas exchange in our lungs decreases**

Emphysema, Chronic Obstructive Pulmonary Disease (COPD), severe asthma, and shortness of breath are all signs that the gas exchange in our lungs is not functioning properly, which is often due to superficial shallow breathing and smoking. The particles in cigarette smoke congregate in our lungs and clog up the alveoli.

Fundamentally, shallow breathing can be likened to breathing through a snorkel that is too long, since the air only reaches the upper part of our lungs. Most of the air we inhale never reaches the alveoli where the gas exchange takes place. Shallow breathing is a very inefficient way of breathing, and we tend to compensate by increasing the amount of breaths we take.

Finally, shallow breathing prevents circulation of air in the lower part of our lungs. Trapped air in the alveoli increases both our risk of infection, as well as the possibility of parts of our lung tissue collapsing and being destroyed. Damaged lung tissues will, over time, reduce our ability to transfer oxygen to the blood and remove carbon dioxide through the air we exhale. Should this be the case, we may be diagnosed with COPD or emphysema.

**8. Protein performance degrades**

Proteins are our body's building blocks. A human being has more than a hundred thousand different proteins designed to perform various tasks. The secret of life is the movement of these proteins, which give rise to digestion, and muscle contraction etc. The difference between a dead body and a person that is alive is that in the latter the proteins are moving. An optimal pH level is required for proteins to be able to move and function fully, since they can only operate within a very narrow pH range. If a lake is acidified the fish will die while the algae, that like the acidic environment will thrive. In order to restore the pH in the lake lime scale is added to it. In our body it is the breathing that is our primary way to control pH levels. This regulation occurs at every breath by exhaling a larger or smaller amount of carbon dioxide.

Examples of proteins are:

a. **Enzymes:** An enzyme is a catalyst designed to speed up chemical processes in the body and make them perform more efficiently. A good example of this would be digestive enzymes. Our ability to absorb nutrients from the food we eat is diminished when the digestive enzymes don't function fully.
b. **Antibodies:** Antibodies are special proteins that are used by the immune system to identify infections. When white blood cells encounter bacteria, they attack. At the same time, the immune system produces specific proteins called antibodies, so that other white blood cells know what to look for. When the pH level is imbalanced the antibodies can't perform, and it takes longer for the immune system to fight infection.
c. **Hemoglobin:** In the blood, oxygen travels around bound to the protein hemoglobin. When the function of the hemoglobin is impaired, less oxygen is released to the cells—instead the oxygen just passes the cells and we exhale it again.

### 9. Stress increases

Since we can only survive a few minutes without breathing it is prioritized over other functions. One of the most efficient ways to expose our body to stress is to prevent air from passing in and out. When our breathing is threatened, all systems in our body are on red alert. The sympathetic part of the nervous system is more active and redirects blood from the abdominal organs to muscles in the arms and legs in order to prepare our body for fight or flight. The stress hormones, adrenaline and cortisol, increase to insure that your airways are open and ready for running or fighting. This is why adrenaline and cortisol are the most important ingredients in asthma medications.

Adrenaline has a widening effect on the airways and in an anaphylactic shock, a life threatening allergic reaction, we get an adrenaline shot to widen the airways. A study showed that adrenaline increased by a full 360 percent when the subjects hyperventilated, which lowered the $CO_2$ levels significantly. When the same subjects inhaled carbon dioxide-enriched air, in order to keep the $CO_2$ levels at a normal level, their adrenaline levels remained unaffected.[3]

Poor breathing can cause inflammation in the airways. In order to suppress it, the body increases the production of cortisol. When the body is stressed, it requires energy fast, and since sugar produces energy more quickly than fat, more cortisol is produced to increase blood sugar. If the stress is prolonged, the resulting increase in cortisol levels will eventually lead to increased sugar cravings.

When we are continually in overdrive we have problems relaxing, which in turn affects our quality of sleep. Insomnia and restlessness produce low sleep quality in which the body never quite recovers fully, and never feels completely rested, despite many hours of sleep.

## HEALTH PROBLEMS

Since breathing is such an important regulator for our wellbeing, it's not surprising that there is a clear connection between impaired breathing, oxygen deficiency, energy shortages, and many different diseases and symptoms. In Part 3 we will look at health problems such as asthma, allergies, insomnia, low energy, muscle and joint pain, obesity, sexual dysfunction, and heart and vascular problems.

Any health problem we experience is, of course, related to the degree to which respiration is impaired. It is not only one of two extremes: optimal breathing or irregular breathing/hyperventilation; it is a sliding scale where symptoms tend to worsen as respiration gradually deteriorates.

Regardless of whether the problem is caused by impaired breathing or something entirely different, the key to breaking a vicious circle lies in making certain changes—for example, by improving your breathing habit. We will explore how to do this later in Part 2.

# Chapter 2 – How Breathing Works

*Most of us take the act of breathing for granted. In fact, many of us are barely aware of this miraculous process that takes place 24 hours a day, when we are awake and asleep. Without breath there would be no life. Poor breathing habits, such as breathing too much, too shallowly, holding our breath, or feeling as if we are not breathing at all, can cause major stress to our body and result in oxygen depletion and energy shortage.*

There is nothing new about the importance of breathing. Just a few minutes of oxygen deprivation is enough to destroy the brain's ability to process incoming information forever. However, it is not only important THAT we breathe, but also HOW we breathe.

"Why should I care about that?" You may wonder, since breathing is an automatic process that takes care of itself. That's true. But nonetheless, the unique thing about breathing is that you may at any time take control of it and direct it at will. Consciously or unconsciously, we have the ability to regulate our respiratory rate and the way we breathe. We may huff and puff when something is hard or we sigh in resignation or relief.

Our breathing mirrors what is going on in our bodies—our thoughts and feelings, whether we are still or on the move, etc. By taking control of our breathing we can influence our thoughts and feelings, our internal organs, such as the heart and brain, as well as our bodily functions, such as digestion and the immune system.

Since we take around 20–25,000 breaths in a day, breathing is the human body's single most important regulator for maintaining balance (homeostasis). Therefore, there are many good reasons to consider how we actually breathe. The main characteristics of optimal as well as impaired breathing are:

| Optimal breathing | Impaired breathing |
|---|---|
| • Nasal breathing, mouth closed | • Mouth breathing, mouth open |
| • Deep (not big) breathing | • Shallow (chest) breathing |
| • Slow, few breaths | • Rapid breathing rate |
| • Rhythmic, regular | • Lack of rhythm, irregular |
| • Quiet, small | • Noisy, big |
| • Relaxed | • Tense, hunched shoulders |
| • Long, relaxed exhalation | • Short, forced exhalation |
| • Erect posture | • Forward leaning, slumped posture |
| • The diaphragm performs 70–80 percent of the muscular activity | • Overactive accessory muscles in chest, neck and shoulders |
| • Lower part of the chest expands sideways, forward, and backwards | • Only the upper part of the chest expands |

### WHY DO WE BREATHE?

Our body consists of approximately 50,000 trillion cells that specialize in performing different tasks. The cells form organs such as the liver, heart and brain. Although the cells and organs sometimes have very different specialized functions, they all have the same basic needs—oxygen, water and nutrients. We cater to those needs through breathing, drinking, and eating.

The cells in our body and organs constantly consume large amounts of oxygen and produce large amounts of carbon dioxide. Breathing is one of our most fundamental functions since it provides our body with oxygen and removes carbon dioxide.

## WHAT HAPPENS WHEN WE BREATHE?

Oxygen is transported into the lungs via our nasal passages and throat, then into the windpipe which branches off in the lungs into smaller and smaller tubes, which end up in small sacs called alveoli. Each alveolus is surrounded by tiny blood vessels called capillaries that receive oxygen into the bloodstream and return waste. The alveoli are grouped in clusters, like grapes, and each lung has several hundred million of these alveoli. The surface area of the alveoli is equivalent to the size of an entire tennis court, which is needed in order to provide the body with enough oxygen to function.

When we breathe in through our nose, the air is warmed, moistened and mixed with nitric oxide, a gas produced in the nasal passages that helps protect the body from viruses and germs. Once the air reaches our lungs it enters the alveoli, which become inflated with the air we just took in, and oxygen is transferred to the blood to be carried to all the cells of the body. At the same time, the blood drops off carbon dioxide in the alveoli to be eliminated when we breathe out, and the alveoli deflate to empty themselves of the waste they have just received.

Since our lungs are narrow at the top and wide at the bottom, there are many more alveolar sacs and blood vessels in the bottom part of the lungs, thus making blood flow at the bottom of the lungs ten times greater than at the top. So for the gas exchange to be effective, the inhaled air should reach the lower parts of the lungs.

Our brain measures the level of carbon dioxide we breathe out to determine how we should be breathing, speeding it up when we are running, slowing it down when we are sleeping, etc. If we have improper breathing, such as fast ragged open-mouthed breathing, and our oxygen intake exceeds the body's needs, we lose too much carbon dioxide. The negative result is two-fold. Since carbon dioxide dilates blood vessels the deprivation of carbon dioxide causes smooth muscles (involuntary muscles) to constrict. Plus the imbalance between carbon dioxide and oxygen causes LESS oxygen to be delivered to our cells.

In addition to providing our body with oxygen and removing waste, breathing also has other important functions:

- **Pain relief:** Next time you experience pain try to breathe slowly, rhythmically and deeply (not big) and the pain will most likely ease off.
- **Stress reduction:** By calming down our breathing pattern and breathing slowly we can take control of a racing mind.
- **Support organs:** The rhythmic movement of the diaphragm supports the heart, liver, intestines and stomach, as well as the lymph system.
- **PH balance:** The way we breathe has a major impact on our ability to maintain a correct pH balance in the body.
- **Making sounds:** To talk or sing without breathing is impossible. The better we breathe, the stronger and clearer our voice will be.
- **Strength:** We have maximum physical strength when breathing out. The more physical power we wish to achieve, the more forcefully we have to push the air out through retracted vocal cords and/or pursed lips.
- **Stabilizing emotions:** When fear and worry take over, we can calm our emotions down by slow and deep diaphragmatic breathing.
- **Spiritual growth:** Even in the name *spirit*, we can spot the close connection it has to breathing—in*spiration* and ex*piration*. Respiration means re-connection to spirit. Good breathing habits increase our ability to grow as human beings, which for me is the same as spiritual growth.

## BREATHING DOES HAVE A MAJOR IMPACT

My understanding of what happens in our bodies when we breathe is based on having read a significant amount of literature and research reports, as well as having had numerous discussions with people who are knowledgeable on the subject. This is what we call theory, and though it is very interesting, I believe that testing theories in practice is even more interesting. By testing a theory in practice, I am not suggesting staring into a microscope to watch how bacteria multiply. I actually mean testing the theories using my own body.

A considerable amount of research available today shows that many of us breathe too much and that our bodies respond with poor health.[1,2,3,4] Since I am a curious soul I have repeatedly tested hyperventilation, which happens when respiration exceeds the body's needs. For example, once I tried hyperventilating, taking 60 big breaths per minute, with my mouth open for twelve minutes. Does that seem healthy? I can assure you that it really was NOT. Following the test, my face was white, my hands and feet were cold, and my legs and hands shook uncontrollably for five minutes. I appeared as if I were suffering from Parkinson's disease. The amount of lactic acid in my blood had increased by 50 percent, and I was completely exhausted, much like one might be the day after a night of heavy partying. Interestingly, the feeling that someone had pulled the rug from under my feet remained with me throughout the day. When I finally recovered enough to do some physical activity late that evening, using proper breathing technique, no more than five minutes passed before I felt harmonious again. I have repeated the tests on numerous occasions and experienced similar results each time.

**WARNING: PLEASE DO NOT TRY THIS AT HOME!**

We may not breathe as forcibly as I did in our daily lives but that doesn´t automatically mean that our breathing habits are good. Because we breathe as much as we do every day, even breathing slightly irregularly will, over time, have a negative effect. Let us take a look at the six most common breathing patterns at rest:

### 1. OPTIMAL BREATHING

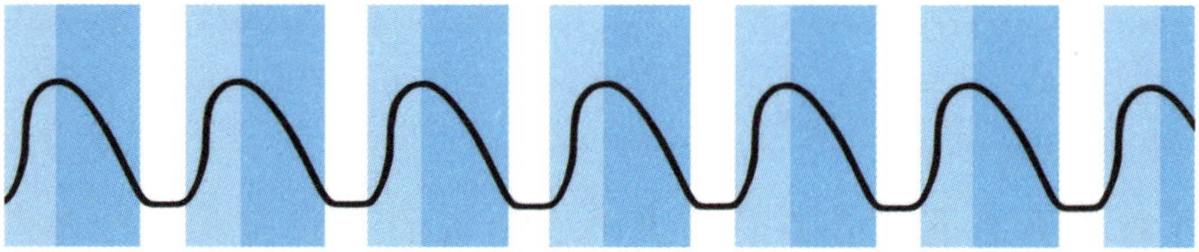

Optimal breathing corresponds to the needs of our body at any given moment. At rest, we breathe in and out through our nose in a slow, relaxed, rhythmic, and silent manner. On inhalation, the upper part of our chest remains stationary while the lower part extends smoothly forward, backward and sideways. The stomach might also extend forward slightly. These movements allow the bottom of the lungs to be filled with air.

Furthermore, exhalation is passive, and the muscles are inactive while the diaphragm, our most important breathing muscle, returns to its original position. The lower part of the rib cage collapses and the stomach recedes. We take around 8–12 breaths per minute when breathing at an optimal level, out of which we inhale 2–3 seconds, exhale 3–4 seconds, with an innate pause of 2–3 seconds before initiating the next inhalation. This, in effect, means that exhalation, including the associated pause, is longer than the inhalation, which increases our ability to recover. Subsequently, inhalation is automatically improved as the air, to a greater extent, is brought deeper into the lungs.

### 2. OVER-BREATHING

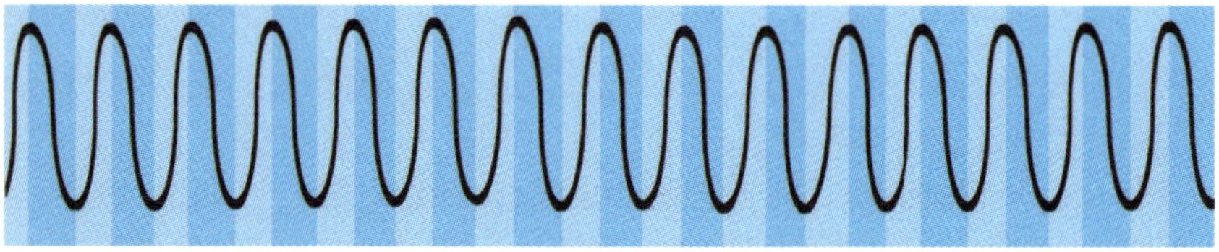

When over-breathing, we breathe 14-18 breaths per minute. The breaths are bigger, with each breath containing 50-100 percent more air than is optimal. Instead of half a liter per breath, each breath contains 0.7

to 1.0 liters. Over-breathing is actually a low-grade, masked form of hyperventilation, and we are usually unaware when we breathe too much.

### 3. PANTING

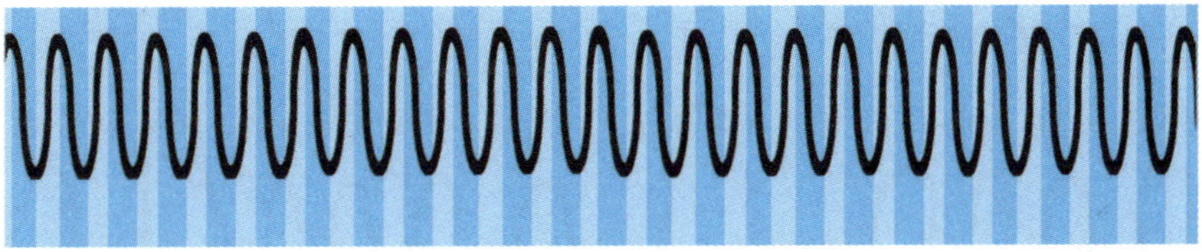

When panting, we breathe 22-30 breaths per minute and are severely over-breathing by breathing fast and high up in the chest. The mouth is often open, and we adopt a hunched posture. When we breathe through the mouth, we generally push the chin slightly forward and upward in order to keep the airways open. Furthermore, the upper chest heaves when breathing and the accessory muscles in the neck and shoulders are active.

### 4. CHEST BREATHING

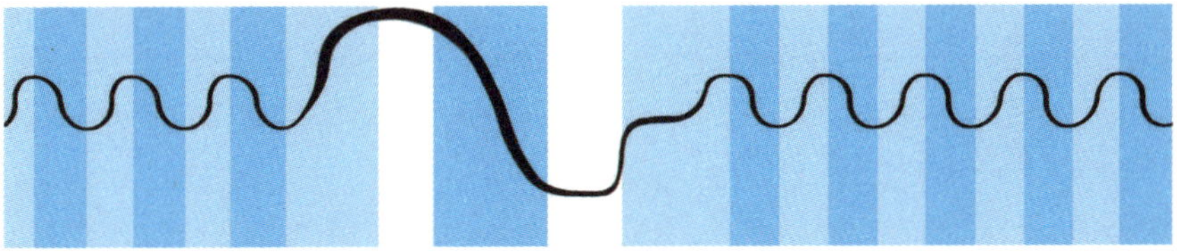

When chest breathing we breathe 14-18 breaths per minute in short, shallow breaths high up in the chest. Each breath is smaller than optimal, and we feel as if we are not breathing at all. Even though we are breathing shallowly, we are still over-breathing because our body compensates for the "nearly non-existent" breathing by sighing, yawning, or taking a deeper breath now and then. These are all big breaths and even if we only take them once every few minutes, they are enough to sustain over-breathing.

When seated we often adopt a slightly slumped posture, and "desk breathe" with the consequence that the space available for the diaphragm to work properly decreases. "Desk breathing" is common in people that work in offices. Over time, a hunched posture becomes our natural upright posture.

### 5. CHAOTIC BREATHING

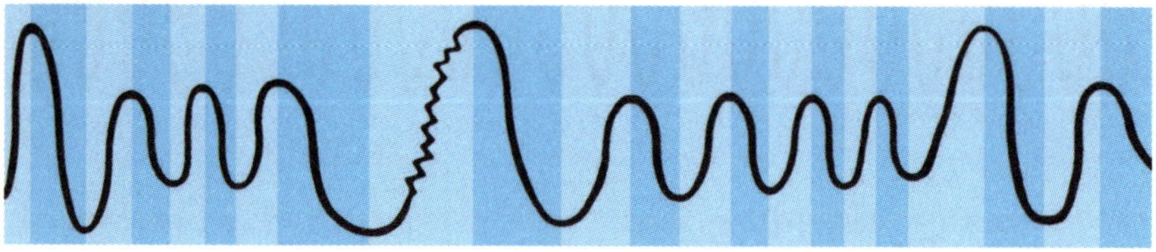

Chaotic breathing is irregular, heavy and loud. Usually we do not realize that when making these sounds we breathe at the same time. It is impossible to make a sound without breathing simultaneously. Noises may be made both when inhaling and exhaling, i.e., throat clearing, sighing, yawning, groaning, huffing and puffing, coughing, snoring and when being stuffed up and sniffling.

Commonly, those of us who breathe chaotically take big breaths before talking and/or gasp for air and speak quickly—what I call "news-reporter-syndrome." Breathing chaotically creates disruption and has a negative effect on our body.

### 6. PERIODIC BREATHING

Periodic breathing is characterized by intermittent breaks in between intervals of rapid breathing when our breathing becomes stuck, i.e., we "forget" to exhale, often when concentrating. The mouth is often kept open. Many of us notice when our breathing is stuck and feel as though we are not breathing at all. What we are not aware of is that when we start to breathe again we will compensate by over-breathing. Sleep apnea is the medical term for stuck breathing when we sleep. Since stuck breathing during the daytime mostly occurs when we concentrate, we could call it concentration apnea. Other terms could be text message apnea, computer apnea or stress apnea.

The two main types of impaired respiration are: a) over-breathing, and b) irregular breathing. Over-breathing comprises all breathing patterns, except for the first one, and means that respiration exceeds our body's needs. Irregular breathing comprises breathing patterns 4, 5 and 6 and involves coughing, sniffling, sighing, holding our breath, taking large breaths before talking, or clearing our throat, etc. We can belong to one or both groups. Additionally, our breathing may be impaired occasionally (intermittently) or often (chronic). Many of us go through periods of over-breathing or breathing irregularly, and breathe normally on other occasions.

My conclusion, after observing the respiration of a large number of people, including counting the number of breaths per minute without them being aware of it, is that very few people breathe optimally. We either over-breathe or breathe irregularly in our everyday lives. This also applies to those who have a long experience of practicing yoga and meditation, although they often have much better breathing habits than most people.

## REASONS FOR INADEQUATE BREATHING

As the quality of our lives improves, our lifestyles become more comfortable, which often has a negative effect on our health and breathing habits. On the following pages you will find some of the reasons why most of us need to improve our breathing habits, and further on in the book I provide some tips and techniques for improving your breathing habits.

### Stress and pressure

Any perceived stress affects our breathing, making it faster and/or irregular. Today, stimuli and activities in our day-to-day lives continue to increase while our ability and opportunity to rest and recover is declining. E-mail, text messages, action movies and video games, news about violence, war and other misfortune, chemicals in the air, water and the food we eat, deadlines at work, expectations of how we should look and dress etc., all lead to stress. Stress in itself is not bad since it makes us grow and develop. Problems arise when the potential for recovery is limited.

Stress produces a fight or flight reaction in the human body, which initiates the secretion of adrenaline and in turn increases our respiratory rate, which makes the heart beat faster. Simultaneously we often open our mouth to inhale more oxygen. The stress response is intended to prepare us for fight or flight from an approaching or perceived hazard. However, much of the stress we experience today is mental and emotional stress, which is not relieved by physical activity. Hence, the increased respiration is not related to what our body actually needs, which results in most of us over-breathing.

### Increased variety of stimuli, giving rise to more thoughts and feelings

Our brain is constantly fed with stimuli, making it almost impossible to relax. When in overdrive mode, thoughts and emotions affect our breathing habits, making our breathing forced and irregular. In turn, our stressed breathing manifests more stress, telling our mind that the stress continues. A vicious circle has been established, and the stressed breathing often continues long after the thoughts and feelings that triggered the process have passed.

### Overly warmed air or clothing that is too warm

If the indoor temperature is too warm, there is an increased risk of over-breathing. Rather than letting some of the heat produced by our body go out through our skin as intended, we must let the heat out by exhaling. We do this by increasing our respiratory rate, similar to when a dog pants (over-breathes) after physical activity because it does not have the ability to sweat. Often we dress our children in clothes that are too warm and they increase their respiration rate in order to get rid of the excess heat. Children carry more of what is called brown fat, which gives them the ability to produce more heat than an adult and, therefore, they do not need to be dressed quite as warmly.

#### Strong odors from exhaust fumes and chemicals

Growing up on a farm, my strategy for dealing with bad smells from the neighbor's pigsty or our barn, was to breathe through my mouth. Feeling smug, I'd think, *Voilà, I got rid of the annoying smell.* Today, I think differently and predominantly breathe through my nose. The ever-increasing amount of exhaust fumes and particles in the air, especially in urban environments, make us breathe through our mouth to a greater degree than before in order to avoid smelling the pollutants. Poor indoor air also contributes to our shallow breathing habits. Since we don't want to bring toxic air deep into our lungs, we unconsciously begin to breathe higher up in the chest.

#### Too much high intensity training

We often have the notion that exercise must be hard in order to bear fruit and, therefore, "we push ourselves to the limit" when we train. Generally, the respiration of an athlete recovering from a hard workout resembles that of a sick person suffering Chronic Obstructive Pulmonary Disease (COPD) or asthma, who experiences shortness of breath.

My soccer coach used to say, "*The way you practice, is the way you play the game. If you train like a sack of hay, you play like a sack of hay.*" If we frequently perform highly intense physical activity, in which we breathe extremely forcefully, there is a risk of adopting the habit of breathing too intensely, even at rest. I have met many athletes, both on elite and exercise level, whose breathing is too intense at rest, i.e., they hyperventilate, often at up to 20 breaths per minute. Such breathing habits do not correspond to the body's needs and have a negative impact.

### Poor eating and drinking habits

When we eat too much the stomach becomes overly full and we are forced to breathe higher up in the chest than is optimal. Precooked and processed foods are generally acid forming, and increased respiration is needed to maintain the correct pH balance in the body after ingesting them. Not only do processed foods and other foods our bodies experience as a burden increase respiration, but they can also lead to increased mucus production in the airways. We begin to cough, and at times our nose is plugged up. Do you clear your throat sometimes after eating or drinking milk, ice cream, or wine, for instance?

Poor eating and drinking habits can also be responsible for a lack of nutrients and water in our body, which is often experienced as stress, and subsequently doesn't give us the opportunity to function as well as we should do. Our breathing is a reflection of such inner stress.

### Too much talk

Many of us who work in sales or teaching have to talk a lot, or we feel the need to process all the new impressions constantly washing over us, by talking about them. A great many of us have also established impaired breathing habits when we speak. We take a big breath before we say something, speak rapidly, or breathe through our mouth. Our voice is a direct reflection of how we breathe, and a hoarse, shrill, intense, strained, or nasal voice indicates that our breathing is not optimal. Don't be surprised if the sound of your voice changes as you improve your breathing.

### Not enough movement

Modern society presents major challenges for the body. Our jobs are often sedentary, and the body is not given the movement it needs because of work, or because we often choose the most convenient option. I'm not suggesting that we should all change our jobs, but by compensating for a sedentary job with physical activity, it is possible to vastly improve our breathing habits and health. An often overlooked physical activity is to stand up. A height-adjustable desk is perfect for office workers and at home.

# PART II

# IMPROVE YOUR BREATHING NOW

# Chapter 3 – Five Simple Principles for Better Breathing

*Since we inhale 20–25,000 times in a single day, we would benefit greatly if we were to establish a breathing pattern that involved "maximum efficiency with minimum effort."*

There are five principles of conscious breathing that will help you, first, become more aware of your breathing style, and second, eliminate tense, stressed breathing and replace it with a healthier, more relaxed and harmonious breathing pattern. Fortunately, you don't have to be a rocket scientist, yoga master, or pay a small fortune to understand and apply these simple principles.

## #1. YOU SHOULD BREATHE IN AND OUT THROUGH THE NOSE

The first principle of breathing is that we should breathe in and out through our nose. It's a fact that most of us prefer cooked food to raw (unless you're on a raw food diet). But few of us wonder how our body would prefer to have its air served. Without a doubt, our lungs would prefer the 10,000–15,000 liters of air we inhale daily to be served in the best possible way. Our nose prepares the air to be used by our body to the best effect while, when inhaling through the mouth, the air reaching our lungs is colder, drier and saturated with viruses and bacteria. In other words, it's as natural to breathe through your open mouth as it is to eat with your nose.

**Better breathing**

It's very difficult to achieve optimal breathing through the mouth. The nose is our fine-tuned breathing instrument, while our mouth is a rather unsophisticated means for inhaling air. Mouth breathing is only intended for particular circumstances, for example during heavy physical activity, and should only be regarded as a back-up option.

When we mouth breathe, we automatically increase the amount of breaths we take, which consequently exceeds our body's need, and per definition, makes us hyperventilate to a degree. In fact, you can hyperventilate slightly without actually being aware of it.

Additionally, breathing through the mouth increases the risk of developing irregular and non-rhythmic breathing patterns since air passes through faster with mouth breathing than it does with nasal breathing, and the faster we breathe, the shorter the breath becomes. Since the entrance to our mouth is considerably larger than the entrance to our nose, not only do we take more breaths per minute, we also inhale a greater volume of air per breath.

**The inhaled air is heated and humidified**

Each nostril has nasal turbines that propel the air down to our lungs. The turbulent airflow is heated and humidified when a significant portion of the air comes into contact with the moist and warm nasal walls. Our nose is fairly similar to a highly efficient heat exchanger, since the nostrils are cooled when they warm up the inhaled air, which is usually cooler than our body temperature. When we exhale, the temperature inside the nostrils is raised, and the area is moisturized by the humid air being returned from the lungs at body temperature.

**Reduced risk of infection**

The air we breathe contains bacteria, viruses, chemicals and other particles. Many of these substances get trapped in the nasal passages when they come into contact with the sticky cilia-coated nasal walls. The cilia bring the particles to the pharynx and we swallow them, so the nose acts as a self-cleaning filter against bacteria. When inhaling through the mouth we miss the body's first line of defense against intruders. The further down our airways inhaled particles descend, the greater the risk of inflammation and infection. Given that the surface area of our lungs is 50-100 square meters, it's essential that it remains free of bacteria. For instance, if we're afraid of catching a cold, to only wash our hands is not enough if we keep our mouth open and inhale 10,000–15,000 liters of unfiltered air each day. It's a bit like filtering mosquitoes and swallowing camels!

Mucus is produced inside our nose each day. If the air entering our nose isn't circulated, the mucus is not cleared out and can lead to infections of the ears and sinuses.

#### The air reaches deeper into our lungs

When the inhaled air leaves the nasal turbines, it reaches the next passage in our nose, which calms the air down and makes it more streamlined, thereby increasing its ability to be transported deep into the lungs. When we breathe through our mouth, however, we breathe faster. This creates a more turbulent air flow, which makes the air swirl around in different directions. And because turbulent airflow is not an efficient way for air to travel, the air we inhale is not able to reach as deeply into the lungs as it should, and hence often ends up higher in the chest.

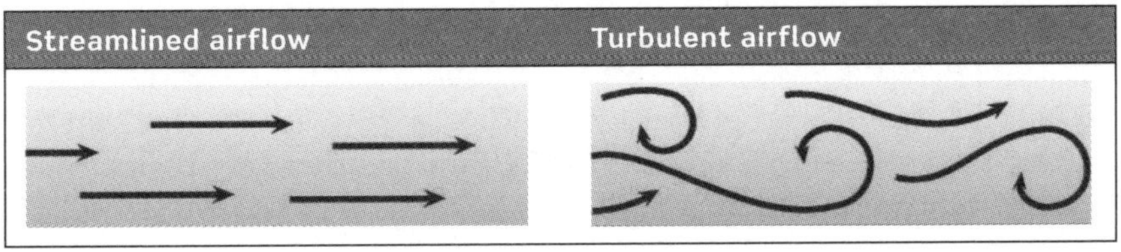


#### Inhaled air is enhanced with Nitric Oxide

Nitric Oxide (NO) is a very important substance produced in large quantities inside our sinuses. NO dilates the smooth muscles of the airways and blood vessels, and accompanies the inhaled air in order to dilate the bronchial tubes to allow the air to pass through easily. NO also causes the blood vessels inside our lungs to dilate, which allows oxygen to be transferred to our blood more easily. When we inhale through our mouth, the air is not spiked with this important substance, which is also antimicrobial and kills viruses and bacteria that have escaped from the cilia inside our nose and throat.

#### Freer airways

Narrow airways make breathing inefficient, as greater effort is required to transport the air into the lungs. When we inhale cold and dry air via the mouth, the strain on the airways increases, and with it the risk of inflammation. Inflammation occurs when our immune system is activated in order to repair damaged tissue, which causes swelling that narrows the airways. Breathing through the mouth leads to more particles reaching our bronchi, which then requires production of more mucus to clear the inhaled particles. In addition, our mucus glands enlarge over time as a result of having to make an effort to meet the need for increased quantities of mucus. Both of the afore mentioned problems can cause narrow airways.

And that's not all. Because there is less NO content in the air inhaled through our mouth, we also miss out on its bronchodilating properties. Our innate response is to increase our respiratory rate in order to compensate for the narrowed airways. When we inhale faster, the airflow automatically becomes even more turbulent. A rapid breathing pattern increases the mechanical stress on our bronchi, which in turn produces even more inflammation. Our chest feels tighter and we breathe even harder, thus initiating a vicious circle. Since breathing is crucial to our survival, the chest tightening will also trigger greater stress.

#### Better and straighter teeth

Saliva evaporates when we breathe through our mouth. Since saliva is necessary to protect our teeth this increases the risk of tooth decay.

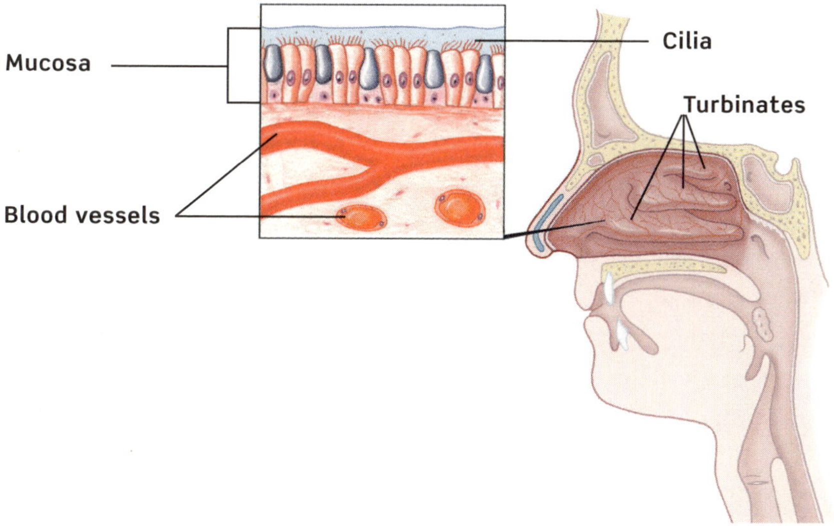


Our nostrils are covered by mucus membrane and cilia. Small particles entering our nasal mucosa are trapped and transported down to our throat by the movement of the cilia. Notice how much space the nose occupies in the cranium. Does it seem likely that the only task for the nose is to smell the flowers and to cultivate boogers? Not really! Our body is designed to operate as efficiently as possible, so when a body part has been allocated as much space as the nose, it's a sign of its importance. Our fantastic nose is probably one of the most underrated and neglected organs we have. It's easy to dismiss a stuffy nose as insignificant, but the consequences are far from insignificant. A stuffy nose should be taken very seriously and action taken so that normal breathing resumes as soon as possible.

Furthermore, our tongue's natural resting place is against the palate, behind the front teeth. When we breathe through our mouth, the tongue stays suspended in the middle of our mouth or falls down into the oral cavity in the lower jaw. Unless the tongue is positioned correctly, there is a risk of the face becoming narrower and the teeth becoming crooked, since the teeth form around the tongue.

### HOW TO FREE A BLOCKED NOSE

"But I can't breathe through my nose," you may say. "It's often blocked or my nasal passages are so narrow." One of the effects of mouth breathing is that a nose that is not being used stops functioning properly. "If you don't use it, you lose it," i.e., reduced airflow through our nose results in lowered air pressure which in turn degenerates and decreases the size of the nasal passages.[1] A clogged or narrow nose is usually an indication that breathing is not optimal. Once we start breathing through our nose, the erectile tissue in the nose will decrease in size and the inside of the nose will feel less crowded. Similarly, it is possible to reduce the size of swollen tonsils since they are part of our immune system. Enlarged tonsils are a sign that the immune system is overloaded. This could be due to inhaling through the mouth, which increases the amount of bacteria and inflammation in the throat, causing the immune system to work harder.

Mouth breathing is one of the reasons why the nose becomes blocked or tight. Excessive breathing, the result of inhaling through the mouth, leads to a lack of carbon dioxide ($CO_2$). Narrowing the nasal passages by increasing mucus production and swelling the erectile tissue can be regarded as our body's way of trying to prevent excessive amounts of $CO_2$ escaping. When we begin to improve our breathing habits, by breathing through the nose and keeping more $CO_2$ in our body, our nose will naturally be less congested.

It usually takes no more than a few days to change the habit of breathing through our mouth to breathing through our nose. When we have switched to nasal breathing, it will probably feel strange to breathe through the mouth again since the air will feel cold and dry. Many people marvel at how it was even possible to breathe through the mouth before.

Decongestant nasal sprays or surgery to widen the airways inside our nose and throat often produce undesirable results, as the root cause—impaired respiration—is not addressed. Prolonged use of nasal sprays may also lead to dependence on the medication because once the mucus membranes become reliant on the decongestant effect of the nasal spray, it becomes difficult to stop using it, for without the spray, the mucus membranes simply swell again.

One of my course participants commented: "I underwent an operation on my nose four years ago without positive effect on my narrow nasal passages. After attending your course on breathing, and a short time of practicing new breathing techniques, my nasal passages felt much wider. Now I am even able to go jogging with my mouth closed without any problem."

**Tip! Rinse your nose with salt and baking soda**

1. Boil 1 cup of water and allow it to cool until it's lukewarm.
2. Add a pinch of salt, preferably sea salt or Himalayan salt, and a pinch of baking soda for each half cup of water. Stir until dissolved.
3. Pour a small amount of water into the palm of your hand and inhale it into each nostril in turn. Alternatively, use a neti pot, Nasaline® or an ordinary 50 cl PET-bottle with sport cork to rinse your nose with water.
4. Repeat several times until your nose feels cleaner and less blocked.
5. Rinse morning and night for a few days.

Bad breath may originate from mucus coming from the nose when it drips into the oral cavity. Nasal mucus is full of dead bacteria, which may cause bad breath. Hence, keeping the inside of your nose clean may improve bad breath.

### #2. BREATHE WITH YOUR DIAPHRAGM—ABDOMINAL BREATHING

The second principle for better breathing is that the inhaled air has to reach the lower part of your lungs, "down to the abdomen." Respiratory muscles are made up of the diaphragm and the muscles in your abdomen, chest, neck and shoulders. At rest, 70-80 percent of muscular activity at inhalation should be with your diaphragm, resulting in deep, abdominal breathing, whereas at exhalation your respiratory muscles are passive. During physical activity or in diseases/disorders that produce labored breathing, the respiratory muscles are also active during exhalation.

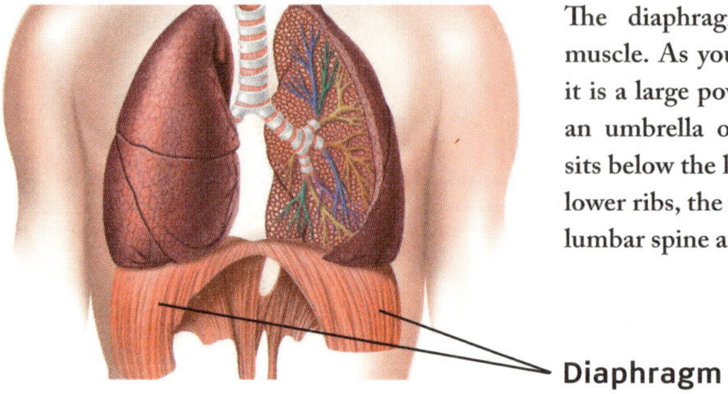


The diaphragm is our main breathing muscle. As you can see in this illustration, it is a large powerful muscle that looks like an umbrella or an upturned bowl, which sits below the lungs. It is attached to our six lower ribs, the sternum, and the back of our lumbar spine at the level of our navel.

## BENEFITS OF ABDOMINAL BREATHING

We use the term abdominal or diaphragmatic breathing because sometimes the term deep breathing is misunderstood, and it is assumed that each breath should be large and powerful, which isn't the case. Optimal deep breathing allows the air you inhale to reach the lower part of your lungs while the actual breath itself is not large.

### Improved gas exchange

One of the most important functions of breathing is to maintain balance between our body's need for oxygen and the need to remove the $CO_2$ produced. The most efficient gas exchange is achieved when the inhaled air reaches far down into our lungs. Shallow breathing, where the inhaled air only reaches the upper parts of the lungs, doesn't just make gas exchange inefficient; the air that is trapped further down in our lungs also becomes stagnant.

### The diaphragm - our very own massage therapist

Have you ever had a massage? Nice, wasn't it? We actually have our very own built-in massage therapist in our diaphragm. When inhaling and exhaling deeply, our diaphragm moves up, down and sideways, while our stomach, lower chest and back, move inward, outward and sideways, in harmony with our breathing. Our liver, stomach and intestines are massaged when our diaphragm moves downwards and.

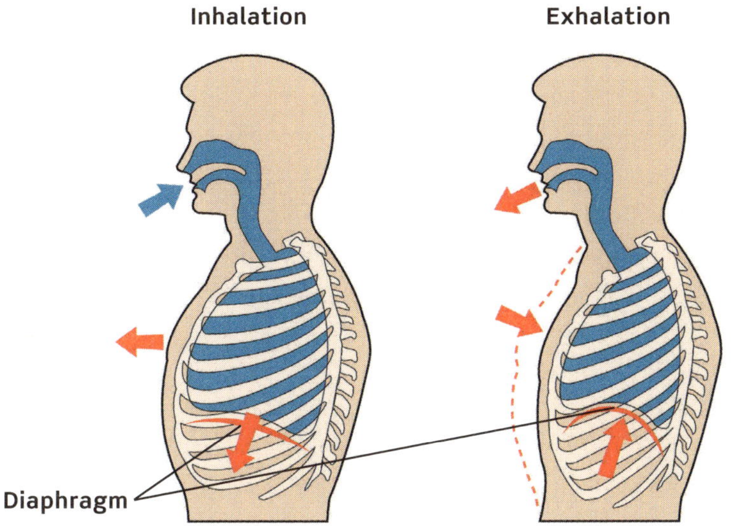


At inhalation our diaphragm moves downwards and is flattened. At the same time it expands laterally outward and rearward, towards our back. These movements expand our chest and lowers the pressure inside our chest cavity. This pushes the air from the outside, where the pressure is higher, into your lungs. On expiration the diaphragm returns to its starting position. A stiff chest prevents the diaphragm from moving in a good way.

outwards on inhalation. The more we improve our respiration, the more rhythmic and relaxed the movement of our diaphragm will be, and the more our internal organs are stimulated.

### The diaphragm - the pump of our lymphatic fluid

The body's lymphatic system which is an important part of our immune system, depends on the movement of the diaphragm. All organs in our abdomen emit waste products, and our lymphatic system has the task of removing the waste. We have more lymphatic fluid than blood in our body, but unlike our blood, which is pumped around the body by our heart; our lymph fluid lacks its own pump, which is why lymphatic fluid is dependent to a large extent on muscular activity. Therefore, the movement of our diaphragm is very important for our lymphatic system, especially since it never rests and is working 24/7.

### Diaphragm motion and the heart

When our diaphragm contracts and expands downwards and outward on inhalation, it lowers the pressure in our chest as well as in our stomach. The interaction between these pressure changes has a squeezing effect on the blood vessels carrying blood to our heart, which makes it easier for our blood to be transported back to our heart. This has a positive impact on varicose veins. Our heart would be forced to work much harder without the help of diaphragmatic movement.[2]

### More efficient muscle activity

Normal breathing at rest is around 4-6 liters of air per minute. However, at maximum exertion, we breathe more than 100 liters per minute, while fit athletes can breathe as much as 200 liters per minute. During physical activity, our abdomen, chest, neck, and shoulder muscles are very active, even when we exhale. At rest, the diaphragm should perform the major part of inhalation muscle activity. When we breathe ineffectively, our diaphragm is less active. The accessory muscles are overused, and each breath requires more energy than necessary, which is not very effective. Since we breathe a considerable amount of breaths each day, breathing should ideally be as efficient as possible, with minimal effort by our body. In economic terms, diaphragmatic breathing should yield a high return on invested capital (minimal effort, maximum return).

### Relaxing the chest, neck and shoulders

Excessive chest breathing results in a tense diaphragm, neck and shoulders, and may cause pain and tension in our back since our chest is connected to the spine. The chest is more relaxed when we breathe deep into our lungs since we don't over exert the chest, neck and shoulder muscles.

## #3. A SLOW AND RELAXED BREATHING

According to the third principle, a good breathing habit is slow, relaxed and harmonious. In comparison to tense and stressed breathing, the respiratory volume is reduced when we breathe well, i.e., when we are taking smaller, fewer and longer breaths that reach deeper into our lungs. When perceived relaxation is low, subjective stress is automatically high. Are there any situations where there is an advantage to being tense and stressed? When we are running for our lives? Prior to an important meeting at work? When we are jogging? Cooking? Doing homework with the kids? I can't think of a single situation when being tense and stressed is advantageous. When I want to achieve something it's obviously good to be alert, focused, concentrated, and relaxed, which is not the same as being stressed and tense.

High stress makes us enter into survival mode, and we progress at high speed with tunnel vision as a result. We easily end up in conflicts, view the world in a way that makes us see everything as threatening, and we are fearful and anxious. Living with high stress for extended periods means that the stress becomes chronic, which leads to disease, injury, and low energy. In the early stages of stress, we naturally breathe faster. Eventually our poor breathing habit becomes chronic, and relaxing becomes more and more difficult.

### Relaxed breathing results in a relaxed body with thoughts and emotions in balance

Regardless of what we wish to achieve, we will perform better if we are relaxed. Since how we breathe reflects our thoughts, emotions and physical body, it means that in situations where we are tense, we also get a tensed and stressed breathing. A high paced life of meetings, deadlines, bills, and many demands will give rise to thoughts and feelings that make us breathe rapidly and irregularly. However, the stress we experience is rarely associated with physical activity, which is why increasing respiration doesn't serve any purpose. The result of stressed and tense breathing is oxygen deficiency, which increases the stress on the body and brain even more.

When we take control of our breathing habits, by making our breathing slower and more relaxed, we encourage our whole body to adapt and be relaxed, and consequently work more efficiently. As we improve our breathing habits, the perceived stress drops and we become more and more relaxed, leaving more time for learning and growth. When our physical body is relaxed, our health is good and our energy is high, we are naturally cooperative, and are happy and loving to others and ourselves.

#### Tense and fast breathing

Some signs that we have a tense body and a fast, labored breathing include:

1. Pulled up shoulders, similar to a highly stressed/fearful/angry cat or dog that raises its hackles.
2. Stiff neck and shoulders; perhaps our seated posture is leaning forward on our office chair, or we lean forward when we walk as if we are in a big hurry.
3. Open mouth.
4. Dilated pupils and "popped out eyes."
5. Stiff and tense facial features; frowning, clenched lips, and making different faces.
6. Stiff and tense movements; moving like a robot, slumped posture giving a depressed impression. Physical stiffness indicates that we are in a phase where we are struggling to achieve balance in life, while a sunken physical appearance suggests that imbalances have gone deeper and we are in a state of exhaustion.

Frequent and extended periods of feeling tension and stress will eventually be reflected in our body. Lines appear between our eyebrows, tense facial expression around the mouth, raised shoulders, or we assume a slumped posture. All of these reflect too much worry and stress. My mum told me when I was young, "Don't pull such a face, it may stick." In fact, that is actually true, especially when it comes to stress.

### #4. RHYTHMIC BREATHING

According to the fourth principle, breathing should be rhythmic. Rhythms are everywhere; everything in the universe has a rhythm—the sea waves, days/nights, seasons, moon etc. The rhythm of the heart can be interpreted by taking an Electrocardiogram (ECG), and to interpret the rhythm of the brain we use an Electroencephalography (EEG) machine. Hormone secretions in the body follow a rhythm, such as when melatonin is secreted when we are about to sleep. Music consists of frequencies or rhythms. Optimal breathing patterns follow a rhythm that is regular, and it is in rhythm that we find comfort.

***Rhythmic movement implies well-being:***

- We are drawn to rhythmic music, and we don't like to listen to non-rhythmic music, as it affects us negatively.
- When we are running or walking at a steady pace we get into a rhythm, and it feels as though the activity flows effortlessly in contrast to how difficult it is when we have to stop and change speed intermittently.

All processes in the body affect each other. The organs interact like cogs in an old-fashioned clock, where each cog engages with each other. If one cog is deteriorating it affects all the other cogs, which can result in the clock slowing down or speeding up. Likewise, the blood circulation and muscle energy supply are affected negatively if the heart beat is out of rhythm, and if the organs in our digestive system are not cooperating fully, it reduces our ability to absorb nutrients from the food we eat. Rhythmic breathing is akin to a football coach or a corporate CEO, who encourage their players and employees to collaborate, cooperate and pull together in the same direction.

Breathing has a direct or indirect impact on all processes and organs throughout the body—heart, brain, digestion, immune function, energy production, etc. Increasing the proportion of rhythmic and relaxed breaths out of the 20–25,000 breaths we take each day will improve how all the different processes in the body interact with each other.

### #5. QUIET AND REDUCED BREATHING VOLUME

The fifth and final principle is that our breathing should be quiet and small, i.e., reduced breathing volume. Sighing, coughing, snoring, sniffling, etc., are all part of breathing. It's easy to overlook the fact that we breathe at the same time as making all of these sounds. Breathing that involves a number of the above problems places a major burden on the body because it becomes non-rhythmic and big, i.e., we hyperventilate. Instead of a healthy breathing volume at rest of 4-6 liters of air per minute it is common to breathe twice to four times as much, which will lead to oxygen deficiency.

Noisy breathing is not natural. Imagine a tiger creeping up on an antelope in the grass while coughing, sniffling and making sounds. Would it get any food? Not likely! Or imagine the reverse, a gnu sleeping in the jungle at night, snoring with sounds that resemble those made by a sawmill. How long will it sleep before a predator gets its teeth into it? Not for long, that's for sure! People today are fortunate to be able to put food on the table and get a whole night's sleep without being eaten alive, even if breathing noisily. But it's by no means natural.

We usually take a big breath before we sigh. When we cough, our breath is large and irregular. Snoring is an indicator of narrow airways. To compensate, we breathe faster and use more power for every breath. Plus many of us inhale rapidly and often loudly before we begin to speak. It's also common for us to breathe through our mouth while talking, which may affect our body negatively since in our society today we generally talk excessively and breathe incorrectly. If your profession involves speaking a lot, it's especially important to consider how you breathe, both at work and privately.

In summary, the five principles of breathing highlight that you should breathe in and out through your nose, and that the inhaled air should reach deep into the lungs while your breathing is slow, relaxed, rhythmic and quiet and the breathing volume is reduced. Now, it's time to examine how you breathe.

## HOW DO YOU BREATHE

You may:

- Clear your throat when you are stressed (throat-clearing is a form of breathing).
- Hold your breath while you concentrate.
- Breathe forcefully when you talk.
- Keep your mouth open while you exercise.
- Snore when you sleep (snoring is a form of breathing).

## BREATHING INDEX

The questions on the next page concern your breathing habits and the state of your airways. Blocked airways, over-breathing, and irregular breathing are all factors that can cause many seemingly unrelated health problems. Hence, there are questions relating to health issues, such as stomach problems, for example. These questions will help you assess your own breathing and become aware of how well your airways work. All questions relate to the past month.

***Circle the option from 1-5 that best describes your current health status.***

| | Very often | Often | Some-times | Rarely | Never |
|---|---|---|---|---|---|
| 1. Overall health: My health status is poor | 1 | 2 | 3 | 4 | 5 |
| 2. Open mouth, mouth breathing, dry mouth, dry lips | 1 | 2 | 3 | 4 | 5 |
| 3. Stuffy/runny/itchy nose, sinus congestion, narrow nasal passages, recurrent colds | 1 | 2 | 3 | 4 | 5 |
| 4. Lump sensation in the throat, difficulty swallowing, irritated throat, sensitive airways | 1 | 2 | 3 | 4 | 5 |
| 5. Shallow breathing, difficulty breathing abdominally | 1 | 2 | 3 | 4 | 5 |
| 6. Heavy breathing/over-breathing, difficulty getting air, chest tightness | 1 | 2 | 3 | 4 | 5 |
| 7. Sneezing, sighing, yawning, taking big breaths prior to speaking | 1 | 2 | 3 | 4 | 5 |
| 8. Daytime apnea/holding breath, forgetting to exhale | 1 | 2 | 3 | 4 | 5 |
| 9. Noisy breathing, mucus, clearing of throat, coughing, sniffling, wheezing | 1 | 2 | 3 | 4 | 5 |
| 10. Forward leaning and/or slumped posture | 1 | 2 | 3 | 4 | 5 |
| 11. Insomnia, restless sleep, snoring, sleep apnea, grinding/clenching teeth | 1 | 2 | 3 | 4 | 5 |
| 12. Low on energy, morning tiredness, tired during the day, poor concentration | 1 | 2 | 3 | 4 | 5 |
| 13. Heart palpitations, extra and/or irregular heart beats | 1 | 2 | 3 | 4 | 5 |
| 14. Internal stress, brain in overdrive, in a hurry, sugar cravings, addictive tendencies | 1 | 2 | 3 | 4 | 5 |
| 15. Feeling anxious, depressed, afraid, avoiding conflicts, "people pleaser" | 1 | 2 | 3 | 4 | 5 |
| 16. Irritated, angry, impatient, conflicts, over-ambitious | 1 | 2 | 3 | 4 | 5 |
| 17. Indigestion, constipation, over-eating | 1 | 2 | 3 | 4 | 5 |
| 18. Stiff and/or tense muscles, pain in the back/neck/shoulders, headache | 1 | 2 | 3 | 4 | 5 |
| 19. Shortness of breath during exercise, low endurance at physical work | 1 | 2 | 3 | 4 | 5 |
| 20. The voice does not carry, hoarseness, squeaky/nasal/strained voice | 1 | 2 | 3 | 4 | 5 |

***Total:*** ____________

The maximum score on the breathing index is 100. A high score indicates a body that is in balance, with ample internal resources, and is capable of handling difficult challenges.

The lowest possible score is 20. A score below 50 indicates that your breathing has great potential for improvement. A low score indicates a body that is out of balance, with low inner resources. There is nothing wrong in having a low score. However, it may be advantageous to lower your level of ambition and try to reduce the severity of the challenges that you face.

It is encouraging to know that improving your breathing habits can help boost your score and assist you in achieving better health.

Below are some breathing experiments you can try:

**Exercise 1 — Hyperventilation**

Even though this exercise is "unhealthy," nothing beats personal experience.

- Inhale and exhale as much air as you can for 30 seconds.
- Take big rapid breaths high up in your chest.
- Let your chest heave and allow your shoulders to move up and down.
- Breathe with your mouth open.

**BE CAREFUL! PLEASE CONSULT YOUR PHYSICIAN BEFORE DOING THE TEST IF YOU FEEL UNCERTAIN.**

What did you experience? Dizziness? Discomfort? Coughing? A dry mouth and/or throat? Pins and needles, or cold hands and feet? If you suffer from asthma, high blood pressure or panic attacks, such symptoms might have made their presence felt, as well.

**Exercise 2 — Breathing into a bag**

Breathing into a bag produces the opposite effect of hyperventilating; it helps you recover quickly and brings your body back into balance.

- Use a standard 3-liter plastic or paper bag.
- Hold the bag a few inches from your nose.
- Inhale and exhale 10 times in and out of the bag.
- Try to breathe slowly and relaxed with your mouth closed, and breathe only through your nose.

**BE CAREFUL! THE OXYGEN CAN DECREASE SHARPLY IF YOU HOLD THE BAG TOO CLOSE TO YOUR NOSE.**

What did you experience? Did your inner peace increase? Did you feel harmonious and/or did the airways in your nose and throat feel clear? Breathing properly can clearly improve your mental, emotional and physical wellbeing.

**Exercise 3 — Count your steps**

One way to free a blocked nose permanently is to increase the amount of $CO_2$ in the body. This can primarily be done through physical activity and by reducing the breathing volume. The best way to reduce respiratory volume is to extend the exhalation. When we move our body and at the same time reduce our breathing, the amount of $CO_2$ in our body is increased, which relieves the blocked nose.

Further, nasal breathing and prolonged exhalation during physical activity increases the pressure and circulation of air in the sinuses. Using the Relaxator will enhance this effect even more. Please note that a slight headache (usually located in the forehead) can occur the first couple of times because of the increased pressure in the sinuses.

- Walk, jog or ride a bike while you count the number of steps/pedal pushes you take on inhalation and the number of steps/pedal pushes you take on exhalation. Since prolonged exhalation promotes relaxation, the goal of the exercise is to take more steps/pedal pushes on exhalation than on inhalation.
- This exercise can also be done when stationary, but it is more powerful in combination with physical activity.

- Keep your mouth closed.
- Find a rhythm that works for you, for example, three steps/pedal pushes on inhalation and six on exhalation.
- The number of steps/pedal pushes may vary during your training session depending on your average fitness and speed, whether you are going uphill or downhill, and if you want to push yourself or take it easy.

**Exercise 4 — Deep (not big), abdominal breathing**

1. Sit upright and place one hand on your chest and one on your stomach.
2. Breathe in and out in a calm and relaxed manner.
3. Strive to fill your stomach first.
4. Maintain a slow, relaxed and rhythmical breathing pattern with a reduced breathing volume.
5. When inhaling, the hand of your stomach should move first, and it should also move more than the hand on your chest.

If the hand on your chest moves first and/or if it moves more than the hand on your stomach, it indicates that your breathing is impaired. Another way to practice abdominal breathing is to lie flat on your back on the floor with a book placed on your stomach. When you have mastered the art of diaphragmatic breathing, the book on your stomach will move upwards during inhalation and downwards during exhalation.

**Exercise 5 — Put your hands behind your head**

1. Sit or stand up.
2. Clasp your hands behind your head.
3. Push your elbows back so your chest extends automatically.
4. Breathe in and out through your nose and note how the inhaled air reaches your abdominal area.
5. Repeat until you feel that your breathing is reduced, abdominal, slow and relaxed.

**Exercise 6 — Clench your fist**

1. Stretch your right arm straight out and clench your fist.
2. Keep it clenched as long as possible until your knuckles turn white. Then keep it clenched a little longer.
3. Now, how is your breathing?
4. Let go, relax your arm and hand, and straighten your fingers.
4. How did you breathe during the exercise? Many hold their breath, as this is a natural reflex during effort and concentration.
5. Repeat steps 1-4 again. This time breathe consciously, inhaling and exhaling abdominally, slowly and regularly through your nose. Did your stamina increase? Was it easier? Were your fingers not as stiff?

Being tense and holding our breath cause oxygen deficiency. It is also common to experience tiredness and pain when we hold our breath. On the other hand, when our breathing pattern is regular, the active muscles receive a continuous supply of oxygen, which allows us to continue to tighten our hand almost indefinitely without getting tired. An additional benefit is that it is not mentally perceived as quite as difficult, either.

**Exercise 7 — Be silent and follow your breath**

1. Set aside some time for yourself, for example, 5–10 minutes or any length of time you are comfortable with.
2. Try to be completely silent—don't talk, don't clear your throat, don't sigh, etc.
3. Observe your breath and observe every breath in and out.
4. Try to make breathing completely silent.

To begin with, this exercise can be a real challenge, particularly if you have a stuffy nose, a cough, or a lot of mucus in the throat. Even so, it's worth doing as it will allow you to develop awareness of the state of your breathing.

# Chapter 4 – Retrain Your Breathing

*Any quest for enhanced health and wellbeing should include improving your breathing habits as a basic component, since breathing is an integral part of us, and is with us wherever we go. We have the opportunity to practice breathing exercises anywhere, at any time, in order to establish improved breathing habits simply, inexpensively, and effectively.*

When we consider improving our lives, we often overlook our breathing habits. Yet this is precisely when our breathing should be our top priority, since everything we do affects our breathing. The reverse is also true. The way we breathe affects our physical body, our thoughts and our feelings. So improving our breathing habits should always be an essential component when striving to improve our health and wellbeing.

Even though breathing is an instinctive process, it is very easy to influence our breathing patterns and change them for the better. Even if we have acquired impaired breathing patterns, to different degrees, we can all improve these habits with a little practice. Since we have our breath with us wherever we go, it's easy to incorporate breathing practice into our everyday lives. Breathing exercises do not have to be done "later" at a specific training session.

Conscious Breathing techniques involve a few simple points that can be used to improve your breathing.

1. **Breathing awareness:** Become aware of how you breathe in different situations.

2. **Closed mouth:** Keeping your mouth closed with your tongue located in the roof of your mouth ensures that breathing occurs in and out through your nose.
3. **Prolonged exhalation:** Prolonging exhalation slows down breathing frequency, increases relaxation and makes inhalation deeper and the whole breathing cycle more rhythmic.
4. **Body awareness:** Become aware of your body and how tense or relaxed it is in different situations. A relaxed body and an upright position make it easier to maintain a rhythmic and relaxed breathing pattern.
5. **Reduce mental stress:** Conscious Breathing helps to soothe a racing mind.
6. **Release emotional blockages:** Improving your breathing habits can reduce, or help eliminate, the feelings of fear and anxiety that often prevent us from reaching our goals.
7. **Physical activity:** Our body is designed to move around. Keeping your mouth closed while in motion will help to improve your breathing, your endurance, and your health.

### 1. BECOME AWARE OF HOW YOU BREATHE IN YOUR EVERYDAY LIFE

To change something, you first have to become aware of what needs to be changed. By observing how you breathe in different situations, you can improve your breathing. Become aware of which of the six respiratory patterns outlined in Chapter 2 apply to you when you are:

- Working or concentrating
- Afraid or angry
- Stressed
- Talking
- Preparing a meal
- Having sex
- Driving
- Feeling depressed
- Using the computer
- Watching TV
- Sleeping

And so on

With a little practice, you will develop a better breathing habit that follows the five simple principles of optimal breathing, even when you're upset or when everything seems to be going wrong.

Many notice a positive and immediate effect from improved breathing. It's almost like taking a magic pill. However, I suggest you try to view it more as a lifestyle approach than a quick fix. Making rapid improvements is not wrong, but if you find that your progress levels out, try to persist and continue to improve your breathing habits even more, since it may take a while for you to become aware of improvements to underlying issues.

The overall aim of breathing retraining is to establish the best breathing habits for you, so that optimal breathing becomes natural. Then you will have come full circle—from an unconscious, impaired breathing habit, to becoming conscious of how you breathe, to finally reaching optimal breathing, which will now have become natural.

***Tips for faster learning:***

Be humble, curious and kind to yourself, and try to make your observations enjoyable as you note and actively strive to improve your day-to-day breathing habits. By being kind to yourself, and grateful that you are actually discovering that your breathing pattern is not good at a particular time or in certain situations, you retain the motivation to keep improving your breathing habits. The things we like and enjoy, we want to do again.

## 2. CLOSE YOUR MOUTH

It is very easy to fall into the habit of breathing through the mouth when it's kept open. To ensure that you breathe in and out through your nose, it's best to keep your mouth closed as much as possible with your tongue dormant in its natural resting position, against the palate. (You can read more about the importance of the tongue in Chapter 8—How Your Breathing Can Affect Your Teeth and Facial Development.)

**Apply tape to your mouth at night for improved sleep**

A simple measure for improving nightly breathing is to apply tape over your mouth before going to sleep. It may sound rather strange, but I really recommend that everyone try it.

A good night's sleep is vital to our health. During sleep our body heals, repairs and regenerates. How we breathe when we sleep is of great importance, especially given the large number of hours we sleep every night.

If you sleep with an open mouth your breathing will automatically exceed your body's needs and you will hyperventilate, which causes oxygen deficiency. Applying tape to your mouth at night is an easy and inexpensive way to ensure that your mouth stays closed and respiration occurs only through your nose. This will make breathing work for you instead of against you. Sleep Tape is a 25mm surgical tape that you can purchase on *www.cbreath.com*.

You may think it sounds barbaric, or feel uncomfortable with the idea of applying tape to your mouth—a common reaction among the participants in my courses. The discomfort is generally just a mental block, and after trying it out for a few minutes most people find they get used to it. If you do feel discomfort, I suggest you start to apply the tape during the day, in order to become more comfortable with the sensation. Apply the tape horizontally or vertically, from the nose to the chin.

Taping your mouth at night is a remarkably simple, yet extremely powerful tool. The feedback I frequently get is that people wake up more alert in the morning, sleep more calmly, don't wake up during the night, and need less sleep. You may think that it's not very sexy, but you can always cuddle first, and then tape your mouth. Some prefer to wait until their partner has fallen asleep before applying the tape to their mouth. Perhaps you can get your partner to tape their mouth too?

**PLEASE NOTE: I DO NOT RECOMMEND THAT CHILDREN UNDER FIVE YEARS OF AGE TAPE THEIR MOUTH.**

### 3. EXTENDED EXPIRATION

Normal exhalation at rest is totally relaxed and occurs without any muscle activity. Exhalation is also longer than inhalation, and a break occurs following exhalation. When breathing optimally, inhalation lasts for 2–3 seconds, exhalation for 3–4 seconds followed by a pause that lasts for 2–3 seconds. A simple rule of thumb is 3–3–3 seconds. Your exhalation is linked to relaxation, so by extending your exhalation and the pause you increase your body's ability to relax and thereby reach deeper relaxation. An additional benefit of prolonged exhalation is that it has a positive effect on your inhalation, since it reaches deeper.

Inhaling is an active process in which your respiratory muscles are actively working to expand your chest so that air can enter. When we inhale, our heart beats faster (the pulse is raised) and the sympathetic part of the autonomic nervous system (the gas pedal) is activated. Expiration is usually passive, where our diaphragm returns to its original position, and our thorax and lungs sink down without any muscle effort. On expiration, the soothing part of the autonomic nervous response, the parasympathetic nervous system (the brake), is more active, which allows the heart to rest and recover, and the pulse to drop. When your body is relaxed it functions better and you can achieve more using less effort.

The exercise *Count your steps* on page 58 is a simple way of prolonging exhalation in different situations.

#### Resistance breathing that trains your respiratory muscles

To force the air out through resistance is called ujjayi-breathing in yoga, but could just as well be called "Darth Vader-breathing" because of the hissing sound the resistance makes when you pinch your throat and squeeze the air through. When you practice ujjayi-breathing, the muscles in your throat tighten, and your vocal cords are pressed together so that the passage becomes narrower. At the same time the stomach and chest muscles are automatically tightened and the air is squeezed out at expiration.

Many people have weak abdominal and diaphragmatic muscles due to persistent shallow breathing, while their chest and neck muscles may be stiff and tense due to overuse. The most important effects of applying resistance when breathing are:

- Upon exhalation your abdominal muscles pushes your diaphragm higher up which makes your diaphragm fall further down during inhalation. This means that the inhaled air reaches further down in "your abdomen," leading to increased oxygen uptake and improved circulation of air in the lower parts of your lungs.
- You develop a more rhythmic breathing pattern, which has a positive effect on your heart and the internal organs in your abdomen.
- Exhalation is prolonged, which results in greater relaxation.
- You take fewer breaths per minute, thus reducing your breathing volume, which increases the amount of $CO_2$ in your lungs, thereby dilating your blood vessels and facilitating more efficient gas exchange.
- Establishing a calmer breathing pattern helps the respiratory center in your brainstem become accustomed to higher levels of $CO_2$. This in turn results in you having to take fewer breaths per minute. The fewer breaths you take per minute, the calmer and more harmonious your breathing becomes.
- The increased pressure in your lungs increases the ability of the alveoli to transfer oxygen to your blood. Lowered pressure in the lungs is very common among those who breathe through their mouths, as air escapes more easily through the mouth than it does through the nose. At worst, lowered pressure in the lungs can lead to the collapse of some parts of the lungs, as is the case in COPD and emphysema.

### Resistance Breathing with the Relaxator Breathing Retrainer

Using a small breathing retrainer in the form of a nozzle that adds resistance on expiration is a good alternative to ujjayi-breathing.

When I first held a breathing retrainer in my hand, I thought it was a ridiculous toy that I definitely didn't need to put into my mouth. At the time, I already held courses where I taught other people how to improve their breathing habits, so I certainly knew how to breathe! When I finally gave it a chance a few months later, I was surprised to discover how good it was. I found it particularly useful when I was working on the computer as it became obvious that my breathing "got stuck" when I was concentrating. When using the breathing retrainer, my breathing pattern became more rhythmic and harmonious. After some time of using and testing other breathing devices, each with its unique design pros and cons, I decided to develop my own breathing retrainer, the Relaxator.

The Relaxator is currently the smallest breathing retrainer on the market. It's easy to carry in your pocket, purse, or around your neck, and it's also very easy to use. The Relaxator only weighs seven grams—light enough to keep in your mouth for a long time without your jaw tensing up. If you decide to use the breathing retrainer, I recommend you start with one 15-minute session or three 5-minute sessions per day. That is enough time to get a better breathing pattern started and to exercise your respiratory muscles, although there is neither an upper or lower time limit for usage. Five minutes is better than none, and some people use the Relaxator for up to one hour or more per day. Practicing breathing retraining several times per day is also very beneficial.

When I work intensively on the computer, as when writing this book, I sometimes use the Relaxator for several hours a day. The respiratory resistance in the Relaxator can be selected on a five-point scale, five being the toughest resistance. There is no need to push yourself to get results when using the Relaxator. Set the resistance at a level where you can still maintain a relaxed breathing pattern. Setting it to 3–3.5 corresponds to breathing twelve breaths per minute for most people.

Breathing retraining can be used to an advantage during periods of high stress, low energy, pain, coughing, anxiety attacks, asthma and allergy attacks, childbirth, and similar situations.

The respiratory retrainer applies resistance on exhalation, which activates your abdominal and respiratory muscles and facilitates a deeper breath. Breathing also becomes more rhythmic with the Relaxator, for example, when you concentrate. When you force the air out, exhalation is extended, breathing volume is decreased and the ability to relax and wind down increases.

You can easily make using the Relaxator part of your daily routine, for instance, in bed a few minutes before getting up, in your car, in front of the computer, when doing homework, while watching television, before important meetings, at meditation, yoga, qigong, before, during and after exercise, on the golf course, and during pregnancy, to practice better breathing.

Some people use the Relaxator in order to train their abdominal muscles. To do this, you would choose a higher resistance so you are forced to make more of an effort when squeezing the air out. The best effect on your abdominal muscles is achieved with interval training, i.e. 10 breaths through the Relaxator where you empty your lungs at each breath, then a moment of rest followed by another 10 breaths. In Chapter 7, you will be given further information on Relaxator training and how to use the Relaxator in order to improve your breathing habits.

Remember that breathing exercises affect all processes in your body and can instigate large and rapid changes in the blood flow to your brain, heart, liver, stomach, intestines and other organs. Therefore, it is advisable to be careful when training with the Relaxator if you are unwell and/or if taking medication.

**PLEASE NOTE! THE RELAXATOR IS NOT A REPLACEMENT FOR MEDICATION. ALWAYS CONSULT YOUR PHYSICIAN BEFORE MAKING ANY MEDICAL CHANGES.**

## 4. RAISE YOUR BODY AWARENESS

It's common to feel tense in different situations. When we are tense our breathing pattern deteriorates and becomes forced, making us use more resources than the situation requires. A relaxed body makes it easier to maintain a rhythmic and relaxed breathing pattern. The questionnaire for breathing habits on page 75 will help you to increase your body awareness and pay attention to whether you are tense or relaxed in different situations. Below are a few additional tips to increase your body awareness:

- Stand in front of a mirror and study your posture. For a good posture, your back should be straight and your ears, upper arms and hips should be in a vertical line. Now, notice how you are breathing. During good breathing, your shoulders and upper chest should be still while your stomach moves slightly outward and the lower part of your chest expands forward, backward, and sideways.
- Be aware of your posture in different situations, when you are seated, standing and walking. Is there a link between your posture, thoughts/feelings and respiration?
- Whenever you notice that your posture is not optimal, stretch your back into an upright position and apply the five principles of Conscious Breathing.
- Enlist the help of friends, family and colleagues to notice and tell you about your posture in different situations.

### An upright posture creates a deeper breathing

Keeping your back straight when sitting, standing or walking, as well as during other daily activities, is a prerequisite for an optimal breathing habit. A slumped posture means that your diaphragm is compressed and its ability to move downward on inhalation decreases, making your breathing shallow and high up in your chest. Most of the work related to your breathing is then performed by the accessory muscles in your chest and neck, resulting in inefficient breathing that requires more of your body's resources than necessary.

In the long run the overuse of these muscles leads to tense and rigid accessory muscles in your neck, shoulders and chest, which further impairs both your breathing and posture. This is particularly evident when we sit down, which many of us do for long periods each day. As discussed earlier, shallow breathing leads to reduced oxygenation of your blood. The diaphragm's massaging effect on your inner organs is also reduced, as well as the lymphatic system's ability to remove residual waste products from your abdomen.

Breathing through your mouth automatically initiates an instinctive forward-leaning stance, which puts a heavy load on your upper spine and neck muscles. A forward leaning stance, inwardly sunk, is very common at the computer, or when performing activities like sending a text message on a cell phone, etc. The long-term effects are permanent vertebral changes in the neck and chest, and changes in the posture of the shoulders. A domino effect will also be triggered that may affect your hips, knees and feet at a later stage. In addition, mouth breathing may also lead to more rigid and tense jaws.

Your posture affects your thoughts and feelings too. A person who is depressed is sometimes described as looking as if the whole world's problems rest on his shoulders, while a person with a straight back radiates power and confidence.

***Try for yourself:***

Adopt a slumped posture with shoulders pointing inwards, your head leaning forward, and with your shoulders sloping. Try at the same time to think positive thoughts and feel feelings of joy. Certainly it's hard! It's easier to think of misery and feel depressed. Now, try doing the opposite. Sit up and align your spine, so that your ears, upper arms and hips are in a vertical line. Try to feel depressed at the same time. It's not very easy is it?

When you straighten your back into a more upright position, your breathing improves automatically, and the inhaled air ends up deeper down in your abdomen. Your thoughts and emotions are affected positi-

| Poor, slumped posture | Erect posture |
|---|---|
| • Mouth breathing | • Nose breathing |
| • Chest breathing | • Abdominal breathing |
| • Negative, depressed, weak | • Happy, harmonious, strong |

vely and it's also easier to breathe through your nose. Remember that improved oxygenation continuously provides more energy in a positive spiraling effect.

### 5-7. REDUCE MENTAL STRESS, RELEASE EMOTIONAL BLOCKAGES, PHYSICAL ACTIVITY

In Chapter 5 we discuss mental stress and emotional blockages and in Chapter 6 we take a closer look at physical activity from a breathing perspective.

### GETTING STARTED WITH BREATHING RETRAINING

While good breathing in our daily lives doesn't always come naturally, it can be learned. By improving your breathing habits there is a great chance that you will also improve your energy levels, sleep quality and overall health. The *28-Day Breathing Retraining Program* will help you to get started in building healthy breathing habits. And it's as simple as following these steps:

1. Learn more about your current breathing habits by answering the questions in the Breathing Index Questionnaire in Chapter 3.
2. Write down three main goals related to your wellbeing.
3. Visualize each goal to engage your emotions.
4. Complete the training schedule for 28 days Breathing Retraining – use the Relaxator, tape your mouth at night, and engage in physical activity with your mouth closed.
5. Complete the schedule for your day-to-day breathing habits at the end of each week – i.e., day 7, 14, 21 and 28.

6. Answer the questions in the Breathing Index Questionnaire once more.
7. Answer the questions in the evaluation and find out how much your health and wellbeing has improved after completing the CBR Program.

### Set your goals

Write down your three main goals related to your wellbeing. To find the purpose in what you do is crucial to success. Setting goals in connection with breathing retraining creates more motivation and meaningfulness. When you set your goals, make sure you're not over-challenging yourself so that you will be able to enjoy the journey. The purpose of the breathing retraining is to reduce stress in your life, not add more. **Please note: To set a goal, you don't need to know how to achieve the goal.**

***Examples of goals may be:***

- Experience fewer conflicts with people around me
- Reduce my medication
- Take better care of my body
- Improve my breathing habits
- Get rid of my recurring colds
- Be able to calm myself more easily when I get upset
- Increase the number of days where I do not drink alcohol
- Have a more relaxed and happy mood
- Have more energy
- Reach my ideal weight
- Increase physical activity
- Reduce my cravings for sweets

### Visualize your goals

The more emotionally involved you are in a goal, the greater the chance that you will achieve it. One way to engage your emotions is to connect it to an image by visualizing your goal. For example:

- *Goal:* To have more energy. *Visualization:* Waking up rested and refreshed, full of energy.
- *Goal:* To reach my ideal weight. *Visualization:* The scale shows my target weight and I'm very happy with my body when I look at myself in the mirror.
- *Goal:* To reduce my alcohol intake. *Visualization:* A party where I'm sober, relaxed and full of confidence.
- *Goal:* To score more goals or come first when I play sports. *Visualization:* See myself crossing the finishing line first, or pumping the air in celebration after scoring the winning goal.

Your visualization should answer the questions: **"How do I know that I've reached my goal?"** and **"How does it feel when I've reached my goal?"**

### MY THREE MOST IMPORTANT GOALS ARE:

1. ______________________________

 Visualization: ______________________________

2. ______________________________

 Visualization: ______________________________

3. ______________________________

 Visualization: ______________________________

### Training schedule

Enter details of your daily workouts in the training schedule on the next page:

- Tape = place an X if you slept with taped mouth.
- Relaxator = the number of minutes you used the Relaxator Breathing Retrainer.
- Physical activity = the number of minutes of physical activity with your mouth closed.

| MON | TUE | WED | THUR | FRI | SAT | SUN |
|---|---|---|---|---|---|---|
| **DAY 1**<br>Relaxator ____<br>Phys. act. ____<br>Tape ☐ | **DAY 2**<br>Relaxator ____<br>Phys. act. ____<br>Tape ☐ | **DAY 3**<br>Relaxator ____<br>Phys. act. ____<br>Tape ☐ | **DAY 4**<br>Relaxator ____<br>Phys. act. ____<br>Tape ☐ | **DAY 5**<br>Relaxator ____<br>Phys. act. ____<br>Tape ☐ | **DAY 6**<br>Relaxator ____<br>Phys. act. ____<br>Tape ☐ | **DAY 7**<br>Relaxator ____<br>Phys. act. ____<br>Tape ☐ |
| **DAY 8**<br>Relaxator ____<br>Phys. act. ____<br>Tape ☐ | **DAY 9**<br>Relaxator ____<br>Phys. act. ____<br>Tape ☐ | **DAY 10**<br>Relaxator ____<br>Phys. act. ____<br>Tape ☐ | **DAY 11**<br>Relaxator ____<br>Phys. act. ____<br>Tape ☐ | **DAY 12**<br>Relaxator ____<br>Phys. act. ____<br>Tape ☐ | **DAY 13**<br>Relaxator ____<br>Phys. act. ____<br>Tape ☐ | **DAY 14**<br>Relaxator ____<br>Phys. act. ____<br>Tape ☐ |
| **DAY 15**<br>Relaxator ____<br>Phys. act. ____<br>Tape ☐ | **DAY 16**<br>Relaxator ____<br>Phys. act. ____<br>Tape ☐ | **DAY 17**<br>Relaxator ____<br>Phys. act. ____<br>Tape ☐ | **DAY 18**<br>Relaxator ____<br>Phys. act. ____<br>Tape ☐ | **DAY 19**<br>Relaxator ____<br>Phys. act. ____<br>Tape ☐ | **DAY 20**<br>Relaxator ____<br>Phys. act. ____<br>Tape ☐ | **DAY 21**<br>Relaxator ____<br>Phys. act. ____<br>Tape ☐ |
| **DAY 22**<br>Relaxator ____<br>Phys. act. ____<br>Tape ☐ | **DAY 23**<br>Relaxator ____<br>Phys. act. ____<br>Tape ☐ | **DAY 24**<br>Relaxator ____<br>Phys. act. ____<br>Tape ☐ | **DAY 25**<br>Relaxator ____<br>Phys. act. ____<br>Tape ☐ | **DAY 26**<br>Relaxator ____<br>Phys. act. ____<br>Tape ☐ | **DAY 27**<br>Relaxator ____<br>Phys. act. ____<br>Tape ☐ | **DAY 28**<br>Relaxator ____<br>Phys. act. ____<br>Tape ☐ |

**Breathing habits in everyday life**

During the *28-Day Breathing Retraining*, once each week (day 7, 14, 21 and 28) you should write down the situations and emotions that you realize trigger stressed breathing, i.e., fast breathing, irregular breathing, periodic breathing, shallow breathing, mouth breathing or noisy breathing—coughing, clearing of throat, blocked nose, sniffling, etc.

***Enter a number between 1 and 5 that you feel best represents how stressed/ poor your respiration has been during the week.***

*1 = very often, 2 = often, 3 = sometimes, 4 = rarely, 5 = never.*

| ***My breathing is poor when I:*** | Week 1 | Week 2 | Week 3 | Week 4 |
|---|---|---|---|---|
| 1. Am driving | | | | |
| 2. Do housework | | | | |
| 3. Concentrate | | | | |
| 4. Do physical activity | | | | |
| 5. Am talking | | | | |
| 6. Use the computer | | | | |
| 7. Watch TV | | | | |
| 8. Am sleeping | | | | |
| ***My breathing is poor when I get:*** | | | | |
| 9. Angry, irritated | | | | |
| 10. Depressed, sad | | | | |
| 11. Stressed | | | | |
| 12. Afraid, worried | | | | |
| **TOTAL** | | | | |

The maximum score is 60. A high score indicates that you have good breathing habits in everyday life. A score below 25 indicates that improving your breathing in different situations and when experiencing different emotions can benefit you greatly.

### *Tips*

In the beginning it may be advantageous to set an alarm to go off a few times per day as a reminder to pay attention to your breathing.

### Evaluation

After the *28-Day Conscious Breathing Retraining Program*, please answer the 20 questions in the breathing index found in Chapter 3 once again. Then complete the evaluation below:

1. Has breathing retraining resulted in any changes in regards to:
   **Breathing Index:** Before: ________ After: ________
   **Breathing Habits:** Week 1: ________ Week 4: ________
2. Has your breathing awareness increased? If so, in what way?
3. How did breathing retraining help you reach or get closer to your specified goals?
4. Do you feel any improvement in the following (skip any that do not relate to you):

| | None | | | | | | | | | Very big |
|---|---|---|---|---|---|---|---|---|---|---|
| Concentration | 0 | 1 | 2 | 3 | 4 | 5 | 6 | 7 | 8 | 9 | 10 |
| Energy levels | 0 | 1 | 2 | 3 | 4 | 5 | 6 | 7 | 8 | 9 | 10 |
| Stress | 0 | 1 | 2 | 3 | 4 | 5 | 6 | 7 | 8 | 9 | 10 |
| Sleep | 0 | 1 | 2 | 3 | 4 | 5 | 6 | 7 | 8 | 9 | 10 |
| Mood | 0 | 1 | 2 | 3 | 4 | 5 | 6 | 7 | 8 | 9 | 10 |
| Pain, ache | 0 | 1 | 2 | 3 | 4 | 5 | 6 | 7 | 8 | 9 | 10 |
| Heart | 0 | 1 | 2 | 3 | 4 | 5 | 6 | 7 | 8 | 9 | 10 |
| Airways (nose, throat, lungs) | 0 | 1 | 2 | 3 | 4 | 5 | 6 | 7 | 8 | 9 | 10 |
| Fear, anxiety, depression | 0 | 1 | 2 | 3 | 4 | 5 | 6 | 7 | 8 | 9 | 10 |
| Physical fitness | 0 | 1 | 2 | 3 | 4 | 5 | 6 | 7 | 8 | 9 | 10 |

## STUDY CONFIRMS THE POSITIVE EFFECT OF BREATHING RETRAINING

In an ongoing study of the effect of breathing retraining it seems evident that it has a great positive effect on our health and wellbeing.[1] The statistics compiled from 40 subjects that have done the *Conscious Breathing Retraining Program* shows that:

- Breathing Index has increased by 25 percent.
- Breathing Habits have improved by 48 percent.

The study further showed that, on average, the participants:

- Slept with a taped mouth during five out of seven nights.
- Completed 36 min of physical activity daily with their mouths closed.
- Used the Relaxator Breathing Retrainer for 29 minutes each day.

The evaluation shows that improved breathing habits have a significant positive impact in a variety of different areas, such as reduced stress, better sleep, increased ability to concentrate, and more energy. On average, a full 88% of the participants experienced an improvement in these areas. 43% experienced a significant improvement relating to sleep, and 35% felt that their energy levels had improved significantly.

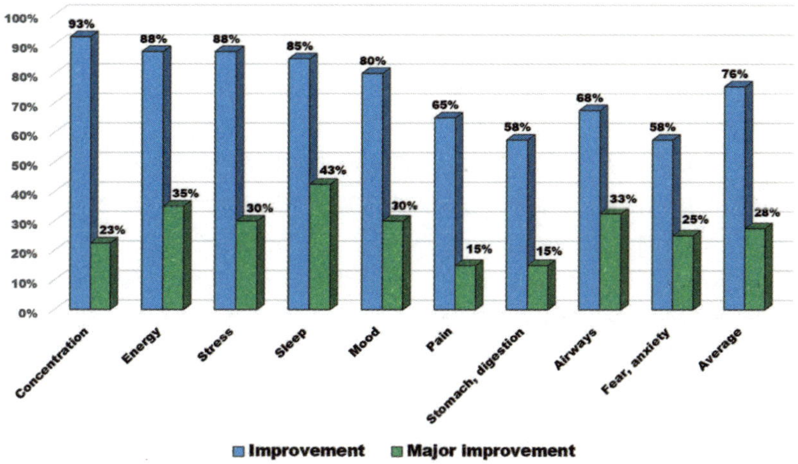


Note: Improvement = everyone that specified 1-10 in the evaluation. Major improvement = everyone that specified 7-10 in the evaluation.

### *Tips*

Do the *28-Day Conscious Breathing Retraining Program* together with a friend so you can inspire each other. You can also appoint a friend as your coach where you call him or her once a week and report about your efforts and progress.

### *More breathing exercises:*

#### Exercise 8 — Observe how you breathe in your daily life

Stop and pay attention to your breathing and note if it's in line with the five principles, e.g., nose, stomach, slow, rhythmic, and silent. You can do this many times a day and in different situations, for example:

- Set the alarm on your mobile phone to go off at intervals throughout the day. When the alarm rings, check your breathing against the five principles.
- Put a note on your computer screen. Each time you see the note, pay attention to your breathing.

Is there room for improvement? What is your posture like when you breathe like this? What are you thinking of? What emotions do you experience? What are your stress levels? Do you breathe in a certain way in particular situations? Is there a connection between the way you breathe, and the thoughts or feelings that you are experiencing?

#### Exercise 9 — Resistance breathing

1. Tighten the muscles in your throat, squeeze your vocal cords, and force the air out through your nose. The muscles of your abdomen and chest will tighten automatically.
2. Squeezing the air through pursed lips is an alternative to tightening the muscles in the throat.
3. Allow the air to enter in a relaxed way on inhalation and just note how it passes down into your abdomen.
4. Keep your breathing calm, slow and relaxed throughout the exercise.
5. Repeat steps 1-3 for 10-30 breaths.

### Exercise 10 — Laugh deep in your belly

To laugh deep down in your belly is a very good way to get the breathing muscles to relax. It's well known that deeper relaxation is achieved when you first tighten a muscle and then allow it to relax, compared with only relaxation. When you laugh deep down in your stomach the muscles are tightened and all the respiratory muscles are activated. After a laugh, the activated muscles are more relaxed, and since a relaxed muscle works better than a strained muscle, your breathing will improve. Many of us also have tense jaws and facial muscles that also get a much-needed dose of exercise when we laugh. Make it a habit to laugh during a few breaths, say 10-20 seconds, a few times per day. Just start to laugh, for no obvious reason. In addition to exercising your respiratory muscles and getting them to relax, feelings of happiness will spread throughout your body. The laughter exercise is much appreciated on my courses, and the participants are often inspired by this movie on YouTube:
*http://youtu.be/9xH0xorgUoI*

### Exercise 11 — Fill up your lungs to the maximum

Breathe big, deep breaths and fill your lungs as much as you possibly can, and then exhale slowly, slowly. You don't need to squeeze the last bit of air out before inhaling again. One way to fill up your lungs to the maximum is to first inhale "down into your abdomen," thereafter filling your chest, and lastly the space near your collarbone. Continue to breathe like this for 2–5 minutes.

This exercise activates all the respiratory muscles in your stomach, chest and neck and makes them relax, as they are first stretched and then released. Furthermore, the circulation of air increases in your lungs, and the old trapped air can be removed. The number of alveoli participating in the gas exchange will increase, since the inhaled air will reach even those alveoli at the bottom of your lungs. The exercise is like spring-cleaning your home, opening all the windows so the old stale air is blown out.

# Chapter 5 - Conscious Breathing for Stress Reduction

*You are stuck in a traffic jam and about to be late to an important meeting. Your kitchen is a disaster, your children are hungry and restless, the phone rings and you discover the dog has stolen from the countertop the meatballs you were defrosting for dinner. You get an unfriendly text message or email. Your partner is upset and yells at you. How is your breathing affected when you read these lines? Does it get stressed or stuck? Taking control of your breathing is the best way to take control of your inner stress.*

In this chapter we shall take a closer look at mental stress, fear, anxiety, and other emotional stressors that can affect your breathing. Let's start with a definition of stress and how it affects your nervous and hormonal systems.

## WHAT IS STRESS?

Hans Seyle, the famous stress researcher, coined the word 'stress' in the 1930's. Stress can be defined as "everything that forces an organism to adapt to new situations." Stress is not bad in itself. On the contrary, it's necessary since it forces us to think in new ways, to grow, to learn new things and gain new insights. Man's ability to handle stress and adapt is unique. It's the reason why the human race has been able to procreate all over the planet and to survive and thrive in very different situations, e.g., the Eskimos in extreme cold, desert nomads in extreme heat, and hill tribes at altitudes of several thousand meters.

| Signs of different types of stress | | |
|---|---|---|
| Physical | Emotional | Mental |
| Symptoms, diseases | Restlessness | Hard to concentrate |
| Injuries | Anger, irritation, hate | Dwell on things in the past |
| Low energy, cravings | Jealousy | No motivation |
| Inactivity/over activity | Grief, depression | Judgmental good/bad |
| Heat/cold | Lack of appreciation | Long "to do" lists |
| Reduced sexual libido | Passivity, apathy | Lives in past/future |

If the stress is too great and lasts too long, however, it breaks down our resources and our ability to adapt, which in turn increases our vulnerability and risk of succumbing to disease.

When we experience problems or adversity in our life it may be attributed to some form of imbalance, which we can also call stress. The stress can be physical, emotional, mental, spiritual, or a combination of all four. When we go through a stressful period in our lives, or experience a trauma, such as the death of a close family member, physical injury, divorce, or unemployment, the stress is reflected in our breathing patterns. If the impaired breathing continues even when the stress has passed, a vicious circle is established in which the new breathing pattern is cemented, which itself becomes a source of trauma and stress over time.

Your body constantly prioritizes what is most important. If you run, muscular activity is prioritized, when you eat it's digestion, and when you are ill your immune system gets a greater part of your body's resources. Providing your body with oxygen is always a top priority. Since we only survive a few minutes without oxygen we need a constant inflow of this gas. An impaired breathing pattern increases our basic stress because it both decreases oxygenation, and places a greater strain on available resources to sustain optimum oxygen levels.

The worse our breathing is, the higher the basic stress, i.e., the higher our mental, emotional and physical stress. Conversely, improving our breathing pattern not only lowers the inner stress, but also increases our overall well being by enhancing our physical and mental strength and improving our ability to concentrate, as well as our experience of harmony, joy and fulfillment.

## STRESS ACTIVATES SURVIVAL FUNCTIONS

The peripheral part of our nervous system that controls functions such as heartbeat, digestion, and the muscles in blood vessels and airways is called the autonomic nervous system. It's divided into a sympathetic, activating part (the gas pedal) and a parasympathetic calming part (the brake). The sympathetic part prepares our body for increased activity and is active in the fight/flight response, while the parasympathetic part influences rest, digestion and energy conservation.

### Examples of functions of the autonomic nervous system

Most organs in our body, including the brain cortex, have nerve fibers from both parts of the autonomic nervous system. These parts work together, always striving to maintain our body in balance, and each has a direct impact on the other. The better they cooperate the better we feel.

| | Sympathetic | Parasympathetic |
|---|---|---|
| Muscles in blood vessels | Constrict | Relax |
| Heartbeats | Increase | Decrease |
| Blood vessels in brain, gut, skin | Constrict | - |
| Movements in the intestines | Decrease | Increase |
| Blood vessels in skeletal muscles | Expand | - |
| Pupils | Expand | Relax |
| Sweat glands | Stimulated | - |

When we experience stress, our body will activate the sympathetic part of our nervous system, which among other things increases our heart rate. Less blood is directed to our brain and digestive system, and more blood is directed to the muscles of the limbs (skeletal muscles). We also sweat, and our pupils dilate.

#### Reducing the perceived stress

Sympathetic activity has been important for our survival throughout human evolution. If we look at life today, we find that we rarely end up in situations that require us to react with our innate fight or flight response. When the adrenaline pumps around our body it alters our breathing pattern to prepare us to run away from danger or defend ourselves. This stone-age reaction doesn't serve us well when we sit on an office chair, and the stress consists of dealing with demanding emails or customers barking at us over the phone. We will neither fight nor flee; instead, we just sit still in our office and think evil thoughts or sigh in resignation. Mental or emotional stress that isn't accompanied by physical activity or abdominal and rhythmic breathing accumulates in our body and will eventually cause a lot of damage.

High sympathetic activity is like driving down the freeway at 80 miles per hour; we have tunnel vision, and to a large extent we react instinctively to what is happening. When I collided with a deer a few years ago, I had no idea that I applied the brakes very hard until I got out of the car and noted the acrid smell of burnt rubber. My reaction was automatic and instinctive, and if we in our daily lives operate mainly from sympathetic stimulation, we will invariably react instinctively to a high degree in different situations. When these reactions are repeated they eventually create firm habits, and stress will, over time, become our habitual way of dealing with life's events.

However, first assessing the situation and then acting in a conscious, creative, and intelligent way can help us handle most challenges in life. Through our breathing we can take control of the

### Sympathetic part (activate)

### Stressed breathing

- Mouth breathing
- Chest breathing
- Fast, tense breathing
- Irregular breathing
- Noisy, big breathing

### Creates imbalance

- Increased stress
- Symptoms, diseases
- "Life is a struggle"
- Repeat old habits
- Cell memories updated

### Parasympathetic part (calm down)

### Conscious Breathing

- Nose breathing
- Diaphragmatic breathing
- Slow, relaxed breathing
- Rhythmical breathing
- Quiet, reduced breathing

### Creates balance

- Decreased stress
- Improved health
- More energy and harmony
- New habits
- Cell memories updated

When we experience incoming stimuli as stressful, the sympathetic part of our nervous system is activated, and our breathing changes. By taking control of our breathing and breathing consciously, we can affect our nervous system in a more parasympathetic direction. This lowers our heart rate, improves our digestion, and relaxes the muscles in our blood vessels and airways. Over time we teach our body to process incoming stimuli in a calmer way. New habits are established and our cellular memories – instincts, life experiences, values, etc. – are updated. It is similar to bringing up a saved document on your computer, changing it, and saving the new, updated information on the hard drive.

autonomous part of our nervous system and stimulate the parasympathetic part with suitable breathing techniques. With increased parasympathetic activity we have a greater ability to make wise decisions when faced with difficult situations, making it easier to calm our nervous system down long enough for our intelligence and creativity to start influencing the way we handle the challenges of everyday life.

There is a reason that the maximum speed outside schools is 20 miles an hour and not 80 miles per hour. At a low speed, it's likely that the parasympathetic part of our nervous system is more active. When we drive slowly, we have a wider perspective and are able to respond consciously instead of reacting instinctively. When we breathe slowly and rhythmically in response to stress, we are better equipped to meet the challenges appropriately instead of letting instinctive responses take over.

## IMPAIRED BREATHING INCREASES STRESS HORMONES

In the body, we have different glands secreting hormones for different bodily functions. The thyroid produces hormones that affect our metabolism, and sex hormones, like estrogen and testosterone, are produced in the ovaries and testicles. Stress hormones such as adrenaline and cortisol are secreted by the adrenal glands, which are located on top of the kidneys and shaped a bit like a hat.

When our body experiences stress, the adrenaline and cortisol levels become elevated. Adrenaline dilates our airways, increases our respiration and heart rate, constricts the blood vessels to the organs in our abdomen, and increases blood flow to muscles in our arms and legs. Our body is simply preparing itself to meet the impending danger that it believes the stress signals indicate.

In a study where twelve medical students hyperventilated normal air, the stress hormone adrenaline increased by 360 percent. When hyperventilation took place with carbon dioxide-enriched air (five percent), the adrenaline levels remained unchanged![1] Hyperventilating with normal air causes a low carbon dioxide level and thus leads to a strong stress response. This is partly because less oxygen reaches the cells (the Bohr effect), and partly because the airways and blood vessels will constrict and impair the gas exchange in the lungs. A vicious circle is established where the adrenaline and the over-breathing reinforce each other.

As mentioned before, another hormone that is secreted during stress is cortisol, which acts as an anti-inflammatory agent. Inflammation is always present in our body. It is created by our immune system to take care of foreign invaders and injured tissues. Inflammation increases when we are stressed and eat too much sugar, unsaturated fats, sodas, and other junk food.[2]

Inflammation also occurs when we expose our airways to polluted urban city air, cold air, dry indoor air, cigarette smoke, bacteria and other particles in the inhaled air. In response, our body increases the secretion of cortisol, since it suppresses inflammation. Eventually, the increased cortisol secretion exhausts the adrenal glands. When they're too exhausted to produce the amount of cortisol needed, we become more sensitive to substances that cause inflammation, and we may start to experience allergic symptoms.[3]

Conscious Breathing reduces stress hormone levels by decreasing inflammation and keeping the airways open. When we calm our breathing down, we also signal to our body that it can relax. Adrenaline production may then be reduced since we don't have to be constantly on red alert, ready to fight or flee.

One of the most efficient ways to reduce stress is to make sure that our airways are open and functioning well.

| Facts about cortisol | |
|---|---|
| **Released under stress.** Cortisol increases when the demand for fast energy is high and when the airways are narrow due to inflammation. | |
| **Effect** | **Anti-inflammatory (regulates activity of the immune system)**<br>**Increases blood sugar**<br>**Reduces formation of skeletal bones** |
| **Cortisol is used in medication (as cortisone)** for the treatment of diseases and problems of the mucosa, in the heart, blood, airways and lungs, in the digestive system, the skin, eyes and the nervous system. Cortisone is used to reduce states of swelling and inflammation, as well as to ease the symptoms of allergies, cancer, viral infections and immune and autoimmune diseases. | |

| Facts about adrenaline | |
|---|---|
| **Prepares the body** for physical activity (fight/flight response). Physical activity can increase the levels of adrenaline in the blood 10-fold and under stress they can increase 50 times or more. | |
| **Effect** | **Increases heart rate**<br>**Widens airways**<br>**Constricts blood vessels to organs in the abdomen**<br>**Dilates blood vessels to muscles in the arms and legs** |
| **Adrenaline or adrenaline-like substances are used** for treatment of cardiac arrest, irregular heartbeat, asthma, anaphylactic shock and low blood pressure. | |

### TOO MUCH STIMULATION CREATES BREATHING PROBLEMS

In one study, participants were stimulated to over-breathe while subjected to low concentrations of specific smells. After only a few repetitions of the test, the smell alone was enough to induce hyperventilation among the participants.[4]

The amount of stimuli you are exposed to today is far greater than it was just 50 years ago. Back then we didn't have cell phones, Facebook, email, computer games, etc. Music, TV and radio were also broadcast significantly less often. The amount of artificial chemicals in our food, air and water were far fewer too. The increase has been dramatic, with thousands of new chemicals being introduced each year, many of them inadequately tested.[5] Moreover, all these types of artificial stimuli intensify stress in the body and distort breathing.

One of the greatest challenges of our time is to be able to handle the huge amount of stimuli we are exposed to every day AND at the same time maintain rhythmic and relaxed breathing. Experiences of war or accidents, in real life or via news, newspapers, and films, amplify thoughts and feelings that change our breathing pattern. We might be sitting still but our breathing is prepared for fight or flight. In the end it might be enough to simply hear the introduction to the news, or see a headline, to trigger stressed breathing, which creates a domino effect where our thoughts, feelings and physical body are influenced negatively, and the impaired breathing habit becomes the norm.

**Our cellular memories control the response to incoming stimuli**

Our brain collects information about what is going on around us and inside our body via our senses, our organs, and the different activities we engage in. The information is processed and reconciled against our cellular memories (information stored in the body's "hard drive" consisting of genetics, instinct, life experiences, values, habits, etc.) The reconciliation answers the question "Hmm, how should I react to these stimuli?" When an appropriate response has been selected our brain sends out signals to achieve the desired results.

The fast way to influence our body is through neurotransmitters in our nervous system, and the slow way is via hormones secreted into our blood. Both the nervous and hormonal systems are constantly active in the endeavor to maintain balance in the body.

We have an excellent opportunity to influence both our hormonal system and nervous system through breathing, which makes it possible to update our cellular memories. By saving new information on our "cellular hard drive," we can create a new response to the same stimuli.

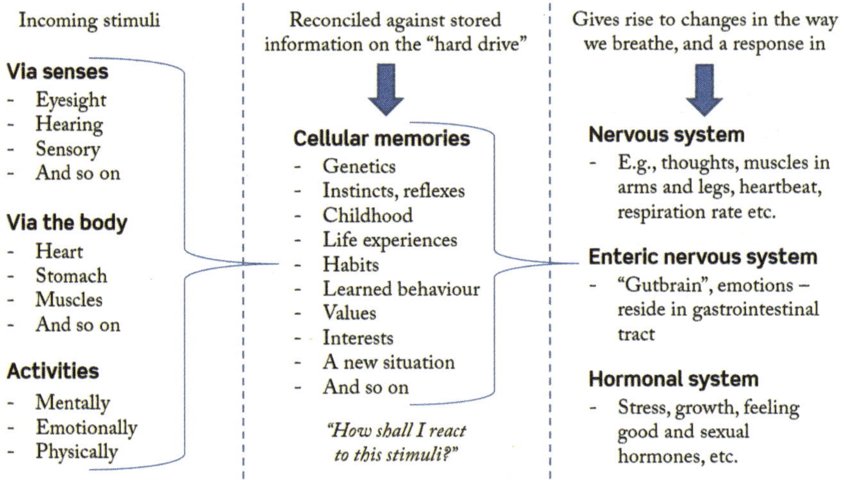


Incoming stimuli are checked against information stored in our cells, which consist of genetics, values, habits, interests, etc. An appropriate response is formed and both our nervous and hormonal systems are activated to achieve the desired results. Problems can arise if our learned behavior, values, etc., are in conflict with our conscious desires. We end up feeling that life is not going our way. Through breathing, we have great opportunities to influence both our hormonal and nervous systems, and update our cellular memories so that the response to incoming stimuli is consistent with what we consciously want to achieve.

## CONSCIOUS BREATHING BRINGS US BACK TO THE BASELINE

Imagine life as a tennis game. Sometimes we are close to the net and on other occasions we are far back in the corner. Sometimes we hit the ball with a volley, sometimes on the rebound, sometimes we have a lot of time on our hands, and on other occasions we are in a rush to hit the ball. Sometimes the ball will pass the net and sometimes we miss the ball altogether. It's just as in life, sometimes you are on an up and sometimes you are on a down.

Any good tennis player knows that the most important action, after hitting the ball, is always to strive to return to the starting position at the baseline so as to be in the best possible position to face the ball again.

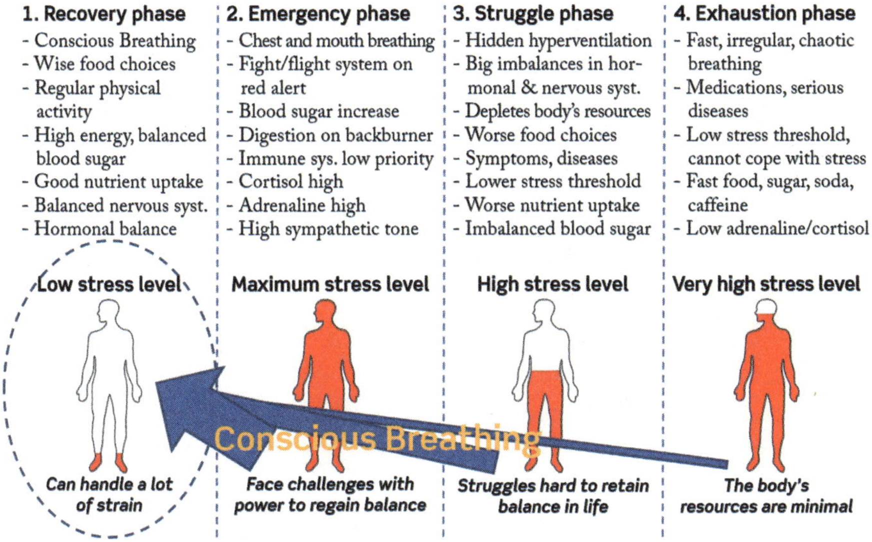


**The problem is that we spend too little time in the recovery phase and too much time in the emergency and struggle phases. The body cannot cope with the prolonged stress and we end up in the exhaustion phase. Conscious Breathing is a powerful tool to take us from the emergency, struggle, and exhaustion phases back to the recovery phase.**

Experiencing stress and/or not feeling well are signs that our body is in a state of imbalance, emotionally, physically or mentally, and we are off the baseline. If we haven't slept during the night or haven't eaten for a long period, the stress can easily be fixed by sleeping or eating.

However, in many situations where we experience stress, the best way to return to the baseline is by reducing our breathing volume and starting to breathe slowly, deeply (not big) and rhythmically. This is the place we need to return to over and over again to regain balance after stress, and to be able to create the life we want. It's actually as simple as that. It works when we are crying or are angry, have a racing mind, or are experiencing pain because we've hurt ourselves.

Positive thinking, or the ability to feel emotions of thankfulness and forgiveness, works best when we feel good, but is not that easy to apply when life seems to have turned against us. The solution is the same as mentioned before—return to the baseline through Conscious Breathing before moving on.

### Catch your breath with Conscious Breathing

If you repeatedly experience life as a struggle and think "Oh, soon the working day/week/year will come to an end so I can catch up on my rest tonight/sleep in this weekend/relax on my vacation," it indicates that you continuously live above your resources and don't achieve the recovery you need. Optimal breathing, on the other hand, provides recovery in every breathing cycle. The quickest way to lower your physical, mental or emotional stress is to reduce your breathing volume and take more and more of your 20-25,000 daily breaths in a slow, deep, rhythmical and relaxed way.

## DARE TO FACE YOUR FEARS

The feelings of fear we experience at the dentist, at the clinic before getting an injection, or when we see a spider, can make our breathing get "stuck," or become fast and shallow, which reduces the movement of the diaphragm.

To release mental or emotional stress we can do something physical, such as laughing, crying, singing, hitting a sand bag to get rid of anger, or go for a run to reduce anxiety. Another way to release stress is to take control of our breathing habits and make sure that we breathe deeply and utilize our diaphragm. The muscle movements that occur in every breathing cycle, when we breathe optimally, also represent physical activity. When we ensure that our breathing is slow, abdominal and relaxed, our fear or feeling of distress will be reduced without too much effort. You can experience this for yourself: put your arms over your chest, grab around your upper arms with your fingers and squeeze the arms towards your chest while holding your breath. This exercise makes you feel tense and stressed, and you may notice that sensations of worry and fear may follow. If you let go of the pressure against the chest, exhale, and start to breathe in and out through your nose as slow, relaxed and rhythmically as possible, the difference is unmistakable. The expression, "The danger is over, now you can breathe and relax," reflects this well.

Your breathing can act like a friend who is always there for you, making you feel more confident and allowing you to dare to face your fears to a greater degree, instead of running away from them. As you reduce your fear of forgiving, of talking in front of people, or of standing up for what is important to you, your self-esteem grows.

At the same time we do have fears for a reason. Fear's purpose is to help us avoid danger, although quite often we would benefit from overcoming our fears so they are more in proportion to the actual danger it represents.

## NASAL BREATHING CONTRIBUTES TO A BALANCED NERVOUS SYSTEM

Did you know that we breathe through one nostril at a time when our body is in balance? It's well known in both Eastern wisdom and Western research that our nose behaves in a cyclical way. The size of the erectile tissue inside the nose increases and decreases to make the airflow alternate between the nostrils. After a certain amount of time, the erectile tissues shift in size, and we begin to breathe through the other nostril. In a study of 20 participants, it was found that the nose showed cyclical behavior in all participants. The cycle where the shift from one nostril to the other occurred lasted between 30 minutes and two hours and 30 minutes.[6]

Other studies have shown a clear link between the nasal cycle and alternating dominance throughout the body. When coal dust was breathed in through the left nostril, much greater quantity of coal dust was stored in the right lung and vice versa.[7]

Another study showed how the shift occurs in the brain. When the airflow goes in and out through the right nostril, the left part of the brain is more active, and vice versa. In the study, 20 participants were subjected to a test before and after breathing in and out through a) the left nostril, b) the right nostril, c) alternating nasal breathing, and d) a control test where they breathed normally. The test consisted of various left-brain dominant tasks and the results showed "significantly improved results, with fewer errors, when participants breathed through the right nostril and alternated nasal breathing." [8]

***Try for yourself:***

You can easily test what impact breathing has on your fear, anxiety and panic. The next time those emotions are about to take over, you can:

- Use the Relaxator to take control of your breathing, or;
- Breathe in and out through a bag. Since exhaled air contains a hundred times more carbon dioxide than inhaled air, breathing through a bag lets you inhale a portion of the carbon dioxide you just exhaled. By doing this, you will build up the carbon dioxide levels that drop when you over-breathe. When patients experiencing panic attacks seek medical help at a hospital they are often told to breathe slowly in and out of a paper bag to help them calm down.

**Exercise 12 — Breathe through your fears**

This exercise help you face your fears and reduce them or make them disappear altogether. First, write down a list of five or more situations and persons that challenge you and make you scared, upset, angry, annoyed or stressed out. Examples of fears are: Poverty, criticism, poor health, loss of love of someone, old age, death, public speaking, failing, standing up for myself, losing my job, getting hurt, spiders, flying, the dentist, getting a shot, asthma attack, heart attack, accident, etc.

1.________________________________________

2.________________________________________

3.________________________________________

4.________________________________________

5.________________________________________

Secondly, do the exercise below for 5-10 minutes

1. Think about the listed situations and persons and make them as vivid as possible by visualizing them. Add colors, sounds, moving images and other people to the scene. Allow your emotions to become stronger and stronger. You are fully attached to your fears, in the midst of the "hurricane" facing them.
2. Notice how you breathe when you think about those terrible situations. If your breathing is stressed and you tense up, it's natural and perfectly okay. If you have problems getting in touch with your fears, try breathing fast and shallow, or hold your breath altogether.
3. Now, make your breathing slow, rhythmic and abdominal by extending the exhalation. Your friend, the breath, is with you all the time to make you feel comfortable and safe in the midst of the hard situation. (If you happen to have a Relaxator, this is a perfect time to start using it.)
4. As you apply Conscious Breathing, change perspective and detach yourself more and more from these harsh feelings. Imagine sitting at the cinema watching yourself and your fears on the screen. Imagine the room bigger and bigger and distance yourself further and further from the screen.

After some practice it's common that fear and anger is transformed into curiosity, understanding, humbleness, relief, etc. At this point you may be able to see the true nature of your challenges—an invaluable source to help you grow as a person. If we want to be stronger, we'll face challenges that makes us stronger when we overcome them. If we want love, we'll meet people to forgive. If we want to be braver, we'll get opportunities to challenge our fears. So to grow we need to face our fears, not run away from them.

I did a similar exercise in a Neuro-Linguistic Programming course (NLP) a few years ago, and it was such a strong experience that it helped me overcome my fear of public speaking. At that point I didn't have any special knowledge of the importance of breathing, but still today I can remember how my breathing pattern became very powerful, rhythmic and deep during the exercise. I'm convinced that my breathing helped me to challenge and eventually conquer one of the biggest fears of my life.

### Exercise 13 — Calm your body and your mind with three prolonged exhalations

This exercise is suitable in situations when you are about to lose control. If possible, find a place to be alone or step back for a moment, as this will increase the chance that you will not say or do anything that you will later regret.

1. Take three (or more) deep breaths (not large ones).
2. Breathe in and out through your nose.
3. Draw the air into your abdomen by focusing on your exhalation and exhale slowly.
4. It's important that your exhalation is longer than your inhalation.

Prolonged exhalation has three important effects:

- It increases the oxygenation of your brain. A brain with too little oxygen is a stressed brain, and this can cause us to find ourselves in fight/flight mode, focused on threats and survival. When our brain is supplied with more oxygen it reduces brain stress, which leads to more consciousness and the ability to find solutions to the problems at hand.
- The diaphragmatic movement in our abdomen calms down upset feelings.
- Focusing on your breath opens up new perspectives. It's easier to gain a wider perspective on what is happening and see the bigger picture. You've heard it said, "We will laugh about this ten years from now." So why not laugh about it now?

### Exercise 14 — Keep cool

This exercise is a challenge designed to improve your ability to remain calm under stress.

- Choose a situation or person that makes you stressed. It can be a "pushy" telephone sales person, a demanding boss, or being stuck in a traffic jam when you are about to be late to a meeting.

- The challenge is that you should be able to remain calm in a situation that normally makes you feel stressed.
- Follow your breathing and see it as a friend who is with you, supporting you. Breathe in and out through your nose and extend your exhalation to enhance relaxation, reduce your breathing volume, and to make your breathing abdominal and rhythmical.

When you manage to stay calm, do you notice a difference in the other person? Does the other person also calm down? Do you experience the situation differently than usual? How do you feel afterwards, when you've managed to stay calm?

Conscious Breathing has helped me many times to remain calm when things get tough. In the past, being irritated, and having a short fuse, has led to many unnecessary verbal conflicts in my life. Nowadays, thanks to being able to stop myself before I let the old learned behavior take over, I hardly ever lose my temper. When we choose a different path enough times, we establish new automatic habits and behaviors—our cellular memories have been updated.

**Exercise 15 — The benefits of alternating nasal breathing**

We have established that we can affect the autonomic nervous system and increase the parasympathetic activity using Conscious Breathing, and if we want to enhance the effect of nasal breathing further, we can apply the exercise of alternating nasal breathing.

1. Close your left nostril with your finger and inhale through your right nostril.
2. On exhalation, close your right nostril and breathe out through your left nostril.
3. Again, breathe in through your left nostril before you switch again so that exhalation occurs through your right nostril.
4. Left in, right out, right in, left out, left in, right out, etc. Continue for 10–20 breaths, or until you feel relaxed.

**Exercise 16 — Coming Home**

This exercise helps you become centered and get in touch with your true self.

1. Sit comfortably with a straight back and close your eyes. Breathe slowly in and out through your nose, or in through your nose and out through the Relaxator. Focus on your breathing and notice how, as it becomes more relaxed and rhythmical, a nice feeling of warmth and relaxation spreads throughout your body.
2. Place your hands on your belly, just below your navel. When you inhale, imagine that the air ends up here.
3. Imagine that the center of your body is here, just below the navel. This place is your inner home, your inner core, the center of your primordial force, your true self. You can always return to this place when you feel stressed, sad or angry. Here you'll find peace and comfort.
4. Your breathing volume is reduced and with each abdominal inhalation, your connection with your inner core increases, and you feel yourself becoming increasingly calm and centered. With every slow exhalation, this feeling of harmony and calm spreads throughout your entire body – your legs, your stomach, your chest and your head.
5. It's your thoughts, feelings and dreams that make YOU unique. When you are in touch with your inner core you can be who you really are. You feel safe, and you dare to express your true self more and more often.
6. On the next deep inhalation, allow the connection with your inner core, your true self, your primordial force, to become twice as big.
7. On the next exhalation allow the sense of calmness and harmony to spread throughout your body, expanding and becoming twice as big. notice how these wonderful feelings reach every single part of your body, completely without effort.
8. You can use this abdominal, slow, rhythmical breathing exercise to access your inner core – this safe, protected place that is always within you – any time you want.

# Chapter 6 – Conscious Breathing for Sports and Exercise

*Breathing well when you exercise ensures that your energy production is efficient, while keeping the consumption of available energy low, so you will consequently achieve more with less effort. This leads to increased endurance and faster recovery.*

Our body performs in amazing ways if we provide the right conditions. Balance between exercise and rest, mental training, good nutrition, proper techniques when running etc., and good exercise programs are all key ingredients for good athletic performance.

However, a very important piece of the puzzle—how we breathe—seems to have been abandoned in many sports. Breathing is critical to your survival. It's the first thing you do when you are born. When exercising, your breathing patterns are important, because you can't run, swim, cycle or maintain concentration, strength and endurance at an optimum level if your breathing is impaired. Yet, how many of us are actively focusing on improving our respiration when running, cycling, playing football, golf, tennis or basketball? From what I've found in my research, the knowledge of how to breathe effectively is relatively forgotten, or simply unknown.

### Breathing and endurance

Evidence suggests that before we were able to create weapons in the form of spears and bows, we hunted by running animals to the ground. We can't run as fast as a deer or an antelope, but our endurance power lets us run for many hours, which was a critical factor in our survival, since animals we chased eventually became overheated and died.

In the fascinating book, *Born To Run*, the author Christopher McDougall brings up the fact that in all the running mammals except man, breathing and movement are intimately interconnected: one step, one breath. However, human beings have the ability to adapt our breathing pattern and choose to take more or fewer breaths per step. We are also the only mammals that eliminate most of our body heat through sweating, whereas other mammals eliminate the major part of their heat via the lungs and breathing. These two factors are directly related to our breathing, and this is the foundation for our superior endurance.[1]

## CONSCIOUS BREATHING SPORTS TRAINING

Regardless of whether we are recreational exercisers, elite athletes, attend the occasional dance class, have a physically demanding job, or enjoy pottering in the garden, we can all benefit from improving our breathing habits during activity. Even for an inactive person wishing to commence physical activity, it's of great advantage to strive to breathe well as part of the training set-up.

Practicing Conscious Breathing during a workout ensures that you not only produce energy efficiently, but also reduce your overall consumption of energy, which in turn enables you to achieve more with less effort. In addition to increasing endurance and speed recovery, many also report an improvement in their overall results.

Applying Conscious Breathing puts your health and breathing first. In all its simplicity it means that you should a) strive to have your mouth closed as often as possible when you train, and try to breathe as rhythmically, abdominally, slowly and relaxed as possible, and b) listen to your body and view it as your best friend.

Many of us belong to one of two categories: those who are not naturally active and exercise too little or not at all, and those who exercise too much or are suffering from high stress levels. Over time neither option is particularly good for the body. Expressions such as "it takes a lot of effort to stay on top," or "no pain, no gain" reflect the cultural belief that training must be hard, associated with a high degree of will power, and be painful in order to yield results. Muscle pain the day after a workout is taken as proof that the training session was good. However, injury, pain, disease and recurrent colds are all indications that we have pushed ourselves too hard or that our body is out of balance. Perhaps we all too frequently focus on performance—winning the game or setting a new personal best. It creates an inner stress, often making us tense, which, ironically, reduces our ability to actually achieve our goal. Plus, we end up running on willpower, which doesn't make the process particularly enjoyable.

How many times have we heard athletes proclaiming after a sensational performance, "*I've just been sick/injured, and couldn't prepare myself the way I wanted to, so I went into the race/match without any expectations*"? A positive effect of focusing on how you breathe is that your inner stress is reduced; you become more relaxed, and are left with the feeling that the training session was fun. Your mental state will also be in better balance, and it will be much easier for you to deal with the pressure to perform. In the long run, mental and physical balance will lead to fewer sick days and fewer injuries, which provides better continuity in training.

The six most important effects of good breathing habits during exercise are:

**1. Nasal breathing promotes health and reduces stress**

An open mouth will always create greater stress for the body regardless of whether it's kept open at rest or during physical activity. Breathing through your mouth means that cold, dry air, full of bacteria and other airborne particles enter your lungs, while breathing through your nose increases your odds for staying healthy since the air you inhale through the nose is prepared for your lungs. Before entering your lungs, the air is warmed up, moistened and cleared from bacteria and viruses in your nose. When air is inhaled through your mouth, however, it does not reap the benefit of this finely tuned cleaning service.

As we inhale and exhale much more air during physical activity than when we rest, an open mouth during exercise represents an even greater stress to the body than when we are at rest. When our breathing volume jumps from 4-6 liters per minute to 100–200 liters per minute, the increased flow increases the mechanical wear and tear and irritates the airways. Inhaling cold and dry air when breathing through the mouth is another factor that contributes to narrowing of the airways. During physical activity, while breathing through your mouth, your airways will become narrower. A 50 percent reduction in the diameter of your airways means that 16 times more effort is needed to push the air in and out.[2] Narrow airways also increase the secretion of adrenaline, since it is this stress hormone that dilates the airways. When you breathe through your nose your airways stay wide, hence the perceived stress is reduced. The benefit is that since less adrenaline is required you can accomplish more while making less effort.

**2. Nasal breathing increases oxygen absorption**

The Nitric Oxide (NO) produced in your sinuses also dilates your airways, reducing airflow resistance, and making breathing more efficient. In your lungs, NO dilates the blood vessels so that more oxygen is transferred to your blood. Studies have shown that NO increases the oxygen uptake in your lungs.[3]

Moreover, nasal breathing creates a more streamlined airflow that reaches deeper into your lungs. However, when we breathe through the mouth, the airflow becomes more turbulent and the air whirls around in all sorts of directions. This is an inefficient way for air to travel. Transporting turbulent air requires more effort, and the inhaled air stays high up in the chest.

### 3. Prolonged exhalation increases relaxation

Exhalation is a passive process associated with relaxation, during which time your heart rate drops. A relaxed body is a requirement for good sports performance, since all the processes in your body work together optimally when relaxation is deep and the ability to perform and recover is at a peak level. Calm breathing relaxes your body and improves athletic performance. If you hold your breath, or exhale quickly and forcibly, your body may tense, which in turn causes your muscles to tense up. This reduces coordination and increases your risk of muscle cramps and injuries.

### 4. Power in the out-breath

On exhalation, you possess maximum relaxation, strength, concentration and precision. Your best result when striking a golf ball, tennis ball, football etc., is therefore achieved on exhalation. To increase your power, tense your stomach muscles, tighten your throat and force the air out. Did you notice that simply tightening your abdomen and holding your breath does not produce the same strength? This is why you will often hear a boxer, tennis player, or javelin thrower make a sound, which is a clear sign of exhalation, while the abdominal muscles are tense and the vocal cords are tightened simultaneously.

Try to strike a blow against a pillow while a) keeping your mouth open and just letting the air out, compared to b) squeezing the air out through pursed lips or through your nose while tightening your throat. Please feel free to make a sound, since it gives a much greater force when your abdominal muscles are tightened and the air is forced out.

### 5. Focusing on your breathing maintains concentration

By observing how you breathe, you are able to quieten the endless ping-pong game of thoughts that take you away from the present and the zone of focus and concentration. When you observe your breathing you are not "in your head," hence your body instinctively does what it has been trained to do without your intellect getting in the way. Connecting the activity you are focusing on with how you breathe at the time, for example, when shooting a free kick in soccer or hitting a golf ball, provides a greater opportunity to achieve the same results every time.

In the classic book *The Inner Game of Tennis*, the author Timothy Galloway writes that the most critical time for the player to stay focused is between the ball duels. It's far too easy to lose concentration when your intellect takes over and starts planning tomorrow or dwelling on yesterday. The best way to maintain concentration, according to Mr. Galloway, is to focus on your breathing. When your intellect accompanies your breathing rhythm in and out, it's kept occupied, and you tend to experience relaxation and inner peace.[4]

**6. Nasal breathing speeds up recovery and increases fat burning**

Compared to breathing out through your mouth, exhaling through your nose increases the pressure in your lungs, which provides better oxygenation. Consequently, more energy can be produced and your muscles can work for a longer period of time without getting tired. When oxygen supply is good, more carbon dioxide and less lactic acid is created. High levels of carbon dioxide reinforce your pH buffer, also called the bicarbonate buffer, which makes it easier to maintain balance between calcium and magnesium. Lack of both calcium and magnesium is closely related to tight muscles, cramps, spasms, tingling legs and long recovery after exertion. When we die, our body becomes stiff, because inflow of calcium ions to the muscles is increased as the energy production ceases. It is the imbalance between calcium and magnesium that makes the muscles stiff. Also, since fat can only be burnt in the presence of oxygen, more fat can be used as fuel when oxygenation is good.

| Optimum oxygen levels in cells | Oxygen deficiency in cells |
|---|---|
| • High $CO_2$ levels in the blood | • Low $CO_2$ levels in the blood |
| • Low levels of lactate in the blood | • High levels of lactate in the blood |
| • Relaxed muscles | • Stiff, tense muscles |
| • High energy and endurance | • Lack of energy, poor stamina |

The response is very positive from those who have started to apply nasal breathing during exercise or other physical activity. The recurring theme in their comments are:

- Increased stamina and strength
- Reduced stress, more harmony and faster recovery
- Lower pulse.

## PILOT STUDY SHOWS THE BENEFITS OF NASAL BREATHING

Thanks to all the positive feedback I have received, I decided to do a study in the spring of 2011.[5] Ten subjects, both athletes and recreational exercisers, trained for a few weeks with their mouths closed. They also used the Relaxator breathing retrainer. The tests were done on two occasions, one week apart, when they cycled with all their might. During one of the tests the subjects' noses were taped, so they were only able to breathe through their mouths, and in the other test their mouths were taped, breathing only through their noses. The results showed in particular:

- 22 percent fewer breaths during nasal breathing (mouth breathing 40 breaths per minute compared to 31 during nasal breathing).
- Eleven percent less lactic acid with nasal breathing.
- When breathing through their noses, four out of ten subjects managed to cycle at a heavier load and four subjects managed the same load as when they were breathing through their mouths. Only two subjects managed a lesser load, although that was not due to exhaustion. One had a headache and the other had the feeling of not getting enough oxygen. Both were really frustrated at not being able to perform at maximum level, as they felt very fit and their legs were doing just fine.

These tests were conducted by knowledgeable and well-educated staff in a professional test lab. I would like to emphasize that I'm not an experienced researcher, but I've done my best to set up a good study. In my opinion, however, the most interesting result is that all participants have opted to continue with nasal breathing in general, as well as during exercise as they find it more natural and beneficial.

#### Comments from participants

One of the participants in the study, Ulf Dextegen, a free diver with two World Championship bronze medals to his name who is capable of holding his breath under water for nine minutes, commented: "*During a one-hour workout I usually swim 20 x 50 meters in laps under water. I'm recovering a lot faster when I start breathing through my nose as soon as possible after exercising under water. The difference is striking.*"

Clas Björling was another subject in the study. He has been awarded a number of national championship gold medals and is a former Swedish triathlon, Ironman distance (8 hours and 15 minutes) record holder. In the study, Clas reduced his pulse by 10 percent from 155, while breathing through his mouth, to 139 during nasal breathing on a 295 watt* load, which is a significant decrease considering he's so fit. The lactic acid registered 38 percent lower with nasal breathing – 3.4 mmol/L (millimoles per liter) compared to 5.5 mmol/L during mouth breathing. Six months after the study Clas had also raised his maximum heart rate with nasal breathing from 139 to 162.

Some comments from other subjects in the study showing the benefits of nasal breathing:

- "My breathing is smoother, quieter, and my mouth is less dry. I also get less exercise-induced asthma."
- "It felt easier to push myself during nasal breathing. I also feel more relaxed afterwards and was able to calm down faster."
- "I feel like I do during meditation—more centered, more focused. It feels less mentally challenging."
- "Big difference. It felt like my legs and arms have more endurance when breathing through my nose."

* When Clas breathed through his mouth, he managed a 365-watt load, but during nasal breathing he "only" managed 295-watt, and therefore the comparison with heart rate, lactic acid, etc., is made at a 295 watt load in both his tests.

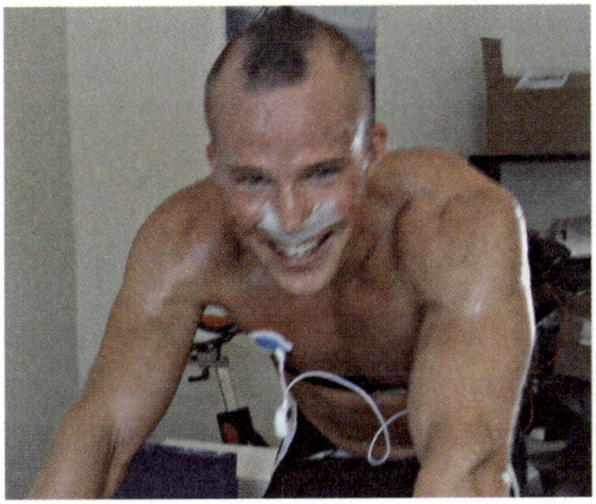

"When I exercise I breathe through my nose as much as I can, since it feels so damn good! I feel more stable, and I have more harmony and rhythm in my workout. When the load is too intense I also breathe through my mouth, but when I, for example, reach the top of a hill I start breathing through my nose again as soon as possible to lower my heart rate and recover faster."

- Clas Björling, March 2011

## WITH NASAL BREATHING WE REPLACE QUANTITY WITH QUALITY

In my breathing courses, I encounter many skeptical athletes and recreational exercisers who say they have narrow nasal passages or a stuffy nose and claim it's impossible to breathe through the nose during physical activity. Once they try, however, they usually discover that nasal breathing works beyond their expectations.

### What you can do

- **Improve your day-to-day breathing:** Become aware of your daily breathing habits and apply the principles of Conscious Breathing. Train with the Relaxator, as it's a great way to improve your diaphragm muscle and gain an abdominal, rhythmic, and relaxed breathing pattern. A good breathing pattern at rest increases your chance of breathing well even when you are doing physical activity.
- **Clear a stuffy nose:** Use a solution of water, salt and baking soda; see instructions on page 47, to cleanse a stuffy nose. During a transition period you could also use nasal strips, like Breathe Right®, to widen the nostrils. Nasal strips widen the nasal passage by up to 30 percent and can ease the transition from mouth to nasal breathing if you have a narrow nose.

- **Get started:** Some people choose to fully adopt nasal breathing from the first moment while others do it step by step. There is no right or wrong way to do it, so just do what feels right for you. If you take it step by step, you may want to strive to wait longer and longer during exertion before you give in to the need to open your mouth and start breathing through it. Don't be surprised if you are soon able to exert yourself at a far higher level with your mouth closed, than you ever thought was possible.
- **Slow down and see yourself as a beginner:** There are two common mistakes made when trying to establish nasal breathing during physical activity a) the person only tried once and b) the person trained at the same intensity as they normally do using mouth breathing. The key to succesfully establishing nasal breathing is that, regardless of how fit you are, be humble and see yourself as a beginner, and slow down and exercise at a lower intensity than usual.

Some people experience difficulty adapting to nasal breathing during physical activity, even after 2–8 weeks of practice. For some, it's a mental issue, since they are overly aware of the huge amount of air inhaled when they exert themselves during physical activity and, therefore, find it hard to comprehend that it would be possible to inhale the same amount of air through small nasal passages. But with nasal breathing, we replace quantity with quality. With each breath we are able to extract a greater amount of energy, so we need fewer breaths. With a little practice, it's possible to adopt nasal breathing during almost any sport, so please don't give up if it feels hard at first. Try to be patient and give yourself time to get used to switching to nasal breathing.

Another reason why people have trouble breathing through their nose has to do with nasal passages and pharynx that actually ARE tight. Minor defects such as blocked sinuses and nasal passages, adenoids, and enlarged tonsils can be tackled fairly easily, since these problems are often reduced or may even disappear completely once you start to improve your breathing habits.

"To show that nose breathing works excellently I ran a half marathon (21 kilometers) with duct tape over my mouth. The tape was on during the entire race, which means that I didn't drink anything, despite the fact that it was 25 degrees Celsius and bright sunshine. A reason for this is that nose breathing allows us to retain more water in our body."

- Anders Olsson, June 2012

A defect that is somewhat more difficult to overcome is when the upper and lower jaws haven't developed forward as they are supposed to. Underdeveloped jaws may lead to narrow, upper airways, which actually limit physical ability. Successful athletes usually have a broad jaw and firm chin, which indicates that the upper airways are well developed, thus assuring effective oxygenation of the muscles.

**Replace quality with quantity**

When jogging with a friend I have noticed that he breathes 2-3 times as much as me, i.e., while I take 20 breaths per minute he takes 40-60 breaths. I breathe through my nose and he is breathing through his mouth. My breaths are regular and abdominal while he is huffing and puffing irregularly high up in his chest. On a 5 km jog (3 miles) I counted the number of times we spit, and cleared our throat and noses. I did it four times while my friend did it a full 61 times. Although these findings are anecdotal, it confirms what I've seen when others exercise—mouth breathing leads to a) an ineffective breathing where we have to compensate by breathing more, b) creates irritated airways, which leads to increased mucus production, and c) creates narrow airways, which increases stress. I have noted that if I jog when I'm stressed out, have slept poorly, or have eaten junk food, I have to clear my throat my often.

### How I learned to swim

I grew up by the sea and have always loved water, and to be able to do the crawl stroke has always been high on my wishlist. However, to swim using the crawl stroke more than 25 meters without feeling completely exhausted was still impossible only a year ago. Half a year ago I realized that I was holding my breath and started to apply rhythmic breathing and managed to swim 50 meters, before panic and lactic acid took over. That was my limit until just a few weeks ago when I climbed down from my high horses and decided to increase my breathing frequency (breathing every 3rd arm stroke instead of every 4th, 5th or 7th). Suddenly I managed to swim 100 meters, 150 and then 200 meters. Yes, finally I cracked the code, and I thought that maybe next time I will be able to swim even a little bit longer.

I certainly did—I crawled 1,000 meters without stopping, and the next time after that I managed 2,000 meters! Indeed, quite a steep learning curve where I went from 200 to 2,000 meters during the last three swim sessions. Interestingly enough, my fitness is not better or worse than it has been before.

My interpretation is that a good, rhythmical breathing pattern with a breathing frequency and breathing volume that matches the needs of our body is the foundation for good physical performance, no matter the activity, as it helps us gain access to our body's enormous inner resources. Also it's important to be humble and not believe, as I did that, "I'm a breathing expert who has taught people how to breathe for the last five yeras, so for sure I know how to breathe when swimming."

## BREATHING IN DIFFERENT SPORTS

Thanks to his successful work with hundreds of patients with severe emphysema, a disease which destroys lung tissue and alveoli, breathing expert Carl Stough, author of the book *Dr. Breath*, had the opportunity to work with the US Olympic team prior to the Olympics in Mexico City in 1968. Mr. Stough became interested in respiration among athletes when he found that many of his patients diagnosed with emphysema had a background in elite athletics. It became clear to him that the breathing pattern of athletes recovering from vigorous effort resembled the breathing pattern of someone with emphysema (destroyed lung tissue).

Mr. Stough taught the athletes to breathe in a relaxed, coordinated, and rhythmic way in both training and competition, as well as during warm up and cool down. The breathing retraining led to a significant increase in both performance and recovery. At higher altitudes, such as in Mexico City, the oxygen pressure is reduced, and it becomes evident how ineffective breathing negatively affects performance. The American athletes took advantage of Mr. Stough's knowledge and the US won more gold medals than they ever had before.[6]

Whatever the sporting activity, it is possible to use Conscious Breathing in a number of situations:

- **Warm up:** A good warm up aims at slowly increasing your heart rate through any activity that is similar to the activity you are about to perform. Breathing only through your nose while warming up with a few speedy rushes, will provide your body with a carbon dioxide boost that will increase your ability to perform. The sharp increase in carbon dioxide increases the pH buffer. The pH buffer consists of bicarbonate ($HCO_3^-$), which in turn is made up of carbon dioxide ($CO_2$) and water ($H_2O$). A high pH buffer prohibits lactic acid from forming in your muscles and reduces or avoids the soreness often experienced after a training session.
- **Cool down:** To cool down means that your body recovers from exercise actively, and the level of intensity is gradually reduced so that your heart rate slowly decreases. At the start of the cool down it's an advantage to do a few speedy rushes adapting nasal breathing only, just like during your warm up.
- **Interval training:** Interval training involves intensity activity followed by recovery and it is used to increase your performance. Nasal

breathing during interval training can be varied in many ways. For example; in a few 50 meter sprints during a jog; 70/20 exercise—70 seconds effort at 70–80 percent of full capacity, followed by 20 seconds rest; 15/15 exercise—15 seconds of effort at full capacity, followed by 15 seconds rest, every other time only breathing nasally.

- **Recovery:** You should close your mouth and breathe through your nose during breaks and recovery periods, since this provides for a faster recovery. You can also speed up your recovery with diaphragmatic breathing, which is best achieved by a) keeping your hands behind your head and pushing your chest out, b) extending your expirations, and c) slowing down your breathing frequency.
- **During the activity:** Tape your mouth closed during some training sessions in order to get accustomed to breathing only through your nose. For example, a Norwegian soccer team uses the mouth taping technique with great success, as the players notice less soreness and experience faster recovery.

Below are a few tips on how to improve your respiration in different sports:

#### Jogging/cycling

Jogging and cycling are probably the two sports that are easiest to participate in while breathing through your nose. Counting your steps/pedal pushes during inhalation and then increasing the amount of steps/pedal pushes on exhalation amplifies the effect even more. Doing this has several advantages: a) it keeps your brain busy so that your mind doesn't wander off to things you are worried about, i.e., if you are tired or that it's a long way to go, and b) prolonged exhalation increases your relaxation, providing relaxed concentration and an increased ability to stay focused.

#### Ice hockey/floorball/handball/basketball

Practice nasal breathing as soon as possible after a highly intense performance for a faster recovery, and even at times when the intensity is lower. Nasal breathing in the bullpen/on the bench also facilitates increased oxygenation and faster recovery. If possible, try hitting the puck/ball or shoot/throw the ball on exhalation.

### Football/soccer

Hit the ball on exhalation as this is when your power and focus is at a maximum. This is particularly applicable at goal kicks, corner kicks, free kicks, penalty kicks and throw-in. It may be more difficult when passing the ball and shooting, although it's probably just a matter of simply getting used to it. A study of Danish elite football players (soccer) concluded that as much as 90 percent of the activity during a football match is low intensity. After some practice, you will spot the great nasal breathing opportunities during the majority of the time on the field. If you adopt the nasal breathing technique, your recovery will be faster and you'll ultimately have greater endurance and increased concentration, even at the end of the games.

### Cross-country skiing/biathlon

Since competitions and training often occur in cold weather, there are many advantages to be gained by improving your ability to breathe through your nose. The large amount of cold, dry air being inhaled is probably a major reason why the vast majority of the world's top elite cross-country skiers have asthma. While racing down hills, and on flatter sections of the track, it is likely that nasal breathing may be applicable. For efficient performance during a biathlon, it's advantageous to adopt nasal breathing when coming into the shooting wall as it lowers your pulse more quickly and your body becomes calmer. You'll get the best result from the shot if it's done during exhalation.

### Track and field

In disciplines such as high jump, long jump, three-step jump and pole vault, the performer will gain more power when jumping on exhalation while forcing the air out at the same time. Focusing on respiration while practicing these sports also helps clear negative thoughts. In running events, the same tips apply as when jogging/cycling. On the starting blocks, it's best to exhale while waiting for the race to be started as this would increase the chance of rhythmic breathing during the race. Holding the breath at this time is common and can easily set off non-rhythmic breathing and a tense body during the race.

### Golf

A good golfer strikes the ball on expiration but may not actually be aware of it. Your swing will automatically improve if you pay attention to and focus on improving your breathing pattern during the swing. The keys to a successful golf stroke can be tied to your breath, and can form a routine where your golf swing may become as simple and natural as baking a cake, i.e., using the same recipe gives the same result. You can vary the force of your exhalation by tightening your throat to different degrees depending on how hard you want to hit the ball. An excellent way to stay fully oxygenated and focused during a round of golf is to count your steps between strokes, and then take more steps on exhalation.

### Tennis

A talented tennis player strikes the ball on exhalation. For example, some players groan when they hit the ball, which means that exhalation occurs through a tightened throat where the air is squeezed out. Another technique for keeping your concentration up between rallies is to follow your breath and try to have a longer exhalation than inhalation.

### Swimming

Inhalation is usually fast during swimming, so exhalation is the main thing to focus on. If inhaled air is retained and rapidly exhaled, just before the next inhalation, the tension in your body will increase. Aim for a continuous outflow of air through your nose, so when it's time to inhale you have already emptied your lungs. It is important to make sure that the airflow in and out is as rhythmic and calm as possible as it will provide more efficient oxygenation and a better rhythm when you swim. Nasal breathing in between exertion speeds up recovery.

### Boxing/Martial Arts

A skilled boxer or martial artist knows that it basically comes down to two things to win a match; first, do your utmost to upset your opponent's breathing pattern, and second, try to keep your own breathing as balanced as possible. When your breathing is balanced, your body is in balance. You are relaxed, your senses are operating at the peak of their ability, and it's easier to predict and prevent your opponent's next attack. The most power in your strikes is achieved when air is forced out through pursed lips or through your nose while your throat is tightened.

## CARBON DIOXIDE TRAINING INCREASES YOUR WELLBEING

Physical activity is frequently associated with the secretion of endorphins and other substances that make us feel good. Another effect of moving our body is that our carbon dioxide levels increase. As we discussed earlier, there's a clear link between low levels of carbon dioxide in our body and poor health. Knowing this, it's easy to see that higher levels of carbon dioxide (to a certain degree) are associated with health and wellbeing, energy, and endurance.

Some people who are used to regular training don't feel well if they miss a workout. The positive effect of training has created a strong dependence on the positive after-effects of training, and to miss a workout is almost out of the question. In my experience, it's common for such individuals to have poor breathing habits that cause their carbon dioxide levels to drop between workouts. Training then becomes a way of raising their carbon dioxide levels and achieving greater harmony in their lives.

At rest, we produce about 250 milliliters of carbon dioxide per minute, and during exercise it increases to up to 1.5 liters per minute. When training with a closed mouth, the levels in our body increase even

| We can increase the level of $CO_2$ in our body by | | |
|---|---|---|
| • Physical activity | • Nose breathing | • Breathing into a bag |
| • Prolonged exhalation | • Intake of baking soda | • Holding our breath |

more as the outflow of carbon dioxide decreases due to the nose serving as a narrow passage, thus reducing the volume of air that passes in and out with each breath. By breathing through our nose while extending exhalation (Exercise 3 – *Count your steps*, page 58), we can increase our carbon dioxide levels even further.

I have done "$CO_2$ Training" on numerous occasions when jogging, cycling, Nordic walking and normal walking. When I challenge myself considerably while jogging—for example, by keeping my mouth closed and taking 3–4 steps on inhalation and 10–12 steps on exhalation—I feel incredibly harmonious afterwards. I personally believe that the increased level of carbon dioxide in our body is a significant reason why we feel so good when exerting ourselves during physical activity.

NOTE! Be careful as powerful carbon dioxide training can cause a headache, usually in the forehead, although it's transient and decreases/disappears as your body learns to tolerate higher pressure in your sinuses. The increased air circulation decreases the risk of sinus and ear infections. In the beginning, you may also experience a runny nose, so keep a handkerchief handy.

***Tips***

To increase your $CO_2$ levels further, you can mix two pinches of baking soda with a glass of water and drink it before, during or after training.

## IMPROVING YOUR DAILY BREATHING IMPROVES YOUR SPORTS PERFORMANCE

If we have a breathing pattern at rest that isn't optimal, we will end up with the same poor breathing habit when training and competing.

Training and competing with high intensity and an open mouth may further reinforce poor breathing habits and the establishment of a vicious circle where the breathing may deteriorate even further.

Impaired breathing reduces oxygenation of your muscles, as well as performance and endurance. Eventually, it will also lower the pH buffer, which makes it more difficult for your body to take care of the lactic acid produced during exercise.

Our most important breathing muscle, the diaphragm, is an often forgotten muscle that is not trained frequently enough. Many athletes have a weakened diaphragm because they breathe higher up in their chest during exercise as well as when they are resting. Such excessive shallow breathing will also lead to stiff chest muscles, so when we get a stitch during exercise it's usually down to a weakened diaphragm muscle. A stitch could also occur if we eat too much or just before our activity starts.

In the same way that an inefficient car engine uses more fuel than an engine in good condition uses, we breathe more when the effectiveness of each breath is reduced. Apart from needing more fuel and oil, an inefficient car engine won't go as fast, is slow to start in the morning and to accelerate at a red light, can't go as long without a break, and needs servicing more often because the parts wear out faster, and hence has a shorter life span. Exactly the same applies to our body. Continuing an inefficient breathing pattern is like driving around at half speed or with the parking brake slightly engaged. We are tired in the morning, often have to be refilled with fresh fuel, get sick more frequently, and may even die prematurely. By taking control of our breathing habits, it's possible to break poor breathing patterns and increase oxygen uptake, as well as boost our concentration and performance, both in and outside the training arena.

### WHICH IS THE BETTER FUEL, SUGAR OR FAT?

We generally hold the belief that exercising has to be very intense to yield results. Sure, many studies show that we burn more calories if we run quickly rather than slowly. That is because our body needs energy quickly when it perceives a situation as stressful, and our body then uses sugar/carbohydrates as fuel, to a greater extent.

However, we don't take into account that a highly intense activity resets our body to use more sugar, both during and after the exercise. During high intensity activity most of us increase our breathing rate too much, meaning that we are over-breathing and exhaling too much carbon dioxide. The result is low levels of $CO_2$, which impair the oxygenation of our cells (the Bohr effect). In order to oxygenate our muscles so that we can continue our high intensity activity, our body then prioritizes the production of $CO_2$. Since it takes 40 percent less oxygen to create carbon dioxide using sugar than fat (see more on respiratory quotient in Chapter 13), sugar is predominantly used as fuel when we over-breathe. If we instead keep our mouth closed during exercise our breathing is normalized, which increases the carbon dioxide levels in our blood and thereby improves the oxygenation of our muscles. Nasal breathing results in an increased ability for the body to burn fat, as more oxygen is delivered to the muscles, not only during the training session but also afterwards. Over time, training with a closed mouth will lead to your body being programmed to use more fat as fuel.

To store energy in fat is six times more efficient than to store it in sugar. The amount of energy in body fat is 50-300 times greater than the energy of the stored sugar. Therefore, it is desirable to use fat as fuel as much as possible since it's an almost inexhaustible energy source.

## WHY DO WE EXERCISE?

Exercising becomes a whole different experience when you are able to tap into your inner motivation for doing it, rather than relying on pure willpower. You may work out because it feels good, because you "know" it's good for you, to get rid of anger and other emotions, to lose or maintain weight, to build muscles, to prepare for a race like the New York Marathon, or simply because you like activities such as tennis, handball or football, or even because you are an athlete and that is your profession.

Regardless of why you are training, I would like you to reflect for a short moment on the reasons why you actually work out. Are you exercising only because you should or you have to? If so, maybe it is possible to find reasons that also provide motivation, happiness and a passion for exercising.

**The three main reasons why I exercise**

1.____________________________________________

2.____________________________________________

3.____________________________________________

**Customize your training and enjoy reaching your exercise goals**

When you plan an exercise program, it is important that you take into account your body's unique needs. A workout giving great results for one person may be awfully stressful for another. Remember also to customize your training according to your life situation. If you have a lot going on in your life—a deadline at work, sick children, etc., then it may be wise to avoid scheduling intensive training sessions. Listen to your body, what does it tell you? Increased body awareness improves your chances of keeping yourself healthy and free from injuries, which also provides greater continuity in your training.

## CHALLENGE FRIENDS AND FAMILY TO SOME HEALTHY COMPETITION

Breathing well can increase your strength, stamina and ability to concentrate, and with this knowledge you can challenge your partner, children or a friend to compete with you. Don't be surprised to find yourself winning over someone who used to be better than you. The

Conscious Breathing Method has helped me to win at lots of different activities, such as bowling, mini golf, long jump, and hitting a punching ball. Below are a few examples of how I have been able to use my improved breathing in sports activities such as:

**Bowling**

Throwing the ball upon exhalation, while cautiously pressing air out of my lungs through a tightened throat in order to achieve more power. The first time I managed to get it right, I made five strikes in a row.

**Miniature golf**

Hitting the ball on exhalation made it easier for me to control the ball's force and direction. If you try this, you probably won't need to press the air out since there is usually no need to create a large force.

**Blows to the punching ball**

Hitting the ball on exhalation while squeezing the air out through a tightened throat and making a sound helped me to make the force very focused.

**Exercise "the plank"**

I couldn't help but notice how much stamina I experienced when assuming the plank pose, keeping my body straight, with only my elbows/forearms and toes touching the floor, while breathing rhythmically in and out through my nose.

**Exercise "90 degrees"**

I noticed how great my endurance was while leaning back against a wall, keeping my legs at a 90 degree angle, and breathing rhythmically in and out through my nose.

# Chapter 7 – Working with the Relaxator to Improve Your Breathing

*Narrow and tense airways limit our ability to live the life we want. Engaging in different physical exercises while using the Relaxator is an efficient way to dilate the airways and strengthen the breathing muscles and help them relax. Soon your normal breathing habits will improve so that the majority of the breaths you take each day serve you in the best possible way.*

The exercises on the following pages aim to open your airways, get them functioning well and strengthening and relax your breathing muscles. Pick a few exercises that appeal to you and put together your own 10-minute workout program. Add a few calm breaths between the exercises, and reflect on how it feels in your body before moving on to the next practice. You can do your exercises daily or at times that are convenient for you. Remember that the goal is to reduce stress, not increase it. If too much is going on in your life at a certain point, just skip your exercises that day.

Keep your back erect and straight during the exercises, as this facilitates the work of the diaphragm and deepens breathing. Breathe in a relaxed way, taking slow, abdominal, reduced, calm, and rhythmic breaths. Using the Relaxator will help you maintain a good breathing pattern during the different exercises. These exercises will help you improve your general breathing pattern so that eventually you take most of the daily 20-25,000 breaths in accordance with the five principles of Conscious Breathing – nose, stomach, slow, rhythmic and quiet. If you manage to maintain an erect posture and relaxed breathing during the exercises, chances are that you'll be able to do the same in different situations you may encounter in your everyday life.

## 1. GET TO KNOW YOUR BREATHING

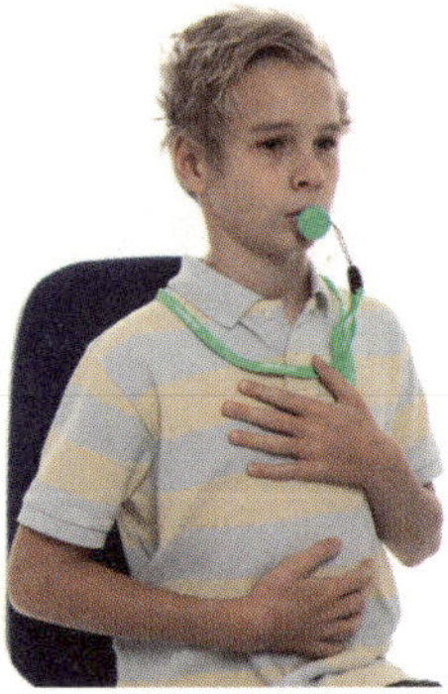

Put one hand on your chest and the other on your stomach. Follow your breaths in and out and notice where the air ends up. Become aware of the different movements that occur in your body when breathing in and out. The hand on your belly should move slightly outwards when you inhale, while the hand on your chest should remain almost still. When exhaling, the stomach should move inwards. Continue the exercise for 2–5 minutes. If you have problems finding a good breathing rhythm, lay down on the floor with a book on your stomach and watch the book move up when you inhale and down when you exhale.

## 2. SPINE FLEX

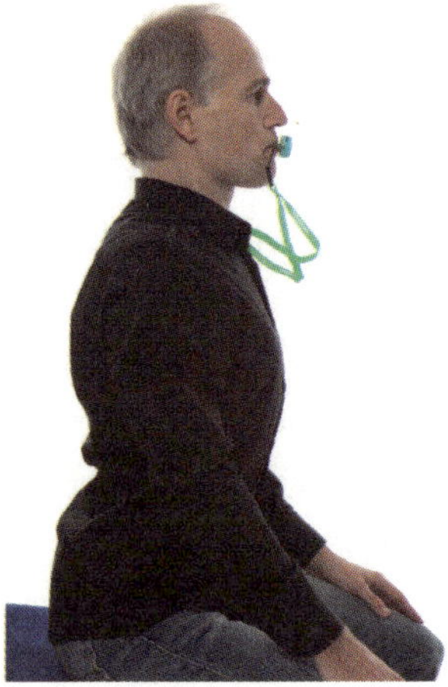

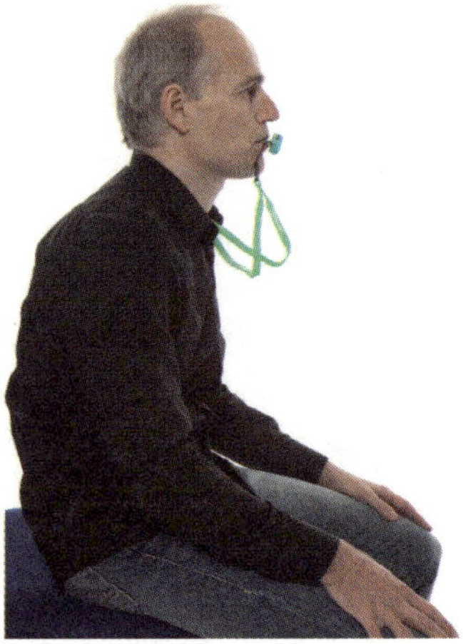

Put your hands on your knees. Breathe in and flex your spine and chest forward, while your shoulders are drawn backward. Breathe out and flex the spine backwards while your shoulders are drawn forward, and your arms are stretched. Repeat ten times. This exercise is good for your lumbar region, abdominal muscles, diaphragm and general body posture.

### 3. SPINE BENDING

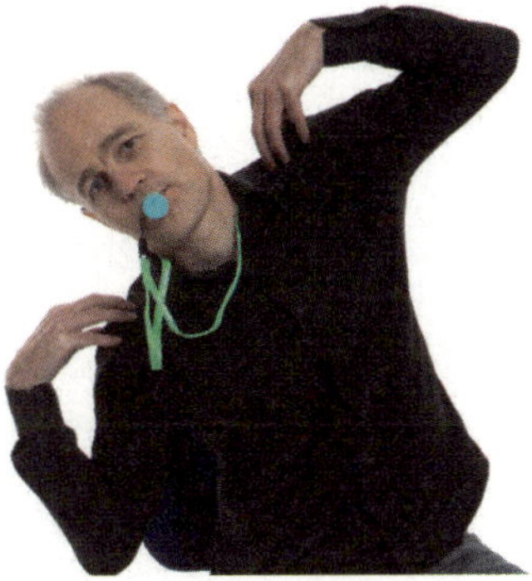

Place your hands on your shoulders, with your elbows at shoulder level. Inhale and bend your head, the upper part of the body, and left elbow towards the floor. Your right elbow should be pointing upwards towards the ceiling. Breathe out and repeat the same action on the right. Repeat five times and then switch, so that you breathe in when bending the body to the right. This exercise is good for your lumbar region, abdominal muscles, diaphragm and general body posture.

### 4. SPINE TWIST

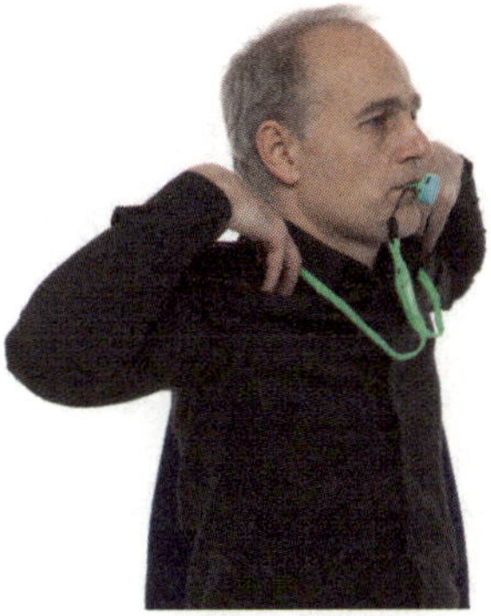

Place your hands on your shoulders, with your elbows at shoulder level. Breathe in and turn the upper part of your body as far left as you can. Exhale and turn to the right. Let your head follow the movement passively, so that your nose is kept in line with your sternum. Repeat five times and then switch so that your inhalation occurs while twisting your body to the right. This movement is good for your spine, scapula, chest, abdominal muscles, and your diaphragm.

## 5. EAR AGAINST SHOULDER

Keep your posture erect and your nose pointing forward. As you breathe in lean your head against your left shoulder. Breathe out as you lean your head against your right shoulder. Repeat five times and then switch to inhale when you bend your head to the right. Good for your neck, shoulders, and lower jaw.

## 6. LOOK OVER SHOULDER

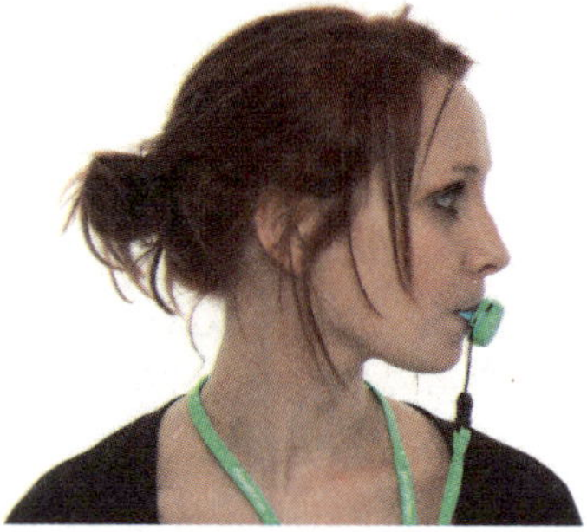

Keep your posture erect and your nose pointing forward. Inhale and turn your head to the left. Exhale and turn to the right. Repeat five times and then switch your inhale to when turning your head to the right. This motion stimulates your neck and shoulders, and helps them relax.

## 7. NECK ROLLING

Let the chin fall towards your chest and then roll your chin via the right shoulder, around, up, back, and then down to the left. Draw a slow, soft, controlled circle with your nose. Don't lean your head backwards too much. NOTE! Your neck should not hurt. Repeat five times and then switch and roll the other way. Good for your throat, neck and jaws.

### 8. BEND BACKWARDS

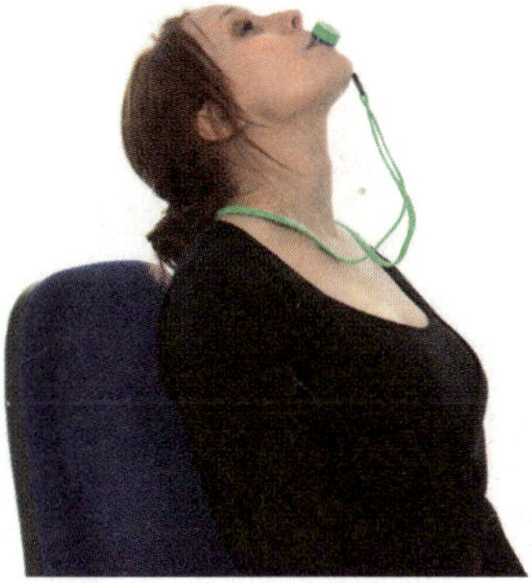

Let your chin fall forward towards your chest. Inhale while leaning the upper part of your body backwards. Let your head and neck fall effortlessly backward as far as possible. Grab your thighs or the chair to let your hands support you. NOTE! Your neck should not hurt. Bring your head back down and let your chin sink towards your chest while exhaling. Repeat 10 times. This exercise is good for your throat, neck and lower jaw.

### 9. TIGHTEN—RELAX YOUR BODY

- Tighten your thighs, calves and feet while inhaling and exhaling three times. Try to maintain a rhythmic and relaxed breathing pattern.
- Relax your entire body while taking a couple of breaths.
- Now, tighten your lower abdomen and pelvis while inhaling and exhaling three times.
- Relax your entire body while taking a couple of breaths.
- End the exercise by inhaling and exhaling three times while clenching your hands and tightening your arms and chest. Then relax.

This exercise is an easy way to make sure that all the muscles in your body are activated and relaxed.

### 10. SHOULDER LIFT

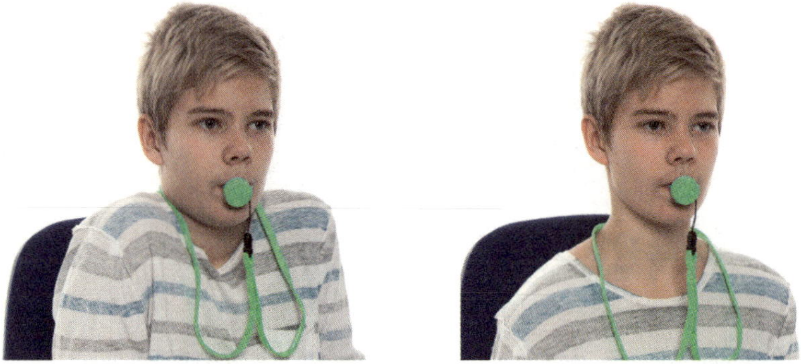

Keep your spine straight. Breathe in, pull your shoulders up towards your ears, and hold your breath for a few seconds while tightening your neck, shoulders and arms. Breathe out as you let the shoulders sink and relax your whole body. Repeat ten times. This exercise helps you become aware of the difference between being tense and relaxed.

### 11. DIAPHRAGM MASSAGE

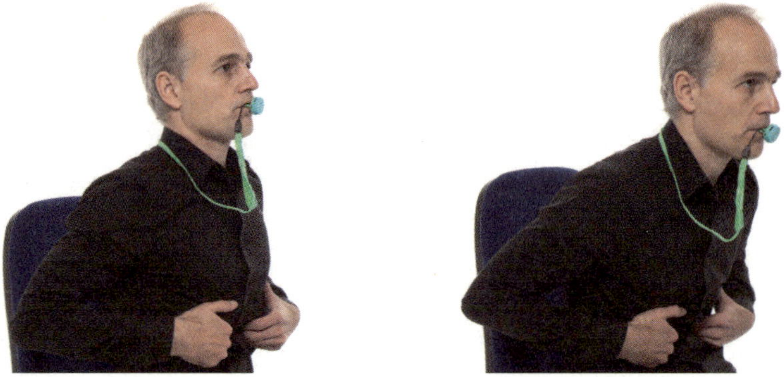

Keep your posture erect and your back straight. Insert your fingers just under your ribs, where your diaphragm is attached. Breathe in and press your fingers against your diaphragm. It's okay to press quite hard. Continue to press on your diaphragm as you exhale. While emptying your lungs, the upper part of your body should collapse a little bit forward. Repeat ten times. This exercise is good for relaxing your diaphragm if it's tense.

## 12. HANDS ABOVE YOUR HEAD

Bring your palms together above your head and maintain a relaxed breathing pattern. The higher you are able to hold your hands, the deeper the inhalations will be. Remember, it's not a competition, so just do your best while maintaining a relaxed breathing pattern. Stay in this position for 2–5 minutes. This exercise is good when your breathing is shallow and you find it difficult to breathe deeply.

## 13. CROSS CRAWL OR "MARCH" IN PLACE

Lift your right knee high and at the same time reach out with your opposite hand and touch your knee. Then shift and lift your left knee high while touching your knee with your right hand. Do the exercises slowly and keep an erect posture. Continue the exercise for 2–5 minutes. By crossing your body's midline, this exercise helps you to integrate the information between your left and right hemisphere. Good brain integration stimulates learning, problem solving and relaxation.

## 14. STAND LIKE A TREE

Stand up with your back straight and bend your legs slightly. Shape your arms and hands in a half circle in front of you, as if you were holding a big beach ball. Pay attention to any tension in your body that may become apparent. Over time, such tension will be released and you will become more and more relaxed. Stand in this position for 2–5 minutes.

## 15. BODY BREATHING

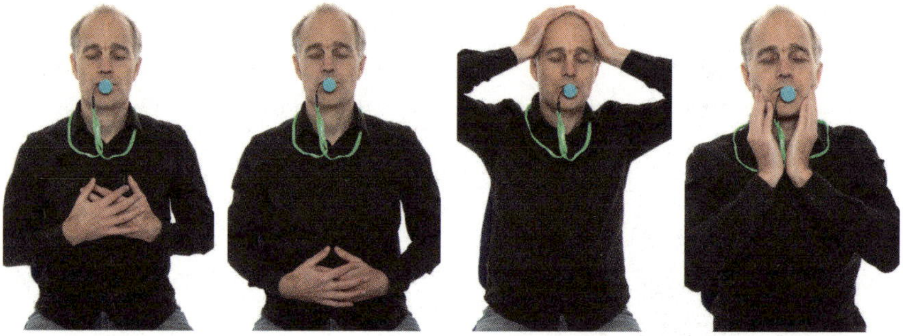

Breathe in and out in a rhythmical and calm manner. Put your hands on your heart and imagine that you are breathing in and out through your heart. You should "feel" how your heart fills with oxygen so that it can work properly on every inhalation. Your heart will recover and rest on the out-breath as it becomes more and more relaxed with each exhalation.

Continue for a few minutes and then move your hands and attention to other parts of your body you may feel need support, like your stomach, head, jaws, knees or lower back. If you work on your jaws you can apply a little pressure to make them relax with ease. This exercise helps you become more aware of your body.

### 16. ABDOMINAL MUSCLES AND DIAPHRAGM TRAINING

Set the Relaxator on a high resistance level, i.e., a high number, so you have to make an effort when squeezing the air through. When you exhale slowly, empty your lungs as much as possible, and at the end let your navel move in towards your lower back. On inhalation, just let the air flow in. This exercise can be used as a form of interval training. For example, exhale and inhale five time, and then rest for three breathing cycles. Repeat over a ten-minute period. This is good for your abdominal muscles and diaphragm, which are often weakened due to shallow breathing.

### 17. CARBON DIOXIDE TRAINING

Use the Relaxator while jogging, cycling, walking, or Nordic Walking as it will extend the exhalation and boost your carbon dioxide levels quickly, which has a favorable effect on your body.

In the beginning, I advise you to avoid doing the activity at high intensity or setting the resistance level too high on the Relaxator, as a quick increase of pressure in your sinuses can prompt headaches and/or dizziness.

When inhaling, try to imagine that the air is reaching all the way down to your navel.

### 18. FORGIVENESS

1. Think of a situation or person that makes you feel upset, angry, or annoyed. Make the situation as real as possible by fantasizing vividly, adding color, sound and moving pictures to the situation. You will notice that the thoughts and feelings you experience will alter your breathing pattern.
2. If you have problems getting in touch with your upset feelings, you may find fast and shallow breathing helpful, or try holding your breath altogether.
3. Now put your hands on your heart and take control over your breathing. Breathe slowly, abdominally and rhythmically.
4. Say, "*I'm sorry,*" to yourself for things you have done or said. When breathing in, inhale forgiveness into your heart, and when exhaling allow this great feeling of forgiveness to spread throughout your entire body.
5. Say, "*I'm sorry,*" to the people who may have upset, annoyed or irritated you. Do the same when inhaling and exhaling, as in point four.
6. Continue the exercise for 2–5 minutes.

If you find it hard to do the forgiveness exercise, try doing the same exercise with acceptance as your goal.

### 19. THANKFULNESS

Put your hands on your heart and breathe in and out in a relaxed manner. On every inhalation, think of different things you are grateful for. Inhale this thankfulness into your heart. On exhalation let this great feeling of thankfulness spread throughout your entire body.

For every breath you take, inhale gratefulness, care and appreciation for yourself, a place, a pet, or something near and dear to your heart. Each time you exhale, every cell in your body will be filled with these great feelings. Continue the exercise for 2–5 minutes.

# PART III

# BREATHING RETRAINING FOR SPECIFIC HEALTH ISSUES

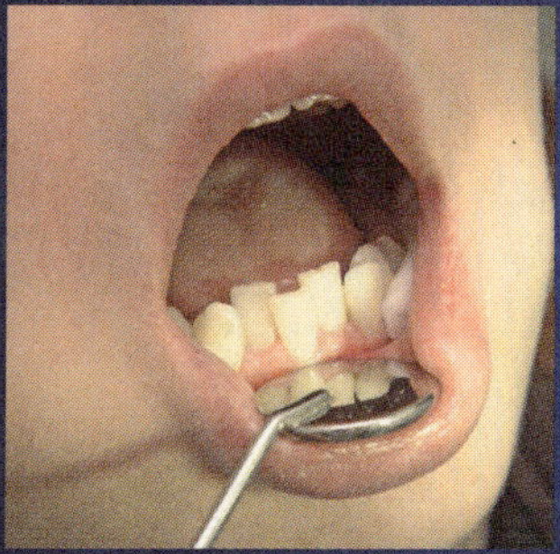

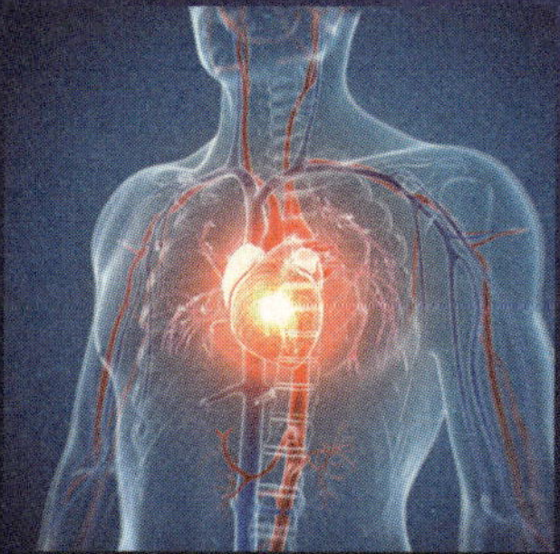
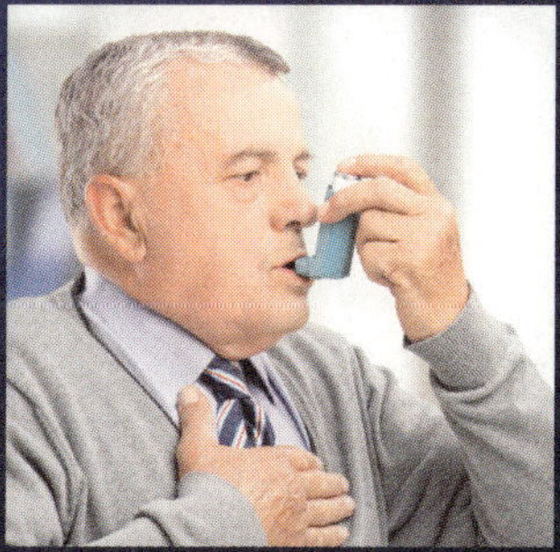

# Chapter 8 – How Your Breathing Can Affect Your Teeth and Facial Development

*Breathing through the mouth creates changes in the jaws, which eventually affects the position of a child's teeth, smile, facial development and upper airways. Dr. John Flutter states, "The single most important thing you can do to improve a child's health is to establish nasal breathing."*

## OUR MODERN LIFE STYLE PROMOTES BAD TEETH AND AN UNDERDEVELOPED FACE

In the 1930s, dentist Weston Price visited many primitive and isolated cultures around the world, such as the Eskimos, Native American Indians, Aborigines, and the Maoris. In his book, *Nutrition and Physical Degeneration*, he explains how a change in diet and lifestyle dramatically affects the teeth and facial development.[1]

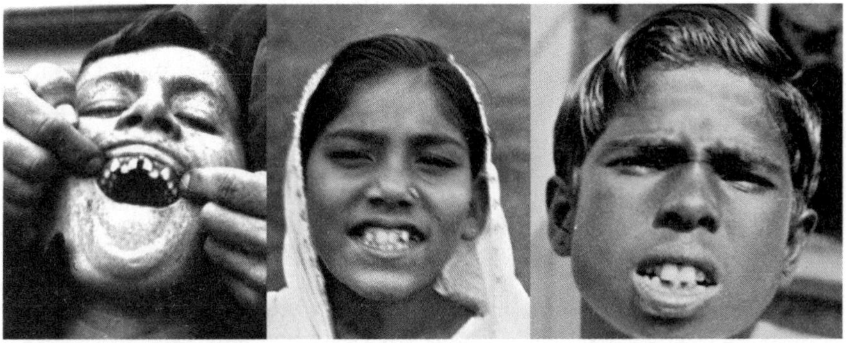

Tooth decay and crooked teeth, narrower face and changes in jaw development, these characteristics were (and are) common among the indigenous peoples that embraced Western eating and lifestyle habits.

**Dr. Price found straight teeth and well developed lower and upper jaws in people who hadn't been exposed to the Western diet and lifestyle.**


Dr. Price wrote: "Among the groups that incorporated a Western lifestyle to the greatest extent, 31-50 percent had tooth decay and 40-100 percent had underdeveloped upper jaws. By comparison, only two percent of the population in the most isolated communities had dental caries. In many places, every single person in the older population had normally shaped upper jaws, while the children of these individuals, however, showed a much higher percentage of defective palates and upper jaws."

The changed lifestyle incorporating new bacteria, diseases, alcohol, etc., resulted in the indigenous population being exposed to more stress. When internal stress increases, our natural reaction is to breathe with our mouths open. Habitually breathing through the mouth can disturb facial development and cause problems such as uneven teeth or narrower jaws.

## BREATHING AFFECTS FACIAL DEVELOPMENT

Dr. John Flutter, a prominent dentist from Australia, noticed that the dental corrections he made on his patients weren't permanent, and he started to look for alternatives to pulling teeth or fitting braces. The conclusion that Dr. Flutter and many other dentists and orthodontists made is that how we breathe and swallow, as well as our posture, affects our jaws, teeth, and facial development. More information on this subject is available from the International Academy for Facial Growth Guidance (IAFGG). The most important factors for optimum development of our face and teeth are to:

1. Always breathe in and out through the nose.
2. Keep the mouth closed and the lips together at rest.
3. Let the tongue rest in the roof of the mouth.
4. No muscle movement on the subconscious swallow.
5. Keep an upright posture.

## THE MAXILLA (UPPER JAW) SHAPES YOUR FACE

Facial structure is largely determined by the development of the maxilla – the large bone situated in the middle of the face that extends from the upper teeth to the eyes. A common consequence of breathing through the mouth is that the upper jaw extends down and back instead of growing wider and more forward as it should do, which leads to a narrower upper jaw and face.

Since our eyes predominantly rest in the upper part of the maxilla, downward growth of this bone offers less support to our eyes, which leave us with the appearance of a sunken face.

### The tongue shapes the maxilla

Our teeth develop around the tongue, and the natural position for the tongue is in the roof of the mouth, behind the incisors. The tongue stimulates the maxilla, making sure it develops forward and in the proper width. The palate of a correctly developed upper jaw is broad with low arches.

When we breathe through the mouth, the tongue doesn't rest in the roof of the mouth the way it should do. Instead, the tongue moves downward towards the center or the floor of the mouth, in order for the air to pass in and out, which has a negative impact on the development of the maxilla. Ultimately, the palate becomes V-shaped rather than

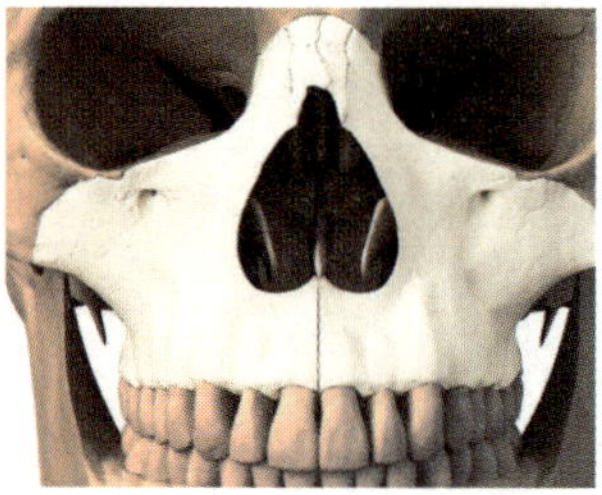

The maxilla shapes your face. An under-developed upper jaw can make the nasal passages narrow.

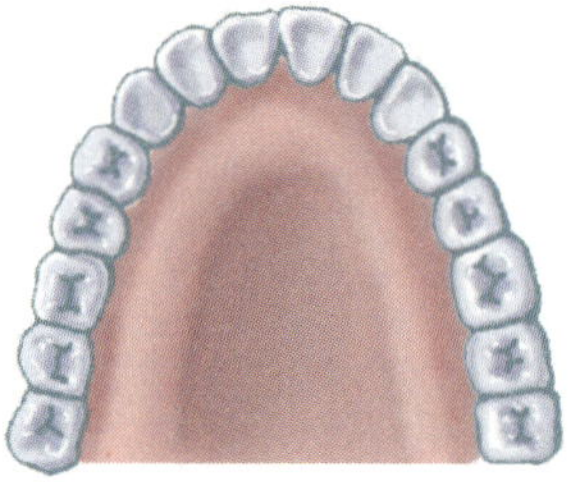

A normally developed U–shaped upper jaw.

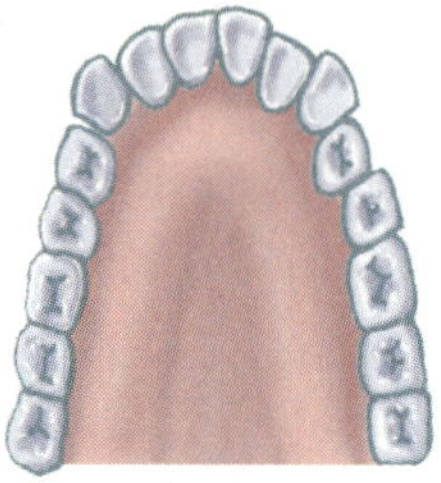

An under-developed V–shaped maxilla. There is not room for all the teeth.

U-shaped, the mouth becomes overcrowded and it becomes difficult to close the mouth tightly when clenching the teeth.

### YOUR TONGUE AND LIPS AFFECT THE POSITION OF YOUR TEETH

Your tongue is one of the most powerful muscles you have in your body, and it can exert a force of approximately 500 grams (1 lb.).[2] Your cheeks and lips are also powerful muscles. The development of skeletal bones is largely controlled by the muscles attached to them, which is why abnormal muscle functions may adversely affect skeletal growth. The muscles in your tongue, cheeks and lips determine the position of your teeth in both the upper and lower jaws. Braces work according to the same principle by exerting slight pressure over an extended period of time to move a tooth.

Every day you swallow around 2,000 times, and your tongue is the most active part of that process. As your tongue is already resting in the palate, the stimulation of your maxilla is reinforced when you press your tongue up against it as you swallow. Given that the force of your tongue could be as much as 0.5 kilo each time it applies pressure against your palate, the total pressure applied to your maxilla by your tongue could amount to many kilos every day.

When you swallow incorrectly, you use the muscles in your cheeks and lips differently, and the force of your tongue is exerted in directions

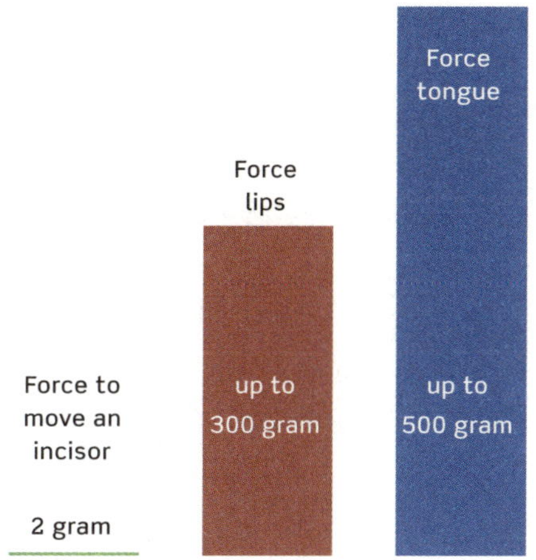


According to a Japanese study, our lips may exert a force against the teeth of between 100 and 300 grams.[3] When we swallow, the force exerted by the tongue may be up to 500 grams. On the other hand it requires only a very small force, applied regularly for a period of time, to move a tooth, which is why braces work. This force is no larger than a few grams.[4]

other than your palate. Not only does swallowing incorrectly leave your palate under stimulated; it also causes your upper jaw to become narrower, and the position of your teeth may be so negatively impacted that they grow unevenly.

## CONSEQUENCES OF BREATHING THROUGH THE MOUTH

In a research study from 2002, 49 children with blocked nasal passages were examined. The report noted that common features of a blocked nasal passage are mouth breathing, enlarged tonsils, a V-shaped upper jaw, a long face, inability to clench the teeth, and an overbite.[5]

Let's take a closer look at some of these negative consequences of breathing through the mouth:

### Tighter nasal passages

85 percent of our nasal passages is created and supported by the maxilla. A narrow upper jaw can produce very narrow nasal passages, which restricts the airflow and the ability to breathe comfortably. Tight airways inside the nose lead to mouth breathing, which eventually causes the diameter of the nasal passages to decrease. The nasal passages of a group of patients who had their larynx surgically removed due to cancer were

examined before and after surgery. Following the surgery, the patients ceased breathing through the nose, and their nasal passages collapsed and became more restricted due to the reduced air pressure inside the nose.[6]

### Overbite, crooked teeth and teeth that don't fit tightly

Underdeveloped jaws can be caused by breathing through the mouth as a consequence of the tongue not resting in the roof of the mouth. Combined with stress, mouth breathing leads to tense jaws, and abnormal muscle activity that may affect the position of the teeth. In many cases, overbite, gaps between the teeth, crooked teeth, or teeth that don't close tightly when you bite together, occur because the upper and lower jaws are developed in a backwards and downwards direction, rather than widening and developing forward.

### Long narrow face and not enough room for the teeth

Instead of growing forward and in width as expected, the upper jaw may grow back and down. When the tongue isn't in place, the force from the lips and cheeks pushes the upper teeth inward and forward, which makes the space in the mouth too narrow for the teeth to fit properly. It also makes the face look flat and slender, and the cheeks appear to be sunken.

### Underdeveloped chin

When the palate is narrow, the dynamics inside the mouth change in order to make room for the tongue. To compensate, the lower jaw generally moves back and the chin doesn't develop as it should do, causing what we call a "weak chin." The development of the mandible (lower jaw) follows the upper jaw. If the upper jaw develops as it should do, the tongue will have enough space to rest in the palate, which will leave better space for the lower jaw to develop properly. In a study of 26 children, Kerr *et al* (1987), showed how the development of the lower jaw began to return to normal when the children went from mouth breathing to nasal breathing.[7]

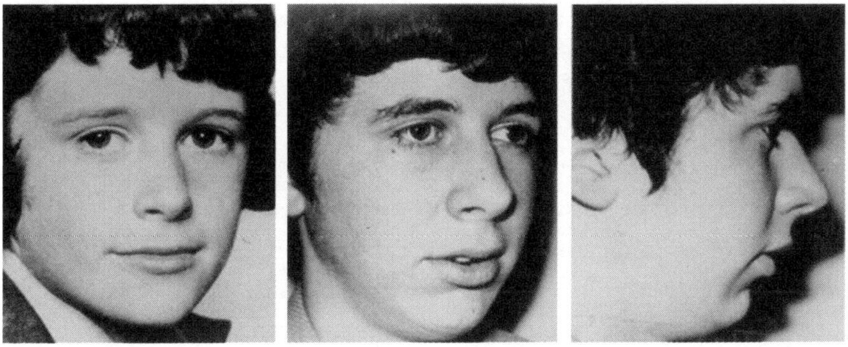

The photo to the left shows a boy at ten years of age. The boy breathes through his nose and has a well-developed face, everything is in proportion, and he has well defined eyes, cheekbones, lips, and chin. When he was 14, he got a gerbil to which he developed an allergy that led to his nose becoming blocked. That is when he began breathing through his mouth. The pictures in the middle and to the right show the same boy at 17. As a result of mouth breathing his face has grown down and backwards, instead of forward and in width. This has made his face elongated. His nose looks bigger, and his chin is small due to the fact that neither his upper nor lower jaw developed forward. This situation results in tighter airways, which eventually can lead to problems with snoring and sleep apnea.[8] *These pictures are published with the permission of professor John Mew.*

### Temporomandibular joint (TMJ) problems

When the maxilla is underdeveloped, the tongue may not fit in the palate. To compensate the mandible generally moves backwards from its normal position to allow more room for the tongue. Consequently, the TMJ may become stiff, which can cause pain and even a clicking sound in the joint. A tense jaw can also create tension headaches.

### Forward leaning posture

When giving first aid to someone, the head should be tilted back to ensure that the airways are open. In general, when breathing through the mouth, we do the same thing by pushing our head forward and tilting it slightly back, which results in a characteristic stooped posture. The lifting of the chin and the forward tilt of the head help to open up the airways when we breathe through the mouth. This particular posture takes more energy than necessary to maintain, as the head weighs 3–4 kilos. You can compare it with carrying a bowling ball either close to or a few inches away from your body.

### Not enough room for the soft tissues

Even if the bones of the upper jaw don't develop to their full genetic potential, the soft tissues of the nose, tongue and throat do. This contributes to the area becoming crowded, which can result in a deviated septum, i.e., the wall of cartilage inside your nose that separates the nostrils becomes displaced. When the septum develops to its normal size and the upper jawbone remains underdeveloped, it's forced to bend in order to fit. A deviated septum prevents a good airflow through the nose and can cause the person to breathe through their mouth most of the time.

### Poorer sleep

When the jaws are narrower because of growing backward, the distance between the throat and tongue is smaller, and the air may have difficulty passing through. There's also less room for the tongue in the mouth, and it may begin falling backward. Being in a horizontal position, especially lying on your back, reduces the space inside your throat. If the pharynx is already narrow due to an underdeveloped jaw, the supine position will add to the problem, and can cause insomnia, snoring and sleep apnea.

It's common for people who snore and suffer sleep apnea to be overweight, and losing weight has often proven to improve sleep problems. Restricted airflow through narrow airways may also result in weight gain owing to a decreased ability to metabolize fat. (You can read more about weight and fat metabolism in Chapter 13.)

Orthodontist Dr. William Hang says, "When I began studying the X-rays of my clients who had received help to expand their upper jaw, I discovered that the gap increased significantly between the back of the tongue and the throat."[9] An open airway in the throat is critical to avoiding the development of sleep problems, such as snoring and sleep apnea.

### Face, neck and shoulder tension

When the mouth is overcrowded, the tongue doesn't press against the maxilla when we swallow as it is supposed to. Such unnatural movement of the tongue and overuse of other muscles in the mouth and face make the muscles tense. The muscle groups of the jaw and face work together when we breathe, swallow, chew and talk, so when they are tense and don't work optimally it makes our face, neck, and shoulders tense, which may also contribute to a stooped posture.[10]

### Stress hormones increase and we "bristle"

Imagine someone put a scarf or their hands around your throat. You would experience an unpleasant feeling, as if you were suffocating, which would trigger a stress reaction. The same thing occurs when our airways are blocked, since a restricted airway caused by mouth breathing and an underdeveloped maxilla will also trigger a stress response. When we open our mouth, push our head forward, and pull up our shoulders in order to be able to open up our airways, it very much resembles the behavior of a stressed dog or cat when they bristle.

### Stuffy nose, sinus infections and ear infections

A narrower maxilla makes the sinuses narrower. Combined with a decreased airflow inside the nose due to mouth breathing, aeration of the sinuses is diminished, which leads to a build-up of mucus in the sinuses that can make them inflamed. Narrow or congested sinuses are common reasons for recurrent ear, sinus and throat infections, and it is usual for children suffering ear problems to have a blocked nose.

### Inability of the child to breastfeed

The consequences of mouth breathing may be evident from birth. All babies are naturally born nasal breathers, which is why they have the ability to suckle and breathe simultaneously. A baby suffering blocked airways may have difficulty breathing through its nose, and therefore prefer a bottle rather than the breast, as it provides faster access to the food.

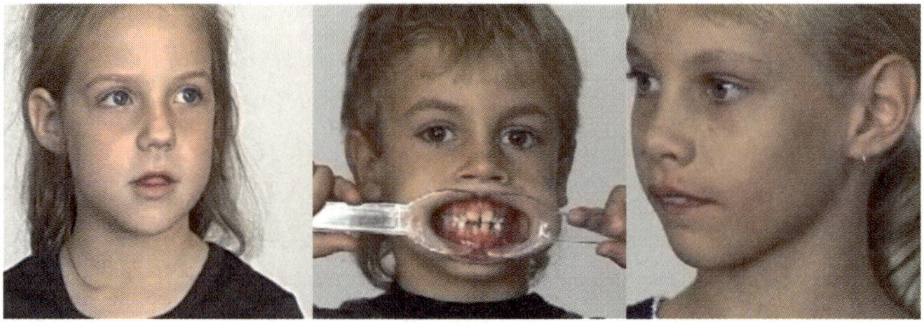

Many children growing up today have jaws that develop down and backwards, which is associated with a long narrow face, sloping forehead, crooked teeth, overbite, underdeveloped chin, underbite, and narrow airways. *These pictures are published with permission by Dr. John Flutter.*

## THE EARLIER NASAL BREATHING IS ESTABLISHED, THE BETTER

The English orthodontist and Professor, John Mew, claims that today, more than 80 percent of four-year-old children have their mouth open most of the day. The earlier in life we establish the bad habit of breathing through the mouth, the greater the risk that our face, smile, teeth and airways will be affected negatively.[11] Ninety percent of our facial development occurs by our early teens.[12] Therefore, the sooner in life we establish nasal breathing, proper swallowing, and a good posture, the better the outcome will be.

Encouraging children from an early age to keep their mouths closed when reading, watching TV and playing computer games will help them develop good breathing habits. They will also be less likely to sleep with their mouth open at night.

You can tell if a child's posture is good if you can draw a straight imaginary line between his or her ear, upper arm and pelvis while sitting or standing.

In *General Dentist*, Yosh Jefferson states, "Children who aren't treated for their mouth breathing can develop long, narrow faces, narrow mouths, high palate arches, crooked teeth, a gummy smile, etc. These children sleep poorly at night because of blocked airways, and a lack of sleep can have a negative impact on their growth and academic ability. Many of these children are diagnosed incorrectly with ADD and hyperactivity." Jefferson further states, "If mouth breathing is treated early, the negative effects on the development of the face and teeth, and the medical and social problems associated with it, can be reduced or avoided." [13]

We may have been told that we've inherited our mother's small jaw size or our father's large teeth, and these are to blame for the lack of space to fit all of our teeth in, as well as for having to have some teeth pulled out. Dr. Flutter argues that this isn't true: "I don't pull out any teeth any more. Every child has the opportunity to develop a face matching their own set of teeth." When teeth are pulled out, there's a risk that the jaw could grow backwards and the airways could become smaller.

During the 1970's and 80's, Professor Linder-Aronsen of the Karolinska Institute noted a relationship between a blocked nose and changes in facial features, such as long, narrow faces, overbites and uneven teeth. Even more interesting was the discovery that facial development returned to normal in those who began breathing through their noses.[14,15,16]

### WHAT CAN YOU DO TO IMPROVE YOUR OWN JAW AND BITE?

Is it too late to affect the shape of the bones when you are an adult? No, it's possible to influence the design of the upper jawbone at all ages. Here are some suggestions for actions to take:

#### Simple tips

- Tape your mouth closed at night. Since the position of the tongue and mouth is so important for the development of the teeth and jaws, your tongue should rest in the roof of your mouth during sleep.
- Rinse your nose with water, salt and baking soda (page 47).

- Do the *Count your steps* exercise (page 58) to release a blocked nose, so that nasal breathing can be established. Usually, 5–10 minutes is enough for your nose to feel freer.
- Chew your food thoroughly in order to exercise your jaws and teeth.
- Become aware of how you swallow and make sure that your tongue naturally pushes gently up against your palate when you swallow.

#### Expanding the upper jaw

The width and length of the upper jaw can be changed at any age, and you can accomplish this by using a so-called expander, which is fitted and placed in the palate by an orthodontist. Another option is to use the Myobrace for Adults™ that can be purchased on the Internet. This is a removable appliance that is placed in your mouth during sleep.

To ensure that the widening remains intact, you need to learn to:

- Breathe through your nose
- Allow your tongue to rest in the palate
- Use your tongue only when swallowing and
- Improve your posture.

If you don't adhere to these recommendations there is a significant risk that your maxilla will retract again after the treatment. The length of time for the upper jaw widening process can vary from person to person, but you can expect the treatment to last for 6–12 months.

#### *Please note*

Make sure you explore all the available options if you plan to visit an orthodontist. Ask questions about the measures that the specialist considers necessary to make room for your 32 teeth, and also ensure that the treatment won't increase the length of your face. If you're not satisfied with the answers, it might be wise to go to someone else. It's not only about straightening your teeth, but also the specialist's ability to see and assess the effect the treatment will have on your entire face. Having uneven teeth is the symptom, not the cause, and the basic problem is that the face has sunken and not developed forward for various reasons. While many dentists and orthodontists are aware of the fact that mouth breathing and how you swallow may affect the development of your teeth, smile, the rest of your face, and especially the airways, the need for further education within this area still remains high. Dr. Flutter advises, "Before deciding to pull teeth, first check to see if there are other options available."

#### Improve your posture

Our head weighs about 3-4 kilos, and when breathing through the mouth, we tilt our head a little backwards and push our chin a bit forward, which changes our posture and affects other parts of our body. The position of our head will also be affected if the position of our feet, pelvis, back, or neck isn't optimal. When a bucket of water is tilted to one side, the water will follow. Given that our head is estimated to contain 85 percent water, we can see that our posture can have a major impact on the development of the 26 cranial bones in our head. A well developed cranium is of great importance for the development of our brain, eyes, ears, etc. If we adopt a posture that is skewed or inclined forward, the bones in our skull need to compensate for the slope. This compensation happens in the bite, where the jaw attaches in front of the ears, and can cause an overbite, an underdeveloped chin, and a tense jaw, in addition to the other problems we have reviewed earlier.

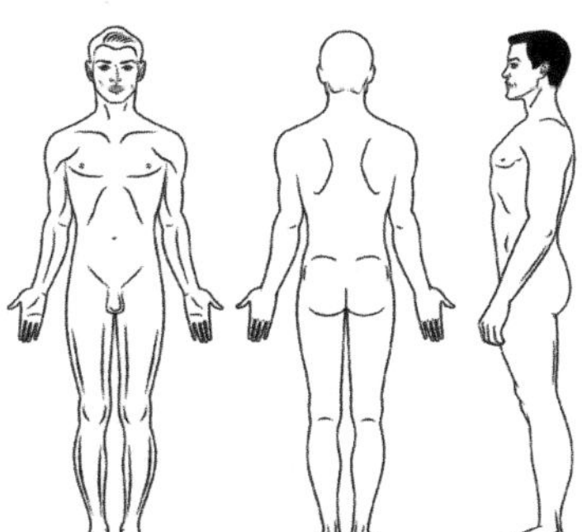

A good, upright posture when we're sitting, standing, walking and running is vital in order for our face, teeth, jaw and the entire cranium to develop optimally.

# Chapter 9 – Breathe Well, Sleep Well

*How we breathe plays an important role in the quality of our sleep, as well as our body's ability to heal, repair and recover during the night. There is a clear link between poor respiration and snoring, sleep apnea, and restless sleep.*

## HOW HAVE YOU BEEN SLEEPING LATELY?

What is the quality of your sleep? Do you have trouble falling asleep, sleep restlessly, and wake up several times a night? Do you wake up too early, find you are unable to go back to sleep, or experience nightmares, sleepwalking, or fidgeting? Does every little sound wake you, or do you sleep like a log and would be able to sleep through an earthquake? Maybe you need to go to the toilet several times each night. Is your mouth dry, nose blocked, throat irritated, or do you need to cough and clear your throat? Do you grind or clench your teeth, or wake up really tired even though you have slept for many hours? Perhaps you snore or take breathing pauses, which is also known as sleep apnea. Or maybe you sleep with a splint or CPAP-mask, which is a device that helps you to breathe properly while sleeping. As you can see, sleep disturbances can have many different faces.

Since we spend about a third of our lives sleeping, the quality of our sleep has a huge impact on our lives. A good night's sleep is essential for our body's ability to heal, repair and recover. We have all been through times when we have slept badly and experienced the negative impact lack of sleep has on our energy, creativity and mood.

Occasional sleeping problems are not a cause for serious concern; however, chronic sleep problems are unfortunately very common. Many of us sleep very lightly and do not get the deep sleep we need, so we wake up in the morning still feeling tired and sleep deprived, despite having had many hours of sleep. Sleep deprivation can also lead to overactivity, not just fatigue, which is basically the flip side of the same coin—a nervous system that is out of balance.

There are two different breathing patterns that affect our sleep negatively. They are snoring and sleep apnea.

### SNORING

Studies show that about 25 percent of the population snore regularly and that snoring is more common among men than women.

Mostly we make jokes about it and otherwise don't pay too much attention to snoring, but the fact is that snoring causes a great strain, not only on your partner whose sleep is also disturbed, but also on your own body. Snoring is a kind of breath that is far from optimum, and it occurs when the pressure in the pharynx (throat) increases so that the uvula and the soft palate begin to vibrate. The sound caused by these vibrations is called snoring, and it can happen on inhalation, as well as on exhalation. Snoring generally happens when breathing through the mouth, but it can also happen during nasal breathing.

The louder the snoring sound, the narrower the openings are in the throat or nose. Hence, the harder it is for the air to pass in and out of the lungs, which automatically makes the breathing shallower. Since the gas exchange is not as efficient higher up in the lungs, the oxygenation of the blood becomes poorer.

To compensate for the reduced effectiveness, we increase the amounts of breaths we take per minute, which increases the pressure inside the throat even further as air is passed in and out more rapidly. Basically, the airways will become narrower and less oxygen will reach the cells, which will cause added stress and ultimately prohibit the deep sleep that would normally allow healing, repair, and recovery to take place. Snoring implies that the sleep is shallow, and the problem

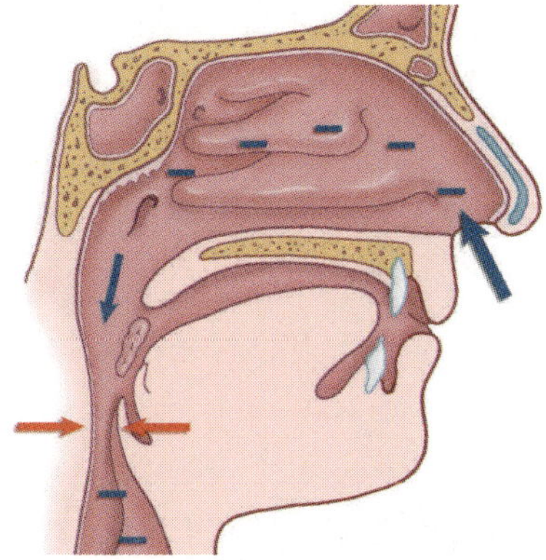

Inhalation. The inspiratory muscles simultaneously make the chest expand and the diaphragm move down towards the abdomen when we inhale, creating a negative pressure in the airways that allows the air to be sucked in. Because of the inferior pressure, the soft parts of the pharynx (throat) are drawn closer to each other. At a fast respiratory rate the negative pressure in the chest becomes heavy, which pulls the trachea down further, making the pharynx even narrower. The more obstructed the airways, the greater the risk for sleeping problems.

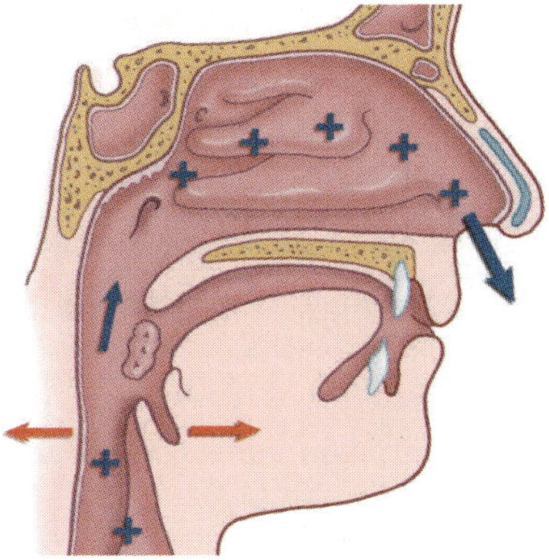

Exhalation. When we exhale calmly, the chest is pressed together by elastic forces, while the diaphragm muscle relaxes and moves up in the chest. During faster exhalation the accessory muscles in the chest assist in expelling the air.

often becomes worse as the years go by, until it eventually produces symptoms of sleep apnea (see next page), i.e., when breathing actually stops intermittently during the night.

Narrow or blocked nasal passages have been associated with sleep problcms in many studics. In one study where eight healthy individuals had their nostrils blocked so that they could only breathe through their mouths during sleep, all the subjects experienced disturbed sleep due to an increased incidence of snoring, sleep apnea, and light sleep.[1]

Other studies have also shown a clear connection between snoring and a blocked nose. In another study, the air exhaled by all the subjects who had their noses blocked and were breathing through their mouths had lower levels of carbon dioxide than when the same subjects slept with their mouths closed and breathed through their noses. A low level of carbon dioxide in the exhaled air is due to prolonged over-breathing that has reduced the total amount of $CO_2$ in the body, leading to oxygen deficiency (Bohr effect).[2]

## SLEEP APNEA

Another sleeping-related problem is sleep apnea, in which sufferers stop breathing during sleep. For various reasons, the airways may be clogged and the apnea occurs when the air can't get through. It's common in sleep apnea to wake up tired, even after sleeping for a long time. Sleep apnea is defined as a breathing pause lasting longer than ten seconds. It generally occurs between 5–30 times per hour, but in some cases it may happen even more often. In the United States, it's estimated that 15 percent of the population suffers from sleep apnea. In an American study of 602 randomly selected people, 24 percent of the men and 9 percent of the women had five or more apneic events during the night.[3]

### Exercise 17 — What sleep apnea feels like

Try holding your breath while awake. Eventually you can't hold it any longer and must open your mouth and take a big, hungry breath. This is what your body does during sleep if you have sleep apnea.

How do you feel afterwards? Is your body relaxed, calm and peaceful? Probably not. Instead, you most likely feel wound up, since your body would have perceived the exercise as a fight for survival.

The body must work very hard when someone suffers from sleep apnea. Breathing shifts like a yo-yo between extended pauses where there is no breathing to heavy breathing, i.e., hyperventilation. During the pause, the oxygen level in the blood decreases, just as it would do during physical exercise. The breathing pause triggers a stress response, which increases adrenaline levels, causing the heart to work harder, which in turn increases the blood pressure. It's also common for many people who experience apneic events at night to be unaware of it, and consequently, to have received no diagnosis.[4]

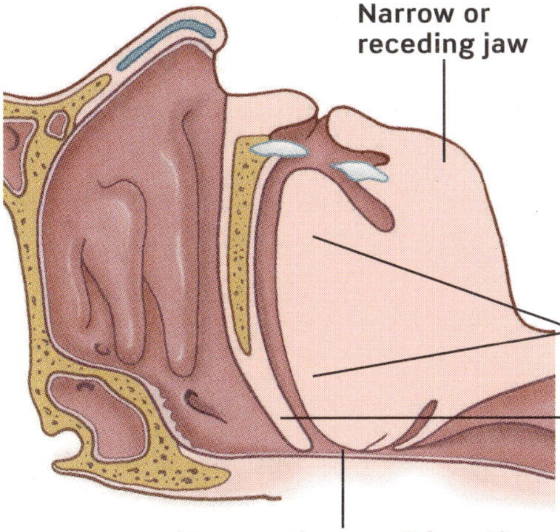


Blockage of the airways can occur in several places in sleep apnea sufferers. An extended and enlarged soft palate interferes with the posterior airway at the level of the upper pharynx. In addition, a receded lower jaw will press the tongue backwards and reduce the space in the lower pharynx.

The basic problem in sleep apnea is blocked airways. One study showed that patients with allergic nasal inflammation had more apneic events during the allergy season when their nose was blocked.[5]

Another study carried out over an 18-year period showed that the test subjects were more than three times as likely to die prematurely if the sleep apnea remained untreated. Sleep apnea increases the risk of high blood pressure, stroke, depression, traffic accidents, asthma, and premature death. When the number of apneic events increases, so does the risk of developing health problems.[6]

If the lower and upper jaws haven't developed forward as they should do, but rather, have developed backwards and/or down, the pharyngeal passage becomes tighter. Even if the skeletal parts don't develop to their full potential, the soft parts like the tongue, palate, and the uvula will. They may then be too large for the underdeveloped skull and the passage of the throat is perceived as narrow.[7] Sleep specialist, Dr. John Remmers, who coined the term, "obstructive sleep apnea," views sleep apnea as a structural problem. According to Dr. Remmers, sleep apnea wouldn't exist if the upper and lower jaw had the right proportions in the face.

Obesity is another factor associated with sleep apnea. Being overweight on the outside equals being overweight on the inside. If the extra weight is situated around the neck and throat, the airways will be narrower. If the fat is located in the abdominal area, the excess weight will be pushed against the diaphragm, which will stop it from working well, and the inhaled air will be forced higher up in the chest. It is estimated that approximately 60-70 percent of those suffering sleep apnea are overweight.

## SLEEP APNEA AID — CPAP

If diagnosed with sleep apnea, a physician may prescribe a breathing device and mask, called a CPAP, for the individual to wear during sleep. The mask is connected to a device that has the reverse effect of a vacuum cleaner, where the air blowing out from the apparatus creates a slight air pressure that keeps the airways in the nasal passages and throat open.

The CPAP mask is an efficient way to help sufferers sleep without apneic events because the improved quality of sleep results in reduced blood pressure as well as less fatigue during the day.[8] The sufferer is able to sleep without breathing pauses while wearing the mask.

Despite the advantage of eliminating the breathing pauses, there are many drawbacks associated with wearing the mask. Most people wish they could stop having to use the apparatus, since both the wearer and their partner are often disturbed by the humming sound from the unit. To have to wear a mask at night can be uncomfortable, and the dry air can also cause the nose to become blocked, irritated and runny.

### Exercise 18 — Withdrawal from the CPAP

Many people who have improved their breathing habits have been able to stop using the CPAP machine at night.[9] The time involved is very individual, but after a few weeks of breathing retraining one may feel ready to, in consultation with his or her physician, try to withdraw from using the CPAP.

***What to do:***

1. Go to bed without wearing your CPAP mask.
2. Apply tape on your mouth so that it is closed during sleep.
3. Set the alarm to go off 2–3 hours after you fall asleep.
4. Take notice of how you are breathing when the alarm wakes you up.
5. If your symptoms are no worse than if you had used the CPAP, you can try to get back to sleep and sleep the rest of the night without the mask. If you wake up in the morning and do not feel worse than you would after a night's sleep with the CPAP, you can continue to sleep without wearing the CPAP. However, as a precaution, continue to set the alarm for the next few nights.
6. If your breathing is loud, fast, or otherwise not optimal, use the Relaxator for 5–15 minutes while sitting up in bed with your back straight, so that your diaphragm is given enough space to carry out its work unhindered. An alternative to using the Relaxator is to breathe slowly, abdominally and rhythmically, focusing on prolonged exhalation, tightening your throat, and gently squeezing the air out. This allows the subsequent inhalation to reach deeper down into your lungs, which calms your breathing pattern and allows you to relax.
7. If your symptoms are worse than usual when the alarm goes off, use the CPAP for the rest of the night. The next night, repeat steps 1–5, and once again go to bed without using the CPAP mask.

**PLEASE NOTE! DON'T MAKE ANY CHANGES TO THE USE OF THE CPAP-DEVICE WITHOUT FIRST CONSULTING YOUR PHYSICIAN.**

### OTHER FACTORS DISTURBING YOUR QUALITY OF SLEEP

Snoring and sleep apnea are common sleep problems, but there are also other issues that can disturb the quality of your sleep:

### Difficulty falling asleep, restless sleep, nightmares, being easily awakened

The more active your brain is during the day, the greater the risk that it will also be active at night, thus making it difficult to relax. The quest to quieten a racing mind is a common reason why people resort to alcohol and sleeping pills to induce sleep. Alcohol and sleeping pills may provide relief for the moment, but they will never solve the underlying problem.

A racing mind can keep you from falling asleep easily, can cause you to wake up in the middle of the night, make it difficult to go back to sleep when awakened, or give you nightmares. These problems indicate that your nervous system is out of balance, and that the sympathetic part, i.e., the gas pedal, is more alert than is required during sleep, i.e., your body is in fight/flight mode. This state results in the elevation of stress hormone levels such as adrenaline, which in turn results in an increased respiratory rate. Unfortunately, this reaction isn't useful when the body is at rest as it instigates over-breathing and results in a lack of $CO_2$ and oxygen. When the brain receives less oxygen than it needs your sleep will be interrupted and you may also suffer nightmares.

### Sleeping too much, sleeping like a log, falling asleep too easily

As sleep problems get worse, insomnia can sometimes be replaced by over-sleeping—i.e., we fall asleep very easily and sleep very heavily. It is often thought that sleeping heavily indicates that the quality of sleep is good, but it's just the opposite. The sleep isn't deep, so we generally wake up tired, even if we've slept for many hours. To sleep like a log may be an indication that you have entered into a phase of exhaustion from a period of sleep deprivation, so that your body isn't able to "sleep lightly." [10]

### Having to pee at night

Just as there are smooth muscles in our blood vessels and airways, there are also smooth muscles in our bladder. When we over-breathe, these muscles contract and become tense, making the bladder smaller. A small bladder may wake us up several times per night, sending us to the toilet, or even causing us to wet the bed, as many children do.[10]

### Tense jaw

The general advice for people who grind or clench their teeth is to sleep with their mouth wide open. Because grinding or clenching your teeth at night is caused by the jaws being tense, which is closely associated with imbalances in the nervous system, it is even more important to keep your mouth closed and breathe through your nose. Grinding and clenching your teeth puts excess stress on your body, which can be alleviated by improving your breathing habits. Cultivating calmer breathing will also reduce any tension in your muscles and jaws, thereby enabling you to sleep better.

## OTHER REASONS FOR SLEEP PROBLEMS

Snoring, sleep apnea, and other sleep problems outlined above indicate a strong correlation with breathing habits that would benefit from being improved. Your quality of sleep is closely related to how you breathe, both when you sleep and when you are awake. Sleep problems occur for many different reasons. In addition to the ones already discussed, here are a few others causes of sleep problems:

### Tight nose and narrow airways

A blocked nose, polyps, sinus congestion, and swollen nasal turbinates (spiral protrusions in the nose that move air more efficiently) make the nasal passages narrow, which makes it harder for the air to pass through your nose. A narrow nasal passage generally leads to mouth breathing, loss of sleep, and swollen tonsils, etc. Narrow airways trigger a stress response resulting in increased sympathetic nervous system activity and increased levels of stress hormones, such as adrenaline.

### Mouth breathing

Breathing with your mouth open has several negative consequences for your sleep, since dry and cold air both increases the risk of the airways being inflamed. When you breathe through your mouth, your respiratory volume automatically increases, as does your outflow of $CO_2$. Decreased carbon dioxide levels leads to constricted muscles in the throat making the passages narrower. When we breathe through the mouth we also lose out on the widening effect of the Nitric Oxide that is produced in the sinuses.

The reason we breathe through the mouth during hard physical labor is because it is easier to inhale air through the mouth than through the nose. Breathing through the mouth when we lie down, however, makes it more difficult to inhale, as our airways will be narrower than they are when we breathe through our nose.[11] A review of available research concluded that poor sleep often was the result of a blocked nose. The authors noted that, "since breathing through our nose seems to be the best way to breathe during sleep, a blocked nose often leads to nocturnal mouth breathing, snoring, and eventually sleep apnea." In the report, the authors recommended that greater emphasis should be put on dealing with problems in the upper airways, and to establish nasal breathing to enhance the quality of sleep.[12]

### Asthma

Inflammation, increased mucus production, and constricted muscles in the throat and bronchi (lungs) cause narrow airways in asthma sufferers. A clear link between asthma and sleep problems has been established. The authors of one study claim that 74 percent of asthmatics experience blocked airflow at night as a result of their asthma.[13]

### Over-breathing during the day causes over-breathing at night

When our breathing volume exceeds our body's needs, the resulting carbon dioxide deficiency causes constriction of the muscles in our airways. If we repeat this pattern long enough and often enough it becomes habitual and eventually will also occur when we are asleep. As we have discussed before carbon dioxide deficiency caused by over-breathing leads to a deficiency in oxygen.

### Late eating habits

For a restful night's sleep our body should be totally relaxed and required to perform only minimal activity. Digesting food demands a lot of resources, so when we eat too close to bedtime our bodies become more active than they should be during the night. Some types of food and beverages may also increase mucus production, which forces us to clear our throat frequently. The more mucus the body produces, the narrower the airways will become.

### Smoking

Smoking irritates our airways, which enhances mucus production and increases inflammation and, therefore, causes narrower airways. The airways are developed to bring air in and out in the most optimal way. Cigarette smoke contains physical particles that get stuck and clog the airways when we breathe; our lungs are not designed to deal with these particles.

### Inactivity

Just a few generations ago we lived a much more active life than we do today. When we have exerted our body really hard for a day and have become completely physically tired, it is easy to fall asleep. Too little physical activity, on the other hand, often has the opposite effect, and we may not be tired when it's time to sleep.

### Sleeping on our back

When we sleep on our back we risk having our tongue fall backwards and block our airway, thus requiring more effort to move the air in and out. This also increases the risk of our chin falling down towards our chest, causing us to breathe with our mouth open.

### Irregular sleeping hours

Shift work or constantly changing bedtimes result in an irregular sleep schedule that can disturb our sleeping rhythm and cause insomnia and shallow sleep.

### Alcohol

All the muscles in our body relax during sleep, except the diaphragm and heart. Problems can occur when the muscles in your throat are too relaxed, as your airways then become narrower. Perhaps you have heard someone say, "I only snore when I've been drinking alcohol." The reason for this is that alcohol increases muscle relaxation in the airways, which may result in them becoming relaxed to the point of collapsing, thus making the diameter of the passage even smaller.

### External interference

A partner who snores is a major reason why an estimated one in ten house owners have separate bedrooms. Parents of young children also often have their sleep disrupted when their children wake up during the night. Plus, there are other external disturbances to sleep caused by traffic or noisy neighbors, etc.

## HOW TO IMPROVE YOUR SLEEP?

Here are a few simple, yet powerful tips to improve your sleep:

### Tape your mouth

A classic tip to ensure that your mouth is closed is to apply surgical tape over your mouth at night. People are surprised at the positive outcome of this technique, which is very simple and inexpensive. Give mouth taping at least a week, in order to allow you to have the opportunity to notice results. Use Sleep Tape or ordinary surgical tape and tape either along or across your lips. More information on mouth taping can be found in Chapter 4.

### Wind down before bedtime

Don't go directly to bed from your PC or TV as your brain will still be fully active and it will be harder to relax. Turn off your computer, mobile phone and TV 15–30 minutes before bedtime to give your brain a chance to wind down and relax. During that time it can be advantageous to take a moment to focus on your breathing. Try to lengthen your exhalations, as prolonged exhalation provides slow, rhythmic breathing and increased relaxation.

### Lower the temperature in your bedroom

If it's too hot in your bedroom there is a risk of over-breathing, because the excess heat produced inside your body can't be removed through the skin. The same applies when we dress too warmly. Since we have to eliminate the surplus heat through exhalation we increase our respiratory rate, which is similar to a dog panting to cool its body down.

### Sleep on your side

The best sleeping position is on your side, as this allows your airways to be kept open and dilated, making the process of breathing less demanding. Sleeping on your side also puts less stress on your circulatory system and reduces your likelihood of experiencing reflux.

If you have trouble sleeping on your side, then lying on your stomach is a better alternative than sleeping on your back. From a respiratory point of view, sleeping on your back is the worst possible option, since your lower jaw may drop and cause you to breathe through the mouth. An added risk is that your tongue may fall back and block the pharynx.

### Open the window

Keep a window slightly open in the bedroom to allow fresh air to enter. Even in wintertime it's an advantage to have a window slightly ajar for the air to circulate.

**Take a break from the noise**

Daily activities provide our brain with a lot of stimuli to process. Many of us have forgotten what it means to be fully relaxed, and we are not aware of how much impact radio, television, newspapers and advertising have on our mental activity. We are constantly fed with problems, violence, and how we should behave and look, which makes most of us feel anxious, fearful, angry, or worried that we are not good enough. Such programming happens in stages and often goes unnoticed, but the effects are very hard on the mind, body and spirit. Try taking a break from media for a few days, or just take a walk without your music or mobile phone. Focus on what you hear and see around you, instead of the thoughts in your head. Then reflect on how it feels to get some distance from the noise.

**Lose weight**

Being overweight is common among people with sleep problems, and it's particularly prevalent in people with a short, thick neck, as the extra weight causes tighter airways in the throat and neck. A big stomach may also contribute to sleep problems as the extra girth leaves less room for the diaphragm and lungs to expand, which results in shallow breathing.

**Increase the humidity**

As the humidity in the exhaled air is always at 100 percent, inhaling dry air makes us lose unnecessary amounts of water with each breath. Try placing a glass of water above the radiator to increase the humidity in your bedroom. It's particularly effective if you have electric radiators as these make the air dry, which in turn can dry out your mucus membranes. If you have floor heaters, wall heaters or central heating you can purchase a small room humidifier to add humidity to the air.

### Stop eating three hours before bedtime

A good rule of thumb is to not eat any food within three hours of bedtime. Digestion demands a lot of energy, and if your digestive system has to work hard while you sleep, your liver and other digestive organs won't get the rest they need.

### Practice Conscious Breathing during training

Any form of physical activity with a closed mouth increases your chances of being physically tired when you go to bed as this type of physical activity has a calming effect on an overactive brain.

### Applying alternating nasal breathing

If you have trouble falling asleep, you can try the alternating nasal breathing exercise to get your nervous system in better balance. More information about this exercise is found on page 97. Alternatively you can close your right nostril with your finger and breathe only through your left nostril. This activates your right brain hemisphere and the soothing, parasympathetic part of your nervous system.

### Become aware of how you sleep

Many people with sleeping problems don't actually know how they sleep. If you want to have a clearer picture of your sleep, you can record yourself on video, mp3 player, use an app on your mobile phone (e.g., Sleep Cycle), or ask someone to observe you for 2–3 hours (an entire sleeping cycle) while you sleep. This will give you a better picture of how you actually sleep, as well as increase your understanding of your sleep quality. If your sleep isn't up to scratch, this knowledge may motivate you to take action in order to achieve better sleep and thereby increase the quality of your life.

# Chapter 10 – Improving Your Breathing Protects Your Heart and Circulatory System

*Tense, non-rhythmic and stressed breathing makes for a strained, non-rhythmic and stressed heart. Relaxed breathing, on the other hand, ensures a relaxed heart.*

## OUR HEART RHYTHM FOLLOWS OUR RESPIRATORY RHYTHM

Our heart is situated right between our lungs, and how we actually breathe has a big impact on it. The normal number of heartbeats at rest is 60–75 beats per minute, therefore a pulse of 70 means that our heart beats 100,000 times in a single day. The rhythm of our heart follows our respiratory rhythm, so if the respiratory rate is high then our pulse is often high too. An example of this relationship is found in infants who normally take 40-50 breaths per minute, while their hearts beat 120-140 times simultaneously. The same happens when we exercise, since both the pulse and respiratory rate are increased.

The renowned Yale Professor, Yandell Henderson, who worked in heart and lung research during the first half of the 1900's, showed in a research project how it was possible to raise dogs' heart rates from 40 to 200 beats per minute by altering the respiratory rate. When the alterations were made to the dogs' respiratory rates, their heart rate rose or dropped accordingly.[1] In another study on 226 patients with heart failure, it was discovered that breathing and heart function followed each other—the more serious a patients' heart failure, the more their breathing deteriorated.[2]

Many of my students testify that breathing exercises have helped them lower their blood pressure, as well as their pulse. Furthermore, they experience fewer problems with a racing heart or palpitations.

Let's take a closer look at high blood pressure, which is a heart and circulatory problem related to breathing:

### HIGH BLOOD PRESSURE

Blood pressure is the pressure exerted on the walls of our blood vessels when blood is pumped from our heart to different parts of our body and then back to our heart. It's measured in mmHg (millimeters of mercury), and blood pressure at rest that is higher than 140/90 is usually considered to be high blood pressure. 140 indicates systolic pressure, i.e., the maximum pressure when your heart pumps the blood out to your body, and 90 shows the diastolic pressure, i.e., the minimum pressure when your heart relaxes and fills up with new blood.

Blood pressure varies throughout the day, just like breathing, and the pressure changes depending on what we do. Normal blood pressure is 110-130/80. The blood pressure of some people is too low, which is generally considered to be 90/60 or lower. Although low blood pressure is not that common, many people with impaired adrenal and thyroid function tend to have problems with low blood pressure.

High blood pressure increases the mechanical strain on our blood vessels and increases the production of cholesterol, which is manufactured to protect the walls of our blood vessels against the higher pressure. Over time, high blood pressure makes the walls of the blood vessels harder and less elastic, and our heart has to work harder to pump the blood through our body.

About a quarter of the adult population in Sweden suffers from high blood pressure, and the majority of those (70-80 percent) take medicine to reduce the pressure.[3] A slightly elevated blood pressure usually doesn't cause any major problems, and medical treatment is normally only commenced when high blood pressure poses an increased risk, especially for stroke, but also for heart attack, heart failure, kidney disease and decreased circulation in the legs.

It's important to remember that medicine only acts as a suppressive and doesn't cure the problem. If we stop taking the medication, the high blood pressure will immediately return, since the root cause of the raised blood pressure hasn't been addressed. Generally, two or three drugs have to be taken in combination. The most prescribed medicines are:

- Diuretics to eliminate water and reduce blood volume.
- Vasodilating agents such as nitroglycerine.
- Calcium blockers that dilate blood vessels to lower the pressure.
- ACE inhibitors that prevent the body from forming the vasoconstrictive substance, angiotensin-2, which increases blood pressure.
- Beta-blockers to reduce the effect of the stress hormone adrenaline, and to lower the pulse.

It's common for people who have high blood pressure and other heart problems to over-breathe as well. Several studies show that the breathing volume per minute in those suffering from heart problems is twice as high or even higher than the normal 4-6 liters.[4,5]

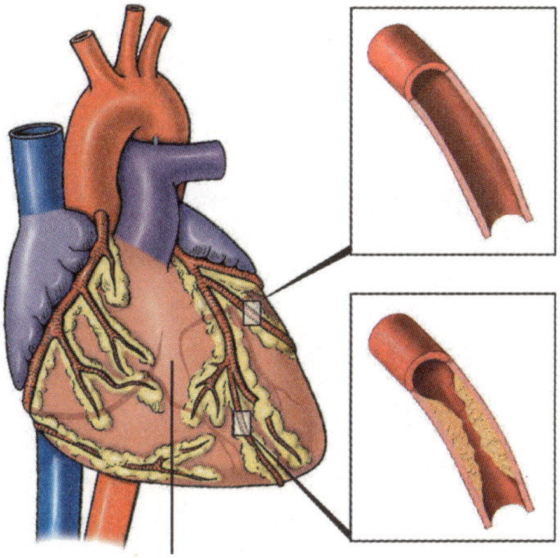


**If you have high blood pressure and other cardiovascular problems, your blood vessels are often narrow. One major reason is low levels of carbon dioxide, which causes the smooth muscles of your blood vessels to constrict.**

**Another reason is low levels of NO, which is produced in the nose, and has the same dilating effect on your blood vessels as carbon dioxide.**

**Lower your blood pressure with breathing retraining**

Our blood pressure depends on:

- How quickly the blood passes through the blood vessels
- Blood viscosity
- How flexible the walls of the blood vessels are
- How wide the blood vessels are.

We often assume that hypertension (high blood pressure) is to a great extent inherited and that we can't do anything about it. However, evidence suggests that it's our lifestyle and the way we act and react in different situations, which we often inherit from our parents, that determines whether we develop high blood pressure or not. The good news is that our lifestyle is something we can affect. Physicians and physiotherapists commonly advise the following lifestyle changes to their patients in order to reduce the blood pressure:

- Regular exercise
- Quit smoking and drink less alcohol
- Improve your eating habits and drink more water
- Practice relaxation
- Lose weight.

All the above suggestions are very good, but breathing retraining, which is a very powerful tool in dealing with high blood pressure, is often overlooked. Since our heart and lungs work very closely together, and most high blood pressure patients suffer from impaired breathing, breathing exercises should really be at the top of the list of treatment advice.[6,7]

Moreover, improving our breathing habits is also a powerful way of reducing our internal stress—physical, emotional and mental.

**Simple tip**

Close your right nostril with your finger and breathe in and out through your left nostril. This activates your right brain hemisphere and the soothing, parasympathetic part of your nervous system and lowers your blood pressure.[8] To raise your blood pressure, simply do the opposite – breathe in and out through your right nostril.

There are also a number of other heart and circulatory problems closely related to our breathing. These include:

**Circulatory problems**

When we eat, most of our blood flow is directed to our stomach/intestinal tract and the capillaries, the smallest blood vessels, are closed in other parts of our body. When digestion is complete, and the need for blood in our stomach/intestinal tract is reduced, circulation will be directed to other areas. An indirect effect of this is that we feel less active immediately following a meal and more alert after a short rest. In other words, there is a mechanism that prioritizes the blood flow to a given area. The order is pre-programmed according to the importance of different functions. Our brain, lungs, liver, kidneys and various glands normally get higher priority for blood circulation than our muscles, bones and skin. A change in our situation, such as a need to run from danger, will shift the priority of blood flow to the most needed functions of the moment. Another example is exercise, which will increase the blood circulation to our muscles.

Cold hands and feet indicate that circulation isn't working optimally and that our body has chosen not to prioritize blood flow to our extremities. In a study where the subjects were asked to hyperventilate, they exhibited such severe constriction in the blood vessels in their hands that it was difficult to obtain blood from the finger for blood tests.[9]

At the Nagoya Kyoritsu Hospital in Japan, more than 200 patients with impaired circulation have been successfully treated with $CO_2$. The patients received footbaths in carbon dioxide-enriched water, which increased circulation in their feet (see photos on next page).[10,11] Carbon dioxide dilates the blood vessels, and when the $CO_2$ levels are optimal,

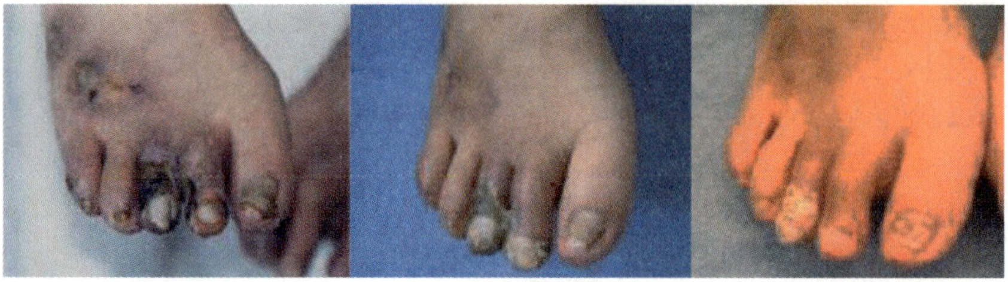

**BEFORE** **1 MONTH** **3 MONTHS**

Pictures of a 48-year old woman diagnosed with hypertension who received dialysis for nine years. She had developed open sores on her feet that made her wheelchair-bound. She was given a $CO_2$ enriched footbath for ten minutes twice a day for three months. After one month, her wounds and pain had diminished enough to avoid the scheduled amputation. After three months, the wounds were almost healed and she was released from the hospital, able to walk unaided.

blood circulation works properly. The $CO_2$ concentration in our body is increased through reduced respiration volume, physical activity, or absorption through the skin.

In the 1920's, a group of American scientists discovered that persons who had undergone surgery under anesthesia recovered faster if they inhaled eight percent carbon dioxide, which stimulated respiration so that the usual problem with cyanosis, indicated by bluish skin, disappeared. The circulation was also improved, and the skin changed temperature and color from cold and grey to warm and rosy. Even the pulse was quickly restored from fast to normal.[12]

Carbon dioxide therapy is a skin care treatment that has long been used in the beauty industry, and it is now starting to receive more attention. Since 1932, more than 500,000 people have received carbon dioxide therapy at the spa center in Royat, France, by either $CO_2$ injections under the skin, or a gel that is applied to the skin. The composition of the gel leads to the formation of carbon dioxide. I've tested a number of different carbon dioxide gels, and all of them produced increased blood circulation. It is the vasodilating effect of $CO_2$ that allows more blood to be transported to the treatment area, bringing oxygen and nutrients, as well as removing waste products. This stimulates collagen production, which in turn increases the skin's elasticity. The treatment is also believed to reduce wrinkles, scars, under-eye puffiness, and uneven skin, as well as reduce the appearance of cellulite.

### Irregular heartbeat (arrhythmia)

There is a clear correlation between low levels of $CO_2$ and the development of cardiac arrhythmia. The lack of carbon dioxide can lead to both insufficient blood flow, due to constricted blood vessels, and lack of oxygen as explained by the Bohr effect. In a study where 474 healthy subjects hyperventilated for five minutes by taking 30 breaths per minute, 15 percent showed changes in heart rhythm even after 10 minutes of rest.[13] It's then conceivable and logical to assume that if over-breathing only a few minutes has that effect, over-breathing, for days, weeks and years can cause the same problems on a deeper level, as was seen in the study.

### Vascular constriction, atherosclerosis

Fatty deposits may form when blood vessels become hardened and stiff, i.e., atherosclerosis or arteriosclerosis, due to high blood pressure, for instance. Sometimes blood clots are formed in blocked blood vessels, too.

In addition, carbon dioxide deficiency caused by over-breathing can accelerate the formation of blood clots because it increases levels of platelets (thrombocytes). Blood platelets are normally formed when the blood coagulates and the increased levels of blood platelets make the blood vessels narrower.

In one study, twelve healthy medical students were asked to hyperventilate for 20 minutes with a respiratory volume of 36 liters per minute. For one of the tests, the subjects were inhaling normal air, while in another test the inhaled air contained five percent carbon dioxide, i.e., over 100 times more $CO_2$ than in normal air. The study was designed to exclude the effect of any extra muscular work required when hyperventilating. The blood platelet levels increased by eight percent when hyperventilating with normal air, and were unchanged when the subjects were breathing air with five percent $CO_2$ added. The results indicated that it was the low levels of $CO_2$ that occurred during hyperventilation of normal air that resulted in the increased formation of blood platelets.[14]

In the case of vascular constriction, the patient is often given a medicine called nitroglycerin to dilate the blood vessels. Nitroglycerin increases our ability to produce NO (nitric oxide), which is exactly the same substance that is produced in large quantities in our nose and transported into our lungs during nasal breathing. NO is produced not only in our nose, but also naturally throughout our body, in the blood vessels, for example, to help them relax and widen. Having relaxed and dilated blood vessels means that our heart doesn't have to work as hard to pump the blood around our body's 60,000 miles (100,000 kilometers) of blood vessels.

### Impaired blood values and increased risk of infection

$CO_2$ has an antibacterial effect, and a study at the Karolinska Institute in Sweden showed that the growth of staphylococci was 1,000 times higher when the bacteria were exposed to normal air for 24 hours, compared with exposure to air saturated with 100 percent $CO_2$.[15,16]

Low levels of $CO_2$ are associated with impaired blood count and increased risk of infection. Several students from my courses testified that their blood count has improved since they started practicing breathing retraining. An 85-year-old man, who had received a blood transfusion every five weeks for many years, improved his blood count sufficiently and no longer requires blood transfusions—all thanks to rhythmic, diaphragmatic breathing in and out through his nose.

$CO_2$ has been used in food packaging since the 1930's. Bread, cheese, chicken, and coffee, are some of the products that have 100 percent carbon dioxide added inside the packaging, while meat usually has 20 percent carbon dioxide and 80 percent oxygen added. One reason that $CO_2$ is used in food packaging is because of its antibacterial effect, which prevents disease-causing bacteria from growing.[17]

If $CO_2$ has an antibacterial effect when used inside food packaging, it is reasonable to assume that it also has an antibacterial effect inside our body. Having low $CO_2$ levels in our body would thus provide a breeding ground for undesirable bacteria, while a higher $CO_2$ content would reduce the risk of infections.

### Reduced sexual ability

Erection difficulties, such as premature ejaculation or loss of libido, are common problems related to breathing and blood circulation. Overbreathing and mouth breathing reduce the levels of $CO_2$ and NO and make the smooth muscles, including the smooth muscles controlling the blood flow to the penis and clitoris, constrict. Reduced blood flow to the clitoris may reduce the sex drive and reduced blood flow to the penis can make it difficult or impossible to achieve an erection. Even if an erection can be achieved, the high underlying stress associated with impaired breathing habits may lead to a premature ejaculation.

An erection is associated with the body being relaxed, which is also when the parasympathetic part of the nervous system (the brake) is more active. Ejaculation, on the other hand, is activated by the sympathetic part of the nervous system (the gas pedal). During tantric sex, a technique used to increase sexual ability and pleasure, a lot of emphasis is placed on breathing in a relaxed and rhythmic manner.

In the book *The Multi-Orgasmic Man* the author writes, "Learning to control ejaculation and be able to have more than one orgasm starts with strengthening and deepening your breathing. It is well known within the worlds of fighting sports and meditation techniques that breathing is the key to maintaining control over the body."[18]

Except for the ears, the only body parts that have erectile tissue are our nose and genitals. A blocked nose, which may be due to polyps, leads to mouth breathing which has a negative impact on sexual capacity in both men and women. In a study of 29 men who had polyps inside their nose, 34 percent also had erectile dysfunction, compared to only 3 percent in the control group. After the polyps had been surgically removed, and the men were able to breathe through their nose, the figure dropped to 10 percent.[19]

The development of the erectile-enhancing drug Viagra was possible thanks to the understanding of nitric oxide (NO) and its vasodilatory effects on the human body. Although the medication was initially developed for vascular constriction, since it was discovered that enhancing an erection was one of its side effects, Viagra is now being marketed as a male potency enhancer.

The amount of NO is reduced in the air that is transported into the lungs and blood when you breathe through your mouth, so if you wish to improve your sex life it seems wise to breathe through your nose.

### Exercise 1 — Pelvic floor training

Below is a simple exercise for increased sexual pleasure, for both women and men. This exercise will help tighten your pelvic floor. The effect is boosted if you use the Relaxator while you do the exercise:

1. Tighten your perineal muscle, located between your anus and genitals, so that it is drawn upwards.
2. Calmly inhale and exhale twice while keeping the muscle tightened.
3. Relax the perineal muscle for a moment and then repeat the exercise five times.

### Angina pectoris

Angina pectoris is a condition in which the blood flow to the heart is insufficient. It occurs most in situations when the heart muscle is forced to work harder than normal, such as in physical or mental exertion, when a greater blood supply is required. When the blood flow is insufficient, the heart doesn't receive enough oxygen and nutrients.

The delivery of oxygen to our heart muscle is reduced when our carbon dioxide levels are low due to blood vessel constriction. Simultaneously, the heart demands an increased amount of oxygen, as it needs to work harder to pump blood around the body when the blood vessels are constricted. These effects may be contributory factors in the various forms of angina, which is a common problem in people who are hyperventilating.[20]

### Heart attack

Narrow blood vessels or blood clots also affect the organs to which the blood vessels supply blood. When the coronary arteries, the blood vessels that supply our heart with oxygen, become too narrow, due to lack of carbon dioxide for instance, angina or a heart attack may be the result. The lack of oxygen that occurs in the heart when the blood supply diminishes in a heart attack can cause permanent damage, which in turn results in the heart working less efficiently than before, thereby increasing the risk of another heart attack.

During surgery there is an increased risk of the blood platelets clumping together to form clots. In a review of 48 studies, a group of researchers found that the number of blood clots is greatly reduced if appropriate techniques for adding carbon dioxide are used during heart surgery.[21]

If it's the blood vessels to your brain that get blocked, cerebral infarction—temporary loss of oxygen to parts of your brain—may occur.

### Varicose veins

An ingenious system of valves in our veins prevents blood from flowing backwards on its return to our heart. When the volume of blood returned to our heart is decreased for any reason, the accumulation of blood in the veins can result in varicose veins. Your diaphragmatic muscle motion is very important for the venous return flow. Breathing abdominally and allowing your diaphragm to move up and down with each inhale and exhale helps support blood return to your heart.[22] Indeed, several participants in my courses have reported that the appearance of their varicose veins has been reduced since improving their diaphragmatic breathing.

Since muscle contractions in your arms and legs force the venous blood back towards your heart, inactivity due to a sedentary job or lack of exercise will produce less muscle contractions. This also occurs when the oxygen level in your blood is low since your muscles become less active when the amount of oxygen present is reduced.

Regular physical activity where your calf muscles have to work—e.g., standing, walking or running—is important for ensuring that a sufficient amount of blood is returned to the heart. Hence, sitting down for an extended period of time, such as during a long flight, for instance, can impair your circulation, causing your legs to swell. This can be prevented by physical activity, which is very good for your body, regardless of whether you fly or not.

## CONNECTIONS BETWEEN POOR RESPIRATION AND CARDIOVASCULAR PROBLEMS

### Increased respiratory rate increases the heart rate

As your respiratory rate increases, your heart rate must also increase in order to pump more blood to your lungs. Shallow breathing, which is generally a result of over-breathing, leads to ineffective gas exchange because there is less blood and fewer alveoli at the top of the lungs, which results in poor oxygenation of your blood. Inefficient gas exchange in your lungs forces you to increase your respiration rate and make the heart work harder to pump more blood to your lungs for oxygenation. However, when you lower your respiratory rate, and apply the principles of Conscious Breathing, the oxygenation of your blood will be more efficiently accomplished, thus allowing your heart to slow down.

### Over-breathing leads to oxygen deficiency

Your heart is a major consumer of oxygen. While you take in more oxygen when you over-breathe, the carbon dioxide deficiency that occurs actually results in less oxygen being delivered to your organs. In a large emergency unit in the United States, the carbon dioxide levels in the blood of 8,607 patients were measured regularly over an 18-month period. As many as 45 percent of the patients had carbon dioxide levels below 35 mmHg, which implies that they were over-breathing, since the normal level is 40 mm Hg.[23]

### Mouth breathing makes the heart work harder

Recent research shows that Nitric Oxide (NO) increases the amount of oxygen transferred from inhaled air into your blood.[24] You don't get any nitric oxide down into your lungs when you breathe through your mouth, and consequently your heart is forced to work harder.

### Tight blood vessels result in reduced blood flow to the heart

Your heart not only provides your body with blood, but it also needs blood to function. Together with the diaphragm, your heart is one of the two muscles that never rests, even during sleep. Therefore, your heart needs a continuous blood flow to bring it oxygen and nutrients and carry away any waste products. If you over-breathe, your blood vessels constrict due to lack of carbon dioxide, which may reduce the blood flow to your heart.

### Dehydration causes elevated blood pressure

Ninety-two percent of your blood plasma consists of water. A lack of water leads to your blood volume being decreased. As a result, the consistency of your blood becomes thicker and requires higher pressure to pump it around your body. An easy way to verify whether you are getting enough water is to chcck thc smcll and color of your urine. A yellow to light yellow hue, with faint or no odor, indicates that you're getting enough water. In addition to drinking enough water, it's also important not to waste too much water through exhalation. It is worth remembering that 42 percent more water leaves your body when you breathe through your mouth than when you breathe through your nose.[25]

### Increased amount of stress hormones and sympathetic activity in the nervous system

A high pulse and high blood pressure are often an indication that the sympathetic part of your nervous system is active. Since the nervous and hormonal systems work together, increased sympathetic activity leads to increased levels of the stress hormone adrenaline. When your blood pressure must be raised quickly, in response to physical stress, for example, the sympathetic nerves send signals to your heart muscle that increases its ability to pump blood, which raises blood pressure. In addition, sympathetic signals are sent to the smooth muscles in your blood vessel walls to make them contract, which raises your blood pressure further. If the sympathetic part of your nervous system and your stress hormones are more active than necessary, even when you rest, your body doesn't get the recovery it needs.

With improved breathing habits your body relaxes, and your parasympathetic activity increases while your stress hormone levels decrease. Your heart will not need to beat as hard or as often, and your heart will have an easier time doing its job.

In the study described earlier, where twelve medical students hyperventilated, adrenaline increased a full 360 percent. When hyperventilating five-percent carbon dioxide-enriched air, their adrenaline levels were unchanged, implying that low $CO_2$ levels lead to a strong stress response. Mild over-breathing, which sometimes lasts for weeks and months, or may even become habitual, could, therefore, result in increasing your stress levels, due to decreased $CO_2$ levels. Although your stress levels might be lower than for those in the experiment, they would probably be higher than normal and last for a longer period of time.

### Your heart's adaptability is reduced

There's a clear link between a heart with poor adaptability and a stressed breathing pattern. When we inhale, our heart beats faster and our pulse rate increases, and when we exhale our heart beats slower, and our pulse rate drops. Your heart's ability to adapt to active and restful states is called Heart Rate Variability (HRV), and the better your heart functions, the greater the variability between activity and inactivity. A stressed heart possesses very little variability, which means that the pulse is basically the same all the time. The heart then lacks the ability to exert extra force and pump faster when needed, or relax and recover when it should do.

One way to increase your heart's capacity is to extend exhalation, which increases your heart's rest phase. When you extend your exhalations while maintaining a relaxed breathing pattern, your parasympathetic activity increases and you calm down. It also leads to your HRV being increased, and your heart's ability to be active or restful at the right time increases. Plus, as you lower your internal stress, your pulse usually drops.

### TIPS FOR BETTER CIRCULATION AND A HEALTHY HEART

It's hard to lower your heart rate with your thoughts alone, but you can influence it with your breathing habits and lifestyle. Since stress and heart problems are closely related, you should focus the changes you make towards reducing your perceived stress.

- Apply the five basic principles of Conscious Breathing – breathing should be done in and out through your nose, so it feels like as if the air reaches your stomach while at the same your breathing is slow, rhythmic and quiet.
- Extend your expirations with the Relaxator breathing trainer or the ujjayi-breathing method to decrease your respiratory rate, increase relaxation, and make your breathing deeper (not bigger).
- Do physical activity with your mouth closed.
- Fear is a major contributor to stress. Do the exercise *Breathe through your fears*, page 94, to reduce your stress.

**Baking soda bath**

To bathe in a hot spring is a fantastic experience that provides physical relaxation and inner calmness. At high temperatures, the release of carbon dioxide from the water into the atmosphere increases. This means that the $CO_2$ level in a hot spring can be very high just above the water's surface. There is about 50 times more carbon dioxide in water than in the air[26], which is one reason why it feels so good to swim. Our body takes up a certain amount of carbon dioxide through the skin when we swim, and hot springs contain even more carbon dioxide than normal water, which increases dermal absorption even further. A German study showed that we absorb an average of 30 milliliters of carbon dioxide per minute through the skin; therefore bathing in a hot spring provides an extra boost of around 10–12 percent of the amount of carbon dioxide of the 250 milliliters per minute that our body normally produces at rest.[27]

Several hot springs are called $CO_2$ baths because of their high carbon dioxide content, and in some places you will also find artificial $CO_2$ baths in which extra carbon dioxide is added to the water. Both natural and artificial $CO_2$ baths are common in Germany and Japan where they are also used to heal skin problems such as eczema and psoriasis, as well as severe diabetes. When in a $CO_2$ bath, your blood vessels dilate to facilitate increased blood circulation by elevating the $CO_2$ level in your body. A Japanese review of available studies concluded that artificial $CO_2$ baths provide similar effects to natural hot springs. Although hot springs contain many other different minerals as well, the research team behind the study believes that it is mainly the high $CO_2$ level in the water that provides the positive effects.[28]

Some of the positive effects that carbon dioxide baths provide are:

- **Heart rate drops:** When blood vessels dilate, the heart doesn't have to work as hard to pump the blood around.
- **Blood flow to the skin increases:** If only a portion of your body is immersed in water, noticeable differences can be seen in the

coloration of your skin, since the skin that is submerged in the $CO_2$ rich water becomes redder. This is caused by the vasodilatory effect of carbon dioxide, which increases blood circulation.

***Try for yourself:***

You can make your own carbon dioxide bath with baking soda. Add 1/2 cup of baking soda (sodium bicarbonate) to a half-filled bathtub, i.e., approximately 50–60 quarts. For a footbath, you can add a tablespoon to about five quarts of warm water. When you put your feet in the footbath, you will notice that they get warmer as you add the baking soda, again, because of the vasodilatory effect. Baking soda can be purchased in eight-ounce boxes at your local supermarket, and you should be able to find larger containers of baking soda at a restaurant wholesaler or on the Internet.

To increase the production of carbon dioxide and enhance the effect further, add 1/2 a cup of citric acid to your bathtub and a tablespoon to your footbath. Pouring the citric acid in the bath a little at a time over a period of 10–20 minutes will prevent too much carbon dioxide from being formed at once as bubbles, and keeps it from escaping the water as gas.

# Chapter 11 - Breathing Better to Reduce Asthma, Allergy and COPD

*Asthma and Chronic Obstructive Pulmonary Disease (COPD) are diseases of the airways. Including improved breathing techniques should be obvious in all forms of treatment of these diseases. According to the Russian Medical Doctor and Professor, Konstantin Buteyko, all asthmatics hyperventilate.*

## THE AIRWAYS ARE CRAMPED IN ASTHMA

Asthma is a disease that constricts the airways, making it increasingly difficult to breathe. The main symptoms include inflammation of the airways, constricted muscles in the airways, an increased secretion of mucus, and increased allergic sensitivity to various agents.

Other common symptoms include chest tightness, coughing, wheezing and hissing sounds in the chest, shortness of breath/difficulty breathing, tight/blocked nasal passages, insomnia, and fatigue. Exhaling is particularly difficult during an asthma attack, and a characteristic squeaking and rattling sound can often be heard during exhalation. An asthma attack can be life threatening, regardless of whether the asthma occurs frequently or rarely.

Asthma can be triggered by hypersensitivity to one or more substances. Other factors, such as breathing through the mouth, chest breathing, respiratory tract infections, stress, physical exertion, cold air, tobacco smoke, or dehydration can trigger or worsen the symptoms of asthma. Acute asthma attacks tend to occur intermittently, with relatively symptom-free periods in between, whereas in chronic asthma symptoms are present all the time, to varying degrees.

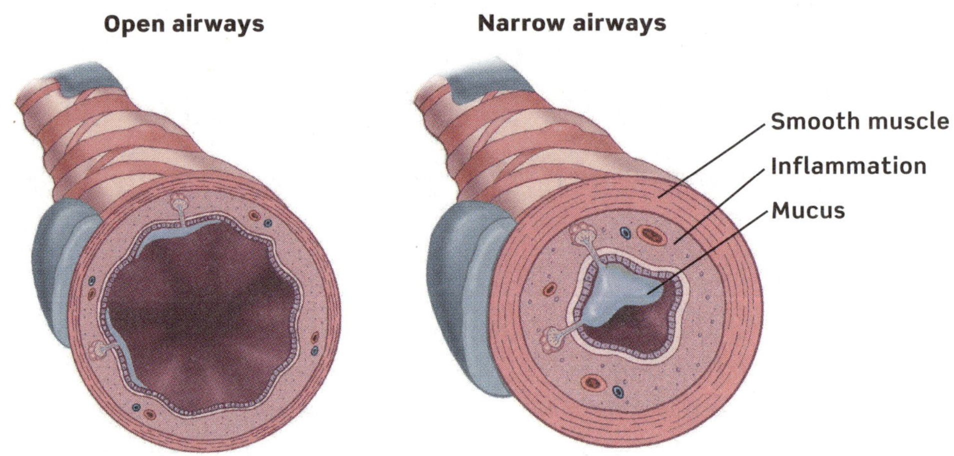


Narrow airways are the result of the smooth muscles constricting, increased inflammation, which causes swelling, and increased mucus production.

## IMPROVED BREATHING AS A COMPLEMENT TO MEDICATION

Currently, asthma patients are generally prescribed two different drugs designed to dilate narrow airways. One is a bronchodilator for use in acute asthma attacks. Bronchodilators contain substances similar to adrenaline that help the muscles of the airways to relax and widen. The second medicine is a steroid used to prevent asthma attacks that contains substances similar to cortisone to reduce inflammation in the airways.

Impaired breathing habits are common in asthma sufferers. In one study of 38 asthmatics, 95 percent had developed impaired breathing habits. By teaching the subjects how to breathe effectively, in conjunction with taking bronchodilating drugs, the respiratory problems were reduced in 90 percent of the asthma sufferers.[1] The results indicate that improved breathing habits would be beneficial as an alternative or complement to traditional asthma treatment. Three studies conducted in New Zealand showed a 66-95 percent reduction in bronchodilator use, and a 41-50 percent reduction in inflammatory steroid (i.e., cortisone) use when subjects improved their breathing habits.[2,3,4] The researchers in one of the studies also noted that: "In addition to a reduction in the use of medication, the participants also experienced reduced symptoms and increased quality of life."

## REASONS FOR BREATHING DIFFICULTIES IN ASTHMA:

### Lack of carbon dioxide

Normal breathing volume at rest is 8-12 beaths per minute and 0.5 liter of air per breath, equaling a respiratory volume of about 4-6 liters per minute. A typical asthma sufferer over-breathes, often taking 15-25 breaths per minute. Moreover, each breath tends to be larger than average and may vary from 700 milliliters to one liter of air per breath, equaling a respiratory volume of 10-15 liters of air per minute.

Carbon dioxide is required to dilate the airways, and an insufficient amount will prompt the smooth muscles in the airways to contract. So when respiration exceeds the body's needs, thus producing a lack of carbon dioxide, it becomes a lot more difficult for the air to pass in and out of the lungs. When the diameter of the airways decreases by 50 percent, the effort needed to transport the air in and out of the lungs increases 16-fold.

Since virtually all the outflow of carbon dioxide occurs through exhalation, it's a natural response for the body to constrict the airways in an attempt to retain optimum $CO_2$ levels. A relaxed breathing pattern reduces the respiratory rate and volume, which in turn reduces the outflow of carbon dioxide.

### Less Nitric Oxide (NO)

As has been stated before, the airborne hormone nitric oxide (NO) that is produced inside your sinuses not only dilates the smooth muscles of your airways, but also is antibacterial. When you breathe through your mouth no nitric oxide is drawn through your airways, and your protection against bacteria is reduced.

### Inflamed airways

Inflammation is a defense mechanism activated by your immune system, and its purpose is to protect your body against perceived intruders. Inflammation is caused by irritants, like pollen, an infection, such as the common cold, and physical injuries, like a sprained ankle, and it produces heat, pain, redness and swelling. Infection has a very stressful impact on your body and causes the release of cortisol, which is an important immune system regulator due to its ability to suppress inflammation. Your ability to secrete cortisol is diminished during prolonged stress, hence your immune system becomes over active and your airways become inflamed.

Air is prohibited from passing freely into your lungs by polluted city air, cold or dry air, cigarette smoke, bacteria and other airborne particles that make the inside of your airways inflamed and swollen. A faster breathing rate, which increases the mechanical wear and tear of your airways, can also produce inflammation. Inflammation may become chronic, and the resulting damage to your tissues can be difficult to repair if your body is exposed to this kind of strain for an extended period of time.

### Increased secretion of mucus

Mucus production inside your airways is an important part of your body's defense system because mucus traps foreign particles in inhaled air, preventing them from entering deeper into your lungs. The composition of the mucus will also neutralize or kill the bacteria.

Mucus is brought up to your throat via the cilia that line your upper airways, and then it is swallowed and travels to your stomach. While mucus is an important part of your body's defense, it also makes your airways narrower. As the number of foreign particles in the air increase, mucus production increases as well, narrowing your airways and making it more difficult to breathe.

If the need for mucus production continues to increase, it will eventually lead to enlarged mucus glands and even tighter airways.

This can be likened to what happens when lifting weights at the gym—increased muscle activity causes the muscles to swell and become larger. Nasal breathing offers better protection against inhaling particles in the air with the benefit of fewer particles reaching the airways and less mucus production.

### Dehydration

Water is needed in your lungs to prevent your airways from drying out when air passes in and out. Each exhalation allows more water to escape than is brought into your body during inhalation. This is because the humidity level in the inhaled air is lower than in the air you exhale. The humidity level is usually 70–80 percent when you inhale, while it is 100 percent when you exhale.

Your lungs are one of the organs through which a lot of water is lost. When you begin to become dehydrated, your body deals with the problem by contracting the muscles in your airways so less water evaporates when you exhale. It is particularly important for asthma sufferers to keep their hydration levels high and to avoid becoming dehydrated.[5,6]

We are at a greater risk of becoming dehydrated during the winter months due to the decreased humidity levels in the cold air. Furthermore, our nose is better than our mouth at keeping the water in our body. We retain 42 percent more water when we exhale through the nose than through the mouth.[7]

We automatically inhale a greater volume of air per minute when we breathe through our mouth, which encourages more water to evaporate.[7] Mucus production is less effective when the available water in the body is at a low level. The reason many of us experience strong reactions to dust, mold, tobacco smoke, etc., is because decreased mucus production, caused by dehydration, leads to even drier airways, which in turn cause our lungs to be more easily irritated. For many of us, dehydration will produce a dry cough as well as reduce our ability to protect ourselves against the bacteria and viruses in the air.

#### Fear

Our breathing pattern is profoundly influenced by our emotions, often creating a vicious cycle. When we are afraid, the feeling of fear will soon be reflected in our breathing pattern. When fear takes over we become tense, our breathing becomes much shallower, and asthma sufferers may experience feelings of suffocation. This causes us to feel even more afraid, we become even tenser, and our breathing deteriorates further.

Fear can provoke an asthma attack, as well as intensify impaired airflow caused by tight airways.

### HOW TO IMPROVE OR OVERCOME YOUR ASTHMA

Many of my own course participants, as well as those of other Conscious Beathing Instructors, have testified to asthma symptoms being overcome, or made less severe, once the participants learned how different breathing habits affected the body and, hence, began improving their breathing.

#### Practice Conscious Breathing

On many occasions, students have been able to reduce the need for medication significantly after using the Conscious Breathing Method, which incorporates nasal breathing, applying tape to their mouth at night, and doing breathing retraining with the Relaxator.

#### Preventing an asthma attack

The key to preventing an asthma attack is to learn to relax when you start to feel the familiar sense of panic associated with a looming attack. The best advice for asthma sufferers is the same given to anyone who needs to calm down: "slow down your breathing and make it rhythmical by closing your mouth and exhaling slowly." This will reduce the breathing volume and increase oxygenation. The respiration of someone about to have an asthma attack is very heavy and fast, and the person often experiences shortness of breath. The problem often lies in their exhalation, since diaphragmatic inhalation is prevented because they don't empty enough air from their lungs. The best way to calm down your own breathing pattern is by lengthening your exhalation to make sure that more air leaves your body. With each inhalation fresh air is then given the opportunity to reach deeper into your lungs, and the vicious cycle of respiratory distress will be broken.

To practice this, breathe deeply (not big) in and out through your nose in a rhythmic and relaxed way, tightening your throat, or using the Relaxator, to ensure that you squeeze the air out. This method prolongs your exhalation and forces your diaphragm upward. The higher your diaphragm is pressed upwards as you breathe out, the further down it goes when you inhale again, which allows the air to reach deeper into your lungs. Prolonging exhalation opens your lungs up for deeper inhalation (not bigger), which will facilitate relaxation.

The benefit you will gain from adopting this method is a reduction in the stress hormones needed to suppress inflammation and to widen your airways. Your carbon dioxide concentration is also reset to normal levels and allows the airways to relax and widen. Furthermore, nasal breathing warms and moistens the air and prevents bacteria and other particles from entering your lungs, which reduces inflammation so that less mucus has to be produced in order to deal with intruders.

Just knowing that you always carry a powerful improved breathing tool with you will give you a sense of comfort and control that further contributes to decreasing your stress and fear.

### Get to know your asthma

Increase your awareness of what things trigger an attack and learn how to avoid them. Notice if attacks happen at any particular time of the day, after certain activities, or during certain seasons. Do certain types of food have a bigger impact? What is your stress level when asthma

**NOTE! ALWAYS CONSULT YOUR PHYSICIAN BEFORE MAKING ANY CHANGES TO YOUR ASTHMA MEDICATION. THE TIPS AND ADVICE IN THIS BOOK ARE NOT INTENDED TO REPLACE MEDICATIONS.**

attacks occur? What is your breathing pattern like before an attack? What makes the symptoms worse? What makes them better?

#### Other tips to prevent asthma

If you have asthma, you should drink plenty of water and avoid or reduce foods that cause inflammation or are mucus forming, such as dairy products, wheat and sugar. Work actively to strengthen your immune system by doing physical activities with your mouth closed. To quickly free your nasal passages during a cold, or if you have a blocked nose, rinse your nostrils with salt and baking soda (page 47) and do the *Count your steps* exercise (page 58) so that you can resume breathing through your nose as soon as possible.

### ASTHMA IS COMMONLY ASSOCIATED WITH SLEEP PROBLEMS

Sleep problems such as snoring and sleep apnea are common in asthma sufferers. When you have asthma, your airways tighten, and when you lie down the airways become even narrower. University of California researcher, WH Bonekat, says that as many as 74 percent of all asthma sufferers have problems with blocked airways at night.[8]

In a study of 244 people suffering from asthma, researchers found that 37 percent snored regularly and that 40 percent were at a high risk for developing sleep apnea. The risk of sleep apnea increased as the asthma symptoms worsened, and also when the use of inhaled steroids was high.[9]

In another study involving 26 patients diagnosed with severe asthma and 26 patients diagnosed with mild asthma, it was found that the prevalence of snoring and sleep apnea is greater in patients with severe asthma than it is with those with mild asthma. The results showed that the number of apneic events exceeded 15 per hour in 88 percent of severe asthma patients compared with only 58 percent of mild asthma patients.[10]

## STRESS HORMONE LEVELS ARE ELEVATED WITH TIGHT AIRWAYS

Considering the huge area available for gas exchange in our lungs (50–100 $m^2$), and the large amount of air we inhale each day (10,000–15,000 liters), it is not surprising that our body should have a strong defense system to protect our lungs in the best way.

Since breathing is so crucial to life, tight airways can quickly trigger a powerful stress reaction prompting the adrenal glands to release the stress hormones adrenaline and cortisol. As we discussed earlier, these same hormones are found in asthma medications, because adrenaline helps to broaden narrow airways and cortisol helps suppress inflammation. The greater the stress response, the higher the levels of these stress hormones will be.[11]

Problems arise when tight airways persist for a long time and the stress response progresses. Adrenaline not only widens airways; it also increases breathing and heart rate, constricts blood vessels to organs in your abdomen, and increases blood flow to your arm and leg muscles. Your body prepares itself to meet a perceived danger by releasing adrenaline, even when the danger isn't real. Constant stress causes extended excretion of adrenaline, which leads to a much heavier demand on your breathing muscles and heart, as well as an increase in your blood pressure.

Moreover, both cortisol and adrenaline elevate your blood sugar levels, which makes sense as you need energy quickly during perceived or real stress and sugar is a more readily accessed fuel than fat. The long-term effect of stress is that your body becomes accustomed to using more sugar and less fat as an energy source.

Stress hormones are secreted from your adrenal glands, which are located on the top of your kidneys. During prolonged stress, your adrenal glands are forced to work hard to produce more stress hormones to meet your body's demands, which can result in them becoming fatigued and enlarged.

In his book, *Adrenal Fatigue*, doctor James Wilson writes that respiratory disease has particularly damaging effects on your adrenal glands.[12] Something that is often described in old medical literature, and which experienced doctors are still seeing, is that adrenal fatigue often begins with recurrent bronchitis, pneumonia, asthma, sinusitis or other airway infections. Severe infections that return frequently put excessive stress on your adrenal glands, thus making bouts of infection last longer.

Adrenal fatigue may occur after just one serious infection, or it can sneak up gradually, as the adrenal glands become increasingly fatigued by persistent or recurrent infections. If there are other contributing stress factors, such as unhappiness, poor eating habits, or stressful work, the symptoms are generally worse and last longer. The reverse is also often the case; people with poor adrenal function often have a tendency to suffer from diseases of the airways.

All these issues addressed by Dr. Wilson are also connected to breathing habits that aren't optimal. It is therefore particularly important for asthma patients to breathe through their nose to prevent diseases that cause narrowed airways.

### ALLERGIES AND HYPERSENSITIVITY INCREASE INFLAMMATION

Allergies affecting the upper respiratory tract are often closely related to asthma and involve a mild or severe hypersensitivity to dust, pollen, mold, animal fur or food. Such over-sensitivity produces inflammation, thus releasing the hormone/neurotransmitter histamine in large quantities.

Histamine, which is part of the immune response to protect your body, contributes to increased mucus production and contraction of the smooth muscles of the bronchi. In most cases, the histamine will make the mucus membranes inside your nose, airways and eyes swell. The skin will itch, and mucus production in your nose will increase. Your airways will constrict, your nose will become runny, and your airways will swell and constrict causing coughing, shortness of breath and asthma.

Allergy medicines containing antihistamine have been used to reduce allergic symptoms since the 1930's. They work by counteracting histamine, which is powerful enough to induce life-threatening constriction to the airways during an allergic reaction. This is known as anaphylactic shock, or allergic shock, and life-saving adrenaline (or epinephrine) must be administered to open the airways quickly.

Another important function of histamine is to ensure optimum hydration levels in your body. Histamine levels are low when your body is sufficiently hydrated. However, as soon as you begin to become dehydrated, the secretion of histamine is increased to contract your airways in order to prevent water from evaporating. It is well known that asthma sufferers have increased histamine content in their lungs, which is most likely due to too much water evaporating when they breathe through their mouth.[5,6]

The problem with medications, no matter if it is antihistamines to reduce allergy symptoms, adrenaline to widen the airways, or cortisone to reduce inflammation, is that we put too much trust in them. We believe that the medicines will make us healthy, when in reality they only have a short-term effect that masks the root problem. If we don't do anything about the underlying cause, we become addicted to suppressing our symptoms with medication, and new health problems often show up later. It's like sticking tape over a red glowing oil warning light in the car or applying paint to rotten planks of wood—we just postpone the problems.

## EXERCISE-INDUCED ASTHMA

Many asthma attacks occur during physical exertion. This is generally called exercise-induced asthma, or sports asthma. When you work hard physically, you increase the amount of air flowing in and out of your lungs. If you breathe through your mouth, large amounts of cold and dry air, full of bacteria, will pass in and out. This raw air acts as an abrasive agent on your airways, making them inflamed since the friction increases sharply during physical activity. The reason for this is that the significant increase in the amount of air we inhale can reach 100 liters per minute or more, in comparison to 4-6 liters per minute at rest. Moreover, the risk of physical activity triggering asthma attacks is increased if your body's hydration level is low before beginning the physical activity.

Sports asthma displays the classic signs of an asthma attack: contraction of the bronchi, inflammation of the airways, and excessive production of mucus, which limits the flow of air to and from the lungs. The asthma sufferer will experience shortness of breath and is often in a state of panic or anxiety during or immediately after jogging, swimming, cycling or other physical activities.

Any physical activity places a huge demand on your body. You may perceive your breathing pattern at rest to be normal, but the deficiencies may not become apparent until you exert yourself. If your breathing pattern at rest isn't optimal it's very likely that it won't be optimal during exercise, either. The level of stress hormones in your body is higher than normal if your breathing pattern at rest is not good, so if you exert yourself too much when you exercise, which is very common, you put additional stress on an already stressed body.

In two studies that compared the effects of mouth breathing and nasal breathing, nasal breathing during exercise was found to provide clear benefits for people with asthma, because the bronchi contracted less, or didn't contract at all. In the pilot study I set up (page 105) we didn't measure the effects that mouth and nasal breathing have on the airways. However, there were clear indications that breathing through the nose was less abrasive on the airways with less exercise-induced asthma and fewer instances of dry airways.

The conclusion is that it is more beneficial for a person diagnosed with asthma, and everyone else for that matter, to breathe through their nose with their mouth closed as much as possible during a workout.[13,14]

It is estimated that most of the world's elite cross-country skiers have problems with asthma, which is also my own experience. A really fit cross-country skier can ventilate up to 200 liters/minute during maximum effort, and with such an extreme exertion it is obviously very difficult to breathe through the nose. As the weather conditions are often harsh and cold, the cold and dry air puts additional strain on the respiratory tract. Hence, it is especially important for cross-country skiers to take every opportunity to breathe through their nose.

The ability to breathe through your nose is a matter of training. Many are surprised to notice that after a period of practicing they can breathe through their nose, even during forceful exertion and interval training. Much of the limitation is really in the mind. It's impossible to inhale 200 liters/minute during nasal breathing, but since nasal breathing is a far more efficient way to deliver oxygen to our muscles we can reduce the amount of air ventilated and thereby replace quantity with quality.

## COPD—CHRONIC OBSTRUCTIVE PULMONARY DISEASE

The characteristics of Chronic Obstructive Pulmonary Disease (COPD) include shortness of breath, mucus, coughing, a wheezing sound when breathing and increased susceptibility to airway infections. Smokers are the most likely to be diagnosed with COPD, and there are many similarities between COPD and asthma since both cause reduced airflow due to narrow airways. An important difference with COPD is that the breathing difficulties develop slowly over many years, whereas in asthma, attacks of shortness of breath occur frequently. Allergies are also more common in asthma than in COPD. Six percent of Americans are diagnosed with COPD[15], and common problems are:

### Accumulation of particles in the lungs

Our lungs are designed to exchange gas between the atmosphere and the blood, not to deal with physical particles. To prevent particles in the air from entering our lungs, our body has a comprehensive defense system located in our nose, throat and the airways in our lungs. The defense consists of the mucus that traps the particles, the cilia that bring the mucus up to the throat to be swallowed and the immune system that creates inflammation to take care of foreign particles. If your airways are exposed to cigarette smoke or dust for an extended period of time, the efficiency of each defense mechanism will deteriorate, and more particles will enter and be stored inside your lungs. In the long term, this will lead to destruction of lung tissue. Your pulmonary alveoli and the larger and smaller airways (bronchi and bronchioles) will all be affected.

#### Stagnant air in mouth and chest breathing

The accumulation of toxins is more pronounced when we breathe through our mouth because the filtering mechanism in the nose is not being utilized and particles can go deeper inside our airways.

Shallow chest breathing is not powerful enough to remove a sufficient amount of air at the bottom of your lungs when you exhale. Since air is refilled from above when you inhale, the air situated in the lower parts of your lungs stays stagnant. Stagnant air increases the risk of lung infections, and the inflammation designed to take care of the occasional infection can, if the infection becomes chronic, lead to destruction of your alveoli.

#### Mucus cough

Normally the cilia manage the transportation of mucus up to our throat so that we can swallow it. Increased mucus production, due to more particles in the air, forces the cilia to work harder. Over time, the cilia become too stressed and start to decrease in numbers. Increased mucus production and decreased numbers of cilia make the task of eliminating mucus too difficult, resulting in a characteristic mucus cough, known as smoker's cough. Because the mucus is difficult to bring up, coughing becomes more frequent.

### Destroyed lung tissue—Emphysema

Over time, a poor breathing habit, or exposure to large amounts of particles in the air, causes chronic inflammation that damages your lung tissue and reduces your lungs' ability to exchange gas between air and blood. These symptoms are indicative of emphysema, which can become widespread and cover large parts of both lungs. Emphysema prohibits you from utilizing the full capacity of your lungs, and shortness of breath is more likely to happen.

### Breathing demands a lot of energy

At rest, breathing normally doesn't use more than 2-3 percent of the body's resources. Since breathing becomes so demanding in COPD, you often have to use extra muscles in the neck and shoulders to force air in and out. With severe COPD, breathing consumes a large amount of energy and may require more than 20 percent of the body's available resources.

#### *Recommendations for improving your breathing if you have COPD*

1. **Quit smoking:** Smokers diagnosed with COPD are advised to try to stop smoking.
2. **Face masks in dusty environments:** Use masks in dusty environments, or even better, avoid dusty environments altogether.
3. **Increase the amount of physical activity:** Often, for those with COPD, the effort needed just to breathe may lead to insufficient energy as well as a lack of strength to move around. Increased physical activity, however, is important to improve the circulation of air in your lungs. Remember to listen to your body and pace yourself. Training too hard for your tolerance level will only have negative consequences. If you are not used to physical activity, a first step could be to go for a short walk while breathing only through your nose. After a while, you can add more time and a deeper level of exercise, including counting steps (see page 58) where you strive to take more steps when you exhale than when you inhale.

4. **Practice breathing resistance:** Improving breathing habits is central to managing COPD. Nasal breathing and diaphragmatic breathing, as well as prolonged exhalations, are the most important measures to take. To achieve diaphragmatic breathing, the best advice is to prolong your exhalation by practicing breathing through resistance. The air in your lungs will be removed to a greater extent, and your diaphragm will move further up on expiration. Consequently, more space will be provided for the inhaled air, while your diaphragm automatically moves further down at the same time. Shortness of breath can thus be countered with resistance breathing. Breathing through the Relaxator Breathing Retrainer, exhaling by tightening your throat, using ujjayi-breathing, or exhaling through pursed lips are excellent ways to extend exhalations (see Chapter 4, pages 65-68). Keep in mind that the goal is to consistently achieve a relaxed breathing pattern, so don't push yourself too hard.

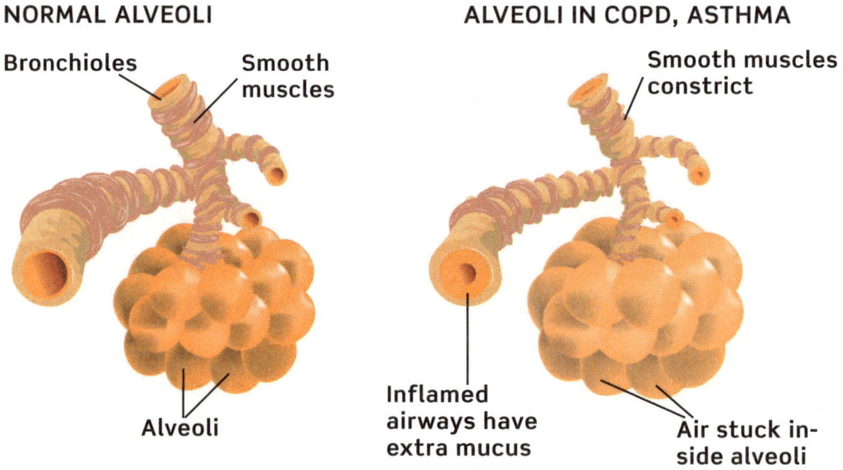


In severe asthma, COPD and emphysema, gas exchange in the lungs is impaired. Constricted muscles in the airways, inflammation, mucus and particles from smoke and dust create narrower airways, which could ultimately lead to destroyed lung tissue. Optimal airflow in our lungs is like water flowing freely in a stream, but when air becomes trapped in narrowed airways, the air is more akin to water in a small pond, stagnant and stale.

## QUIT SMOKING WITH THE HELP OF CONSCIOUS BREATHING

Most people who are diagnosed with COPD are long-term smokers. All COPD patients who smoke are therefore encouraged to give up smoking to keep the disease from spreading further. Stopping smoking may be easier said than done for many reasons. Two of those reasons are:

### Nitric Oxide in cigarette smoke

Regular cigarette smoke contains large amounts of nitric oxide (NO), the same gas that is also produced in the nose and follows the air into our lungs when we breathe with our mouth closed. In one study, subjects inhaled normal cigarette smoke and then inhaled cigarette smoke that was lacking NO. The study had to be terminated when the oxygen saturation levels in the blood of the subjects smoking the cigarettes lacking NO dropped drastically. Although the study was conducted with pigs, it's likely that humans would react in exactly the same way. In other words, if we smoked a cigarette that didn't contain nitric oxide, we would probably feel so bad we'd never want to smoke again.

### Improved breathing when smoking

Smoking a cigarette generally requires that the smoker bothe breathe abdominally, drawing the cigarette air deep down into the lungs, and exhale for a longer period than normal, which actually constitutes a good breathing pattern. When the cigarette is finished, the habitually stressed breathing pattern is resumed, which will soon make the craving for another cigarette in order to "calm down" unbearable.

Quitting smoking may seem very tedious and difficult, especially if you are someone who is a chest and mouth breather. Incorporating Conscious Breathing as part of your "quit smoking" process can be very helpful. Nasal breathing provides your body with the same amount of NO that you'd get from the cigarette smoke. Together with diaphragmatic breathing, this will allow the air to reach deep down into the lungs and will induce a relaxed state, just like when you used to smoke a cigarette.

The easiest way to get into a good breathing habit, and continue to break the smoking habit, is to continue practicing extending your exhalations.

### TIPS FOR CLEARING A COUGH

Our breathing pattern has a bearing on coughing. Shallow chest breathing decreases the circulation of air in our lungs, which will increase coughing attacks. Some tips to help you clear a cough are:

- **Straight posture:** An erect posture makes it easier for the air to enter deep into your lungs.
- **Diaphragmatic breathing:** Diaphragmatic breathing is most easily achieved by extending the exhalations. The Relaxator is an excellent tool to use during a cough to prolong your exhalations.
- **Breathing into a bag:** When we cough, we take larger breaths that increase the breathing volume and the outflow of carbon dioxide, thus creating a shortage of $CO_2$. Try breathing in and out of a 3-liter bag about 20 times. Keep in mind that the bag should be a few inches away from your face so that oxygen depletion doesn't occur in the bag, and therefore in the inhaled air. Doing this will increase the amount of carbon dioxide in your lungs and reduce or stop your cough.

When coughing at night, try sitting up in bed (straight posture) and extend your exhalations, either by yourself or with the Relaxator, or breathe into a bag.

# Chapter 12 - Aches, Pains and Fatigue: How Breathing Right Can Help

*A tense body creates tense breathing habits and more energy is needed to breathe. At the same time, tense breathing habits prohibit oxygen from reaching your muscles and organs. Consequently, less energy is produced, leading to energy deficiency that causes fatigue, pain and a build up of lactic acid in the muscles, which causes soreness. Adopting the Conscious Breathing Method will help you avoid these problems.*

## YOUR BREATHING HAS A DIRECT EFFECT ON YOUR PAIN LEVEL

Imagine that you step into a cold shower. What is your first reaction? You quickly draw in a breath, right? Generally we would take a breath that only reaches high up in our chest, hold our breath, tense up, or breathe quickly and shallowly in an effort to endure the spray of cold water. It's not a particularly pleasant experience, and we tend to want it to be over as quickly as possible.

However, you would have a much more pleasant experience if you made it a point to breathe rhythmically in and out of your nose as you entered the cold shower. Although I don't profess to love getting under cold water, I have had many cold showers, mainly out of curiosity. The effect that the cold water has on me is significantly different when I breathe rhythmically as compared to when I hold my breath.

The same applies when you become tense before an injection or when sitting in the dental chair. Holding your breath will only encourage your body to become like a taut violin string as you anticipate the coming pain, and because you are tense it will hurt more. However, if you take control of your breathing the experience will be completely different. Despite having to keep your mouth wide open when you visit the dentist, it's perfectly possible to breathe regularly and deeply, in and out through your nose, which will allow you to keep calm and help you avoid having the fear of pain take over.

One of my breathing students told me how taking control of his breathing helped overcome his fear of dentists. A few minutes into an acute root canal procedure he had been forced to undergo, which was just as bad as he had expected, he came to realize that he could pay attention to his breathing. The root canal experience changed dramatically once he stopped holding his breath and began to breathe rhythmically with prolonged exhalations. He told me that the discomfort he felt decreased radically, and he soon felt very calm.

An expression used in connection with childbirth is the "fear–tension–pain" cycle. Women who give birth are often worried about the process, so they become tense. A tense body leads to increased pain, which promotes even more fear and tension. Our natural response to feeling scared and tense is that our breathing pattern alters, due to bodily reflexes, and we hold our breath in order to wake our bodies up, or we breathe shallowly high up in our chest in an attempt to "run away" from the unpleasant feelings often situated in our abdominal area.

Unprocessed fears move respiration higher up in the chest, causing the "chest breathing" described in greater detail in Chapter 2. Since the breath changes according to the state of the body, our breathing is likely to become more chaotic and periodic when we are tense. Generally when we are stressed, we will breathe in and hold our breath, which is a natural reflex as our body prepares to meet a perceived danger. At times like this, adrenaline excretion will increase, and the sympathetic part of our nervous system will be activated. It's similar to what happens when we turn the key in the car so the starter ignites the engine. Once the engine is ignited we let go of the key as we don't need to activate the starter anymore. However, should we not let go, and keep the key turned even though the engine has been ignited, we would over-stress and burn out the starter. It is when we continue to hold our breath that problems arise, because we are continuing to "wake the body up" even though it is already awake.

How do you breathe in your everyday life? Does your life consist of one endless to-do list that makes you tense and anxious? Are you constantly forced to concentrate, be on the move, or keep waking your body up? If so, you have a higher risk of developing a tense breathing habit. In the end, you may establish a permanent bad habit of alternating between breath-holding, near non-existent breathing, and over-breathing, in which your breathing pattern becomes increasingly tense, consequently your body tenses, and you tire more easily.

A woman I know who tends to suffer from lumbago every few years says, "What I usually do when I get lumbago is to tense my whole body in an attempt to try to reduce the pain. Thanks to having improved my breathing habits, I have now learned to relax in the middle of the worst pain, and this time the pain disappeared in just a few days instead of lasting a week or more."

Another woman who attended my breathing course confirmed how rhythmic, diaphragmatic, and reduced breathing volume helped her when she was bitten very badly by a dog and wound up in hospital for three days. "When I was bitten, I couldn't breathe properly. I started to hyperventilate and my face went completely white. Soon after the bite, I began to breathe through the Relaxator, which helped me establish a better breathing pattern, and I felt so much better. The difference was striking! To check, I stopped using the Relaxator when I got to the hospital. Right away the pain took over, and almost caused me to go into shock."

## FIBROMYALGIA

Fibromyalgia is characterized by tired stiff muscles and muscle pain, but symptoms also include fatigue, insomnia, anxiety, depression, stomach problems, and joint pain. It is difficult to diagnose fibromyalgia since there are no specific diagnostic tests. The disease is nine times more prevalent in women than in men. A possible reason for the problem being so much more common in women may be the secretion of progesterone during menstruation and pregnancy. Progesterone induces increased respiration, which can eventually lead to permanent changes in the breathing pattern. There are also other breathing characteristics related to fibromyalgia. The most common of these are:

- **Infections in the respiratory tract:** Mycoplasma is a bacterial infection of the lungs. In 50 percent of cases where people have been diagnosed with fibromyalgia, a mycoplasma infection has also been present. Breathing through the mouth increases the number of bacteria in the lungs, and shallow breathing slows down the circulation of air in the lungs. Both ways of breathing increase the risk of airway infections.
- **Increased amounts of free radicals:** Studies show that increased amounts of free radicals are common in fibromyalgia. Free radicals are unstable molecules that strive to gain balance by either gaining from or losing an electron to other molecules. This creates a chain reaction since the attacked molecules become free radicals themselves. When this occurs, the attacked cells and tissues are damaged by the free radicals. When breathing is inefficient, the number of free oxygen radicals increases in the mitochondria of the cells.[1] The vast majority of energy is produced in the mitochondria in a process where fat, sugar, and oxygen are combusted. If the mitochondria are under stimulated, as would be the case in someone who is not breathing well, and less oxygen then reaches the cells, the leak of free radicals increases and the cells will be damaged. Over-breathing will also lead to increased circulation of oxygen that is not bound to hemoglobin as more oxygen is inhaled than consumed, which increases the risk of the formation of free radicals in the blood.
- **Breathing problems:** Fifty percent of people who are diagnosed with fibromyalgia confirm that they have breathing problems.[2]

- **Magnesium deficiency:** A lack of the mineral magnesium is common in fibromyalgia sufferers. Magnesium and calcium are two important minerals that work together in making your muscles work properly. Magnesium relaxes your muscles, while calcium helps with muscle contraction. When the magnesium content in the muscles decreases, the influx of calcium increases and makes the muscles go rigid.
- **Insomnia:** Seventy percent of fibromyalgia sufferers experience sleeping problems, e.g. poor sleep and/or waking up tired and stiff in the morning.
- **Digestive problems:** Seventy percent also suffer from Irritable Bowel Syndrome (IBS).
- **Oxygen deficiency in the muscles:** A common perception among doctors and those suffering from fibromyalgia is that the symptoms begin in the muscles. Lack of oxygen causes energy shortage and increases lactic acid, thus making the muscles stiffer.

### CHRONIC FATIGUE SYNDROME/ME

Chronic Fatigue Syndrome, CFS, also commonly referred to as ME, Myalgic Encephalomyelitis, makes sufferers feel very weak and tired. Many also experience aches, pains, and sleeping problems and several of the symptoms are similar to fibromyalgia. Seventy five percent of the people who develop CFS are women. Currently there aren't any proven tests for diagnosing CFS as general tests don't show any signs of the disease. Many sufferers will, therefore, be dismissed as having phantom symptoms, although, for the person experiencing the symptoms, they are very real. It is likely that a disturbed breathing pattern contributes to the problems. Some common respiratory related features of CFS are:

- **Excessive tiredness and fatigue after exertion:** Despite resting, the fatigue will not go away after physical and mental activity. A good breathing pattern is crucial to counteract the extreme and prolonged fatigue that may occur, and also produce energy in an efficient manner.

- **Sleeping problems:** Waking up exhausted is a common problem in people diagnosed with CFS. If the person's mouth is also dry in the morning, it is highly likely that the person is breathing through the mouth throughout the night. Mouth breathing automatically leads to over-breathing.
- **Aches and pains:** Pain in muscles, joint pain without any redness, tender lymph nodes in the throat or armpits and headache are symptoms sufferers of CFS experience. A disturbed breathing pattern contributes to many types of aches and pains.
- **Throat problems:** Mouth breathing and over-breathing increase the burden on the respiratory tract, which contributes to related throat symptoms and can cause recurrent throat infections.
- **Impaired short-term memory:** Since our brain is a major consumer of oxygen, it's natural that an impaired breathing pattern affects most brain functions negatively and can result in deterioration of short-term memory and/or concentration.

A woman who attended one of my breathing courses immediately experienced increased energy when she kept her mouth closed as much as possible during the daytime and began taping her mouth closed at night. Her need for sleep was reduced with from fourteen to six hours per day, and she had enough energy to go for a one-hour walk almost every day. She managed to maintain the newfound energy levels for almost six months, until she caught an infection that depleted her energy. Consequently, her need for sleep increased again by three hours, but since her body was fragile from having been ill for ten years, that is probably to be expected. Despite the setback, her recovery is now progressing steadily.

We are all unique individuals, and there is no guarantee that improved breathing will produce any positive results with pains, aches, CFS or fibromyalgia. On the other hand there isn't much to lose, as we have our breathing with us all the time and we can begin to improve it straight away. You can test the principles of the Conscious Breathing Method for just the cost of a Relaxator and Sleep Tape.

## BREATHING DURING PREGNANCY AND CHILDBIRTH

Some characteristics related to respiration in pregnancy are:

### Increased respiratory volume and decreased carbon dioxide content

In pregnancy it is common for breathing volume to increase by about 30 percent due to increased metabolism. It's also common for $CO_2$ levels in the woman's blood to decrease from a normal $CO_2$ pressure of about 40 mmHg to 27-32 mmHg, indicating that the breathing volume increases more than necessary. Low levels of $CO_2$ lead to oxygen deficiency and reduced energy production and can contribute to health problems. One reason pregnant women start to breathe more is due to an increased secretion of the hormone progesterone, which has been shown in many studies to increase breathing volumes. The respiratory volume and carbon dioxide levels usually return to normal after childbirth.[3]

### Symptoms during pregnancy are similar to problems at high altitude

Nausea, headache, trouble breathing, loss of appetite, thirst, and fatigue are common during pregnancy. Interestingly, these symptoms are very similar to problems that can occur at high altitude. Respiration rate and volume increases at high altitude, reducing carbon dioxide levels, which is similar to what happens during pregnancy.

### Stuffy nose

It is common to have a blocked nose during the last trimester of pregnancy. Progesterone, which softens the cervix, loosens cartilage and ligaments in the pelvic area, and prepares the birth canal, is also thought to affect the mucus membranes in the nose, causing them to swell. A blocked nose is also a very clear indication of hyperventilation and carbon dioxide deficiency, and can usually be cleared by adopting the Conscious Breathing Methods to increase the carbon dioxide levels.

### Risk of complications during pregnancy and childbirth

The low levels of carbon dioxide during pregnancy indicate that the body's pH reserves—i.e., the bicarbonate buffer—have been reduced over time. It is reasonable to assume that the hormonal changes associated with pregnancy have a greater negative impact when the body's reserves decline. Therefore, if you enter pregnancy with a lowered bicarbonate buffer, you will be more affected by the stress of the pregnancy and be at risk for complications during labor. Oxygen deficiency is the result of over-breathing and leads to higher levels of lactic acid in your body. At the Swedish hospital, Södersjukhuset, researcher and chief physician, Eva Itzel-Wiberg, measured lactic acid in the amniotic fluid during labor and found a clear correlation between high levels of lactic acid, protracted labor, and/or C-section. Lactic acid increases when the uterus is subjected to oxygen deficiency during labor. This impairs the ability of the uterus to produce sufficient contractions and may result in a longer labor.

In America, a third of all births today are prolonged due to ineffective contractions during labor, and the risk of becoming exhausted or succumbing to an infection becomes higher for the mother as well as the child. Furthermore, the mother is at risk of other complications and the baby may be at risk of oxygen depletion.[4,5]

During pregnancy and childbirth, it's of great help to become aware of how you breathe in different situations and to make sure that your breathing is as slow, abdominal, rhythmical, and relaxed as possible.

## REASONS FOR ACHES, PAIN AND FATIGUE

Some common causes of respiratory-issue related aches, pain and fatigue are:

### Impaired breathing

During shallow breathing we overuse the accessory muscles in our chest, neck, and shoulders. Short, forced exhalation is also common. Exhalation is usually a passive process where the breathing muscles are not active, but overuse causes these muscles to become tense and contributes to the development of shoulder and neck tension. Since the chest is connected to the spine, the tension can also spread to the back and contribute to back pain. Moreover, because the neck muscles extends upward into the head, tense neck muscles can give rise to headache.

When breathing shallowly, your diaphragm is activated to a lesser extent than when breathing deeply. Normally, your diaphragm does 70-80 percent of the muscle work on inhalation. When it is used less often it becomes weak. A weakened diaphragm may not be obvious at rest, but it becomes evident during physical activity by producing a "stitch" in our side or making us tire easily. One way to exercise your diaphragm is to prolong your exhalation and squeeze the air out. You push the air out with your abdominal muscles, and your diaphragm is pressed upwards at the same time. The higher up your diaphragm reaches during exhalation, the further down it will go on the subsequent inhalation. See the exercise on page 79.

### Imbalances in your body's minerals reserves

When we over-breathe, the lack of carbon dioxide will initially appear in our lungs, then in our blood, and eventually in our muscles and tissues. A lack of $CO_2$ is detrimental to the functioning of our cells and will elevate our pH level, which is why maintaining an optimal pH balance in our body is so important. To counteract over-breathing and restore the pH balance in our blood and cells, our kidneys begin to secrete more bicarbonate ($HCO_3^-$) in the urine. However, the negative bicarbonate ions will also bring positive ions into our urine, such as the minerals calcium ($Ca^{2+}$) and magnesium ($Mg^{2+}$). Deficiencies in our body's minerals reserves can produce different negative consequences for our muscles, brain, and energy production.

Egg producers are struggling with the problem of eggshells becoming too thin and fragile, especially during the summer months when it's hot. A research group found that when the temperature in the barn increased in the summer, the chickens raised their respiratory rate and hyperventilated because they couldn't eliminate the excess heat through sweating. Over-breathing led to an increased amount of calcium leaving the chickens' bodies, along with the bicarbonate that was excreted in their urine. Calcium is an important constituent of bones and eggshells, and when the chickens were given carbonated water instead of plain water, their eggshells hardened. Carbonated drinks contain carbonic acid, which in turn contains carbon dioxide. The increased amount of carbon dioxide balances the pH levels so less bicarbonate and calcium are eliminated in the urine.[6] However, it's better to improve your breathing habits instead of drinking carbonated drinks, since they usually contain a lot of sugar and other additives that put a strain on your body.

Many studies show that muscle cramps are a byproduct of hyperventilation. In Chapter 2 I mentioned how my hyperventilation test caused the muscles in my arms and legs to shake uncontrollably for several minutes after I stopped hyperventilating. Imbalances in the muscle and cell mineral reserve may be a major contributing factor in the shakes that I experienced.

Analysis of over 250 research papers on hyperventilation showed that hyperventilation increases irritability of nerves and muscles.[6] In other words, the more we over-breathe, the more tense our muscles will be.

### Impaired energy production in the cells

The mitochondria are our energy factories and they are the place where 90 percent of our energy (ATP) is produced as food, and oxygen is converted into energy. We can only be physically and mentally active at the level allowed by our mitochondrial capacity to produce energy. If our mitochondria are few and have poor access to fuel and oxygen, our energy and endurance will be poor.

If the ability to produce energy in our mitochondria is reduced due to the lack of oxygen, for example, we have to rely more on anaerobic energy production where sugar is converted to energy without the involvement of oxygen. This process, called fermentation, only creates a small amount of energy. It is a very inefficient way of producing energy and leads to decreased endurance. The fermentation process also produces increased amounts of lactic acid, which is common in fatigue and muscle pain.

### Low levels of carbon dioxide

According to a Swedish pilot study by chief physician Johannes Lindh, a low level of carbon dioxide in the body is linked to a variety of physical problems, such as muscle, joint and shoulder pain. In the study, Dr. Lindh looked at the overall level of carbon dioxide in 44 patients.[7] The criteria for inclusion in the study were that the participants had at least ten different symptoms, one of which was shortness of breath. Other symptoms included pain in the muscles, joints, neck, shoulders, headaches, unexplained tiredness, and fatigue after exertion. Forty percent of the 44 patients had low levels of carbon dioxide, which is a remarkably high figure. This is not surprising considering all the practical experience and available research that connect low levels of $CO_2$ to illness.

Low levels of $CO_2$ contribute to low levels of bicarbonate and reduce the pH buffer, which is your backup for maintaining the correct pH balance in your body. If the pH buffer is low, our ability to absorb nutrients from food is reduced. This is detrimental, as it is crucial to keep the pH balance appropriate in different parts of the digestive system, because nutritional deficiency will lead to fatigue. A low pH buffer also impairs your body's ability to take care of the lactic acid formed during exercise. The increase of lactic acid in your blood is associated with aches and pains after exercise.

Low $CO_2$ levels in the body can easily become chronic. This became evident in a study in which $CO_2$ levels were measured continuously for one hour while the participants hyperventilated. The goal was to reduce the $CO_2$ pressure by 50 percent to 20 mmHg, which was achieved after 10–20 minutes of vigorous breathing. The interesting thing was that once the participants had reached the desired level it took very little effort to maintain the low carbon dioxide levels. It was enough for them to sigh or draw a big breath here and there, and no one recognized that they were actually over-breathing.[8] This indicates that over-breathing developed during a stressful period can actually result in a permanent pattern that continues to affect us even after the stress has ended.

Some people, such as COPD and asthma patients, may have elevated carbon dioxide levels. Although I have not yet found any research that supports my theory, it is not entirely inconceivable that such patients had lower $CO_2$ levels to begin with and a persistent high level of carbon dioxide was established as their health has deteriorated. What happens is that impaired breathing decreases your lungs' capacity for gas exchange, and when the gas exchange deteriorates too much it prevents carbon dioxide from being released, causing the levels of $CO_2$ in your blood to rise. It is not unlike when you go through the different phases of stress mentioned in Chapter 5—acute stress, struggle and exhaustion. In the acute and struggle phases, your $CO_2$ levels are low, and in the exhaustion phase your $CO_2$ levels rise too high. For those with too high $CO_2$ levels, breathing retraining will help to increase the pressure in the lungs so that the gas exchange improves and the $CO_2$ levels normalize.

#### Inflammation

Acute inflammation is your body's normal response to physical or chemical stress that needs to be healed and repaired. Chronic inflammation, on the other hand, is an abnormal condition that may cause, or be associated with, poor health and disease.

When acute inflammation fails to achieve the desired effect, chronic inflammation results. The transition to chronic inflammation can occur due to continued physical or chemical stressors such as smoking, unhealthy diet, infection or over-breathing. Increased inflammation has also been associated with Chronic Fatigue Syndrome, and in studies where inflammatory chemicals were administered, the result were fever, aches, and fatigue. A lot of people have chronic inflammation without any obvious symptoms, but the inflammation may be a contributing factor to many health problems.[9]

Inflammation is partly due to free oxygen radicals that are constantly produced in your body. The reaction is the same as the oxidation reaction that causes metal to rust or an apple slice to turn brown when exposed to light and oxygen. If oxidation in your body takes place at a higher rate than your body can handle, your ageing process will speed up.

Free radicals are a necessary part of the immune system because they are needed to destroy malignant organisms and faulty cells. The problem arises when we produce too many free radicals and/or have too-low antioxidant levels. The inflammation will then become chronic and cause extreme tiredness.

### The effect of weather on pain

Arthritis, joint inflammation, rheumatism, lower back pain and chronic muscle pain, as seen in fibromyalgia, are often linked to the weather. At Brigham and Women's Hospital Pain Management Center in Boston, USA, they noticed a sharp increase in the number of patients in the waiting room on days when the weather was damp and cold, compared to when the weather was warm and sunny. Professor Jamison and his colleagues studied the phenomenon in 567 patients, and they believe that "changes in barometric pressure are the main link between weather and pain. Low air pressure is usually associated with cold, wet weather and an increase in pain. Clear, dry weather signals a high air pressure and a decrease in pain."[10]

When barometric pressure decreases, as happens in low pressure, or at a high altitude, we increase our breathing rate and volume to obtain the same amount of oxygen. Basically, the lower the pressure, the greater the increase in the respiratory frequency and volume. On the top of Mount Everest (8,848 meters), the atmospheric pressure is only 1/3 of the pressure at sea level. The American Medical Expedition in 1981 recorded a respiratory rate of 80 breaths per minute at the top of the mountain. An increased breathing volume leads to a drop in $CO_2$ levels. If our $CO_2$ reserve is already low, which is highly likely in people who suffer different types of pain, we are more inclined to be affected by weather changes. Sudden weather changes, in which the air pressure changes quickly, can also have a negative health impact on people with different types of pain.

## HOW CONSCIOUS BREATHING CAN REDUCE ACHE, PAIN AND FATIGUE

### Do things in the right order

When your energy is low, it's especially important that you do things in the right order and at a pace you can handle. The first step may be to become more aware of how you breathe in different situations and to ensure that your mouth is closed as often as possible, both during the day and at night. Applying tape to your mouth at night is a simple action that can have a positive effect. Even taping your mouth during daytime (when alone) is beneficial if you are a habitual mouth breather. If your energy increases you can add breathing exercises with the Relaxator, or practice prolonged exhalation on your own. When your energy allows, an additional next step could be to take walks with your mouth closed. In time, you can also strive to adopt a good posture as often as possible, as this will make your breathing deeper and the respiratory work less demanding. (See Chapter 4 for more information.)

### Find relaxation in your daily life

By listening to your body, you can become aware of when you are tense in different situations. If you discover that you're tense, you can easily apply the Conscious Breathing Method to achieve a good breathing pattern and thereby increase relaxation.

When I went skiing a while ago I had a very bad fall. My skis came off when I was showing off, taking a steep slope at full speed. I slid for 40 meters at high speed, but since I was relaxed it went really well, and I didn't hurt myself at all. Instead of getting tense and afraid I managed to stay calm and just observe what was happening. Whoops! One ski fell off. *Okay let's try to slow down with the other ski.* Whoops! The other ski fell off, as well. *Oh now I'm sliding.*

Impaired breathing and stress may be responsible for your body becoming tense, achy and exhausted. Each problem contributes to the others, and a vicious cycle is established causing the pain that makes your body tense up even more. Hence, establishing a breathing habit that will see you through each day can be very helpful in reducing aches, pain, and tiredness.

# Chapter 13 – Fat or Fit: Why Breathing Affects Your Digestion, Metabolism and Weight

*There is a connection between over-breathing and excess weight. Many of us have a respiratory rate twice as fast as is should be, which can be likened to eating twice as many meals as you need, i.e., double breakfasts, lunches and dinners. By putting yourself on an "air diet," slowing down your breathing rate and breathing less, you'll improve your digestion and speed up your fat metabolism.*

Would you like to increase your fat loss but don't know how? Do you keep trying to lose weight but fail again and again? Doesn't the advice to, "just eat less" actually work? Maybe you've tried various diets and actually lost weight, but put it back on again when the motivation floundered, or you got fed up with the diet.

Is it possible to lose weight by improving our breathing habits? Yes it is!

Weight loss advice generally doesn't include improving your breathing habits, although it's a simple yet often overlooked way to both

| Proper breathing results in | Overbreathing or irregular breathing results in |
|---|---|
| • Optimum $CO_2$ levels in blood<br>• A lot of oxygen reaches the cells<br>• High fat metabolism<br>• Decreased sugar cravings<br>• A relaxed body<br>• Effective digestion, good nutrient uptake | • Low $CO_2$ levels in blood<br>• Less oxygen reaching the cells<br>• Impaired fat metabolism<br>• Increased sugar cravings<br>• A stressed body<br>• Digestion on the backburner, impaired nutrient uptake |

increase fat metabolism and improve digestion. When we understand how our body works and give it what it wants, weight loss doesn't have to be a struggle.

## BREATHING-RELATED CAUSES OF EXCESS WEIGHT

There are a number of breathing-related causes of obesity. Below you will find a few:

### Energy crisis leading to inefficient energy production

When we do not breathe optimally, less oxygen reaches our muscles and organs, which in turn leads to less energy being produced in our cells. We often over-compensate by eating more than we need to since up to 19 times *less* energy is produced per glucose molecule when oxygen is not available, and consequently less work can be performed. The energy crisis is perceived by our body as malnutrition when, in fact, we are suffering from a lack of oxygen.

When our ability to produce energy with oxygen decreases, we compensate by increasing anaerobic energy production (without oxygen). If oxygen is lacking, the only source available to produce energy from is sugar, and the vast consumption of sugar in our society can be interpreted as a sign of a deteriorating ability to produce energy, due to oxygen deficiency. A sedentary lifestyle and overindulgence in the consumption of simple carbohydrates combined with over-breathing means that most of us are simply suffering from energy deficiency.

When we hit the all-too-common afternoon energy dip we tend to try to resolve the problem by eating cookies and sweets, drinking tea or coffee, or downing sodas and energy drinks. Many of the simple carbohydrates we eat when we are low on energy creates an acidic environment in our body. For example, sugar creates a favorable breeding ground for bacteria found in your mouth. The waste from these bacteria is acidic, i.e., at a low pH level, which corrodes the teeth. Your body's innate response to acid-producing food and drinks is to increase respiration in order to eliminate more carbon dioxide, which increases pH, in an attempt to restore the pH level in your blood. The risk of establishing poor breathing habits arises and can easily end in a vicious circle.

Next time you crave sugar or feel low on energy, try to focus on your breathing pattern and make it abdominal, rhythmic, slow, and reduce your breathing volume. You can also try drinking water, as increasing your hydration levels can help stave off cravings.

#### Over-breathing leads to excess weight

When we are on an "air diet" we reduce our total breathing volume, i.e. the number of breaths per minute plus breathing volume per breath, so that it's more in line with our body's requirements. By putting yourself on an "air diet"—slowing down respiration and breathing less—you can improve digestion so that nutrient uptake and fat metabolism increase. The "air diet" allows you to breathe less, which puts your body in better balance and stops you from eating as much.

#### Increased waist-hip ratio prevents the diaphragm from working

Excess weight located around the stomach puts pressure on the diaphragm, which may reduce its ability to function properly and tends to promote shallow chest breathing. The same thing happens when we eat too much. The diaphragm, which moves downward during inhalation, is not able to do its work if our stomach is too full.

A British study of 320 people at risk of developing diabetes discovered that there is a close link between increased waist-to-hip ratio and poor lung function.[1]

To calculate your waist-hip ratio, divide your waist measurement by your hip measurement. A value greater than 1.0 in men, and 0.8 in women can be a sign that breathing habits are not at an optimum, and that a significant proportion of the body fat comes from too many carbohydrates in the diet, especially the refined kind that exist in all sugars, white bread, pastries, etc. Fast food and so-called "light" products often contain a large amount of hidden sugar or other unhealthy sweeteners.

### Overweight on the outside means overweight on the inside

If excess weight sits around your neck and throat it is very likely that fatty tissue will also be found on the inside of your airways. This makes your airways narrower and hampers proper oxygenation of your body cells. Narrow airways can also create a greater problem when we lie down as they can cause sleep disturbances, snoring, sleep apnea, and a host of other sleeping issues. Sleeping problems are also linked to poor breathing habits, which in turn may be due to obesity. If we sleep poorly we generally wake up feeling tired. This increases our risk of making bad food choices during the day and indulging in fast, low quality, easily accessible energy.

### Metabolic syndrome and lung functions are closely linked

Metabolic syndrome is an umbrella term for a number of problems including impaired glucose metabolism, hypertension, abdominal obesity, and elevated fat levels in the blood, i.e., triglycerides, which is common in Type 2 Diabetes and cardiovascular disease. In a Taiwanese study, where the link between impaired lung function and metabolic syndrome was investigated in over 40,000 adults, it was found that metabolic syndrome was significantly higher in people with impaired lung function compared to subjects with normal lung function.[2]

### Decreased bowel movements due to over-breathing and stress

Our digestive tract runs from our oral cavity to our anus and is approximately seven meters long. Our small intestine is five meters in length, and our colon is 1.5-meters long. Our intestines consist of smooth muscles that can both contract and relax when functioning well. However, the carbon dioxide deficiency that results from over-breathing only allows the smooth muscles in our intestines to contract. Studies have shown that bowel movements were negatively affected when the subjects hyperventilated, and that improved breathing habits made the smooth muscles relax, consequently increasing bowel movements.[3] Abdominal breathing, where the diaphragm is working actively, also results in increased stimulation and massage of the digestive organs and intestines.

The way we breathe reflects how we feel, so when our body is stressed, our breathing pattern also becomes stressed. During stress, the natural response of our body is to choose survival over fundamental needs like digestion. Blood circulation is directed to our arm and leg muscles first to supply them with the oxygen and nutrients needed to fight or flee, while blood supply to our abdominal organs decreases. Because digestion puts a heavy demand on our body's resources it is put on the backburner at times like this.

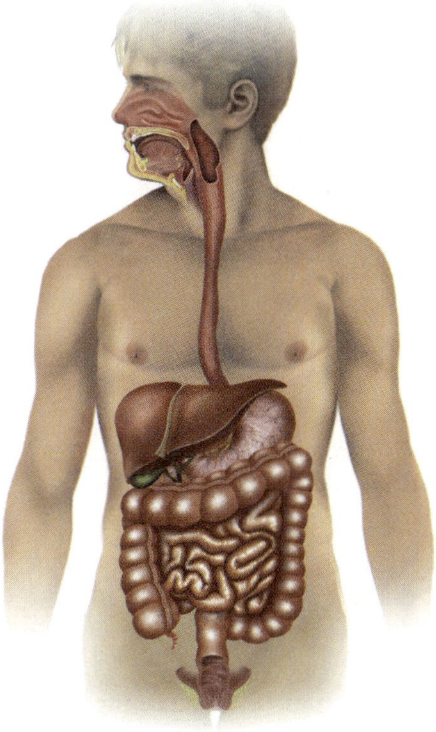

The digestive tract, which runs from the oral cavity to the anus, is about seven meters long. Good breathing habits are important in order for the food to be digested and for nutrients to be taken up as they pass through the intestinal tract.

Conscious Breathing helps the body to relax so that the smooth muscles of the intestines can work in the best possible way.

Using our diaphragm to breathe deeply and regularly stimulates the digestive organs. With each inhalation our diaphragm moves downward and pushes on the organs in our abdomen, giving them a rhythmic massage.

### Digestive enzymes perform less well

An enzyme is a catalyst that speeds up and streamlines various chemical bodily processes. Enzymes are made up of proteins and require the right environment to function well. Our body has a lot of different digestive enzymes that help digest and extract nutrients from the food we eat. A pH imbalance, which may be caused by inefficient breathing, provides an unfavorable environment and inferior enzyme function, resulting in impaired nutrient uptake. When nutrient uptake decreases, we compensate by eating more to satisfy our body's nutritional needs. This makes the digestive organs work overtime, and the increased load can further reduce uptake.

Poor absorption of nutrients can make us become too thin and frail when not enough energy is absorbed. It can also make us obese if we eat more food than our body needs in order to compensate for reduced uptake. A lot of the food we eat, especially the carbohydrates, is not being used and will instead be converted into fat and stored in the fat tissue. It's similar to what happens when a bear prepares for hibernation.

Incomplete digestion will also lead to many of the proteins we eat being only partially broken down. When the undigested proteins enter into our bloodstream, our immune system views them as foreign invaders and creates inflammations in order to eliminate them. Inflammation can occur in different parts of our body depending on where the proteins end up. The inflammation process is active in all kinds of diseases and can produce classic allergy symptoms, like a runny nose, sneezing, and a sore throat.[4]

## FAT OR SUGAR AS AN ENERGY SOURCE

To produce energy your body uses two main types of fuel: fat and carbohydrates (sugar/glucose). Carbohydrates bind a lot of liquid and are therefore an inefficient way to store energy compared to fat that doesn't retain any water. Since fat contains more than twice the amount of energy than carbohydrates, six kilos of carbohydrates are needed to

| Storage of energy | |
|---|---|
| Carbohydrates | 2,000 - 2,500 calories |
| Fat | 50,000 - 300,000 calories |

store the same amount of energy contained in one kilo of fat. Therefore, it is logical that your body only stores a small amount of energy in the form of carbohydrates (glucose), while the remainder is stored as fat. Calories are a way to measure the amount of energy, and in total, around 2,000–2,500 calories of glucose is stored in the body at any one time. The number of calories stored as fat is considerably higher, and depending on whether you are thin or overweight, it can vary from about 50,000 calories up to several hundred thousand.

Your fat reserves contain nearly unlimited amounts of energy. Oxygen must be present in your cells for fat to be broken down at all. When we breathe inefficiently, less oxygen will reach the cells and a greater proportion of carbohydrates than normal will be used to produce energy. The relatively small amount of carbohydrates stored will be used up faster than planned, and that is when we get sugar cravings. When we improve our breathing habits and thereby increase our ability to burn fat, we also reduce the need to refill with simple carbohydrates and other stimulating foods like caffeinated coffee, sodas and energy drinks to keep our energy up during the day.

### Respiratory Quotient

Respiratory Quotient (RQ) is the measure of how much energy is derived from carbohydrates and fats, respectively. At rest, a higher proportion of our total energy consumption usually comes from fat and a smaller share from carbohydrates. The dominant energy source is calculated by using a gas analyzer that measures the composition of the gas in exhaled air. Sugar has a respiratory quotient of 1.0, and for fat it is 0.7. The higher the RQ value, the greater proportion of the fuel in the energy production is provided by carbohydrates.

| Respiratory Quotient (RQ) = Produced $CO_2$ / Consumed $O_2$ | |
|---|---|
| Carbohydrates | RQ 1.0 = 6 $CO_2$ made of 6 $O_2$ |
| Fat | RQ 0.7 = 16 $CO_2$ made of 23 $O_2$ |

In a Finnish study on 16 individuals suffering from hyperventilation syndrome (HVS), the number of breaths per minute, respiratory volume, and the amount of carbon dioxide in the exhaled air were measured and compared with a control group that consisted of 13 healthy subjects.[5] Measurements were taken lying down after a ten-minute rest, and standing up after being in an upright position for eight minutes. At rest there were no major differences between the HVS group and the control group, but when they stood up for eight minutes the differences became pronounced:

- The breathing frequency increased by 4 breaths/minute in the HVS group and was virtually unchanged in the control group.
- The respiratory volume increased by a full 6.5 liters (from 7.7 to 14.2) in the HVS group and only 1.2 liters (from 8.1 to 9.3) in the control group.
- When they stood up, the RQ was high at 0.91 in the HVS group compared with only 0.77 in the control group.

The results confirmed that those with poor respiration use a higher proportion of carbohydrates to produce energy.

A Czech study followed up on the weight of obese people who had started a low calorie diet two years earlier. It was found that those who first lost weight and then gained it back again had a high RQ, i.e., they used more carbohydrates in general to produce energy. Those who managed to maintain the lower weight, however, had significantly lower RQ levels.[6]

The results showed that it is harder to both lose weight and to maintain weight loss when our respiration is ineffective. This is because breathing inefficiently causes oxygen deficiency. Since fat cannot be converted to energy without oxygen, our body will switch from burning fat to burning carbohydrates when our breathing is impaired. So if we're trying to lose weight, and at the same time over-breathe and/or breathe irregularly, it will be more difficult to keep the weight off because our body is set to burn sugar.

### Stable blood sugar is important

Normally, no more than a total of about five grams, a teaspoon, of sugar (glucose) circulates in the blood. Our body consumes approximately 100-150 grams of sugar per day (by comparison a 12-ounce (33 cl) bottle of Coca-Cola or a medium size ice cream contain 30 grams of sugar). When we consume simple carbohydrates that carry a high glycemic index, i.e., white bread, pasta, fizzy drinks, sweets, and other products high in sugar, our blood sugar level elevates rapidly. However, the raised blood sugar only has a short-lived effect and will drop quickly to a level that is lower than before we ate.

Since simple carbohydrates are quickly converted to glucose and enter into the bloodstream, a continuous intake of them may reduce our cells' ability to respond to insulin, which in turn can result in insulin resistance. Moreover, instead of being stored in our muscles or liver, the excess sugar either gets converted to fat for storage (usually belly fat), or continues to travel around our body, which may result in Type 2 Diabetes.

If your blood sugar levels resemble a roller-coaster ride during the day, your mood will be severely affected. When low blood sugar coincides with inefficient breathing, the effect may not only severely affect your mood, but also may drastically impact your cognitive ability, reaction time, concentration, and memory due to carbon dioxide and oxygen shortage.[7]

Some people only get hungry when their blood sugar drops, while others don't feel hungry and will just be in a bad mood. The biggest problem with low blood sugar occurs when the $CO_2$ levels are also low at the same time. Since your brain needs sugar and oxygen to produce energy, it becomes very stressed when the delivery of both are cut off simultaneously. This is when the risk of reaching for a sweet treat or comfort food is the greatest.

### Blood sugar, over-breathing and brain activity

Nerve cells in your brain depend on a continuous supply of sugar and oxygen, as they don't have the ability to store glucose. It is common to feel confused, powerless and/or nervous, and lose the ability to think clearly and focus if your nerve cells go into an energy crisis when blood glucose levels drop sharply a few hours after a sugar high.

In one study, brain activity was measured while participants were asked to hyperventilate at different blood glucose levels. EEG is used to measure activity in the brain, and different names have been allocated depending on the speed at which the brain waves move: Delta (0.5-4 Hz), Theta (4-8 Hz), Alpha (8-13 Hz) and Beta (13-40 Hz). The waves can be compared to gears in a car, because they too are suitable for use at different speeds. In the study, the brain activity shifted significantly depending on whether the blood sugar was high or low. At lower blood glucose levels, hyperventilation led to an increase in delta waves, which is associated with low brain activity and sleep. In other words, the brain's ability to process incoming information deteriorated when the subjects were over-breathing.[7]

### Tips for increased fat metabolism and improved digestion

A few simple tips to achieve greater fat metabolism and improved digestion include:

- **Improved breathing habits:** Conscious Breathing ensures that plenty of oxygen is delivered to the cells in our body so that fat can be used as an energy source. An excellent time to practice breathing retraining is when our energy feels low, as it may make it easier to resist the impulse to eat something sweet.

- **Perform physical activity with your mouth closed:** The most beneficial way to increase fat metabolism is to do low intense physical activity with your mouth closed. This ensures that enough oxygen reaches the muscles to maintain a high level of fat metabolism, both during exercise as well as afterwards.
- **Reduce stress:** If we constantly are in a hurry and live our life as if it was a series of 100-meter races, the need for access to quick energy increases, which means that the craving for sugar and simple carbohydrates increases, and fat metabolism decreases. However, if we relax and calm down, by improving our breathing habits, for example, the oxygen content in our cells will increase and more fat can be used as a fuel.

  Our digestive system receives a smaller proportion of our body's resources when we experience stress. Calm and relaxed breathing will reduce the internal stress and help improve digestion.
- **Do breathing retraining for a better pH balance:** It is important that our digestive system is at the correct pH level so digestive enzymes can function properly. Breathing is our most important system for regulating pH levels in the body, and over-breathing reduces the pH buffer. By practicing Conscious Breathing the pH buffer is raised, so our body can create an optimum environment in our stomach and intestines. Breathing retraining can be done either a while before or in between meals.
- **Eat in peace:** Taking three nasal, abdominal breaths with prolonged exhalations is an easy way to calm down at the table before eating. Much like saying grace, this short breathing exercise centers you, and increases your presence in the "here-and-now," which will also improve nutrient uptake.
- **Drink water before meals:** A lot of water is needed to digest food. For instance a liter of saliva (consists of 99.5% water) and up to two-liters of gastric juice are produced each day. It is best to drink a glass of water a little while before eating, which allows enough time for the water to be absorbed.

- **Invest in quality food:** "We get what we pay for" is an old proverb. Cheap food often hides poor ingredients, chemical flavors, and other artificial additives. A simple rule of thumb, even if it is completely unscientific, is that the longer the ingredient list, the more processed with preservatives, dyes, and other additives the food is likely to be.

# Chapter 14 – The Science of Breathing

*For many, a basic understanding of how breathing works is sufficient to understand why breathing well is so important. This chapter is for those who want a more in-depth understanding of the mechanism of breathing.*

## STEP 1: OXYGEN'S PATH FROM THE ATMOSPHERE TO THE LUNGS

Oxygen is transported into your lungs via your nasal passages and throat. The upper respiratory tract comprises your nose, sinuses, mouth and throat. It is here, particularly in your nose, that the air is being prepared for your lungs by being warmed up, moistened, and cleansed of bacteria and other particles. The lower respiratory tract begins below the larynx and consists of the trachea and bronchi in your lungs.

Your windpipe, i.e., the bronchi, branch off in the lungs into smaller units and become minute pulmonary vesicles, called alveoli. The alveoli are grouped in clusters, much like clusters of grapes, and several hundred million alveolar sacs are located inside each lung. When you inhale, your lungs fill with air and the alveolar sacs inflate like tiny balloons. When you exhale, the balloons are emptied of air and become compressed. The surface area of the alveoli is 50-100 $m^2$ in total, which is equivalent to an entire tennis court. The purpose for this gigantic lung surface is to satisfy your body's enormous need for oxygen.

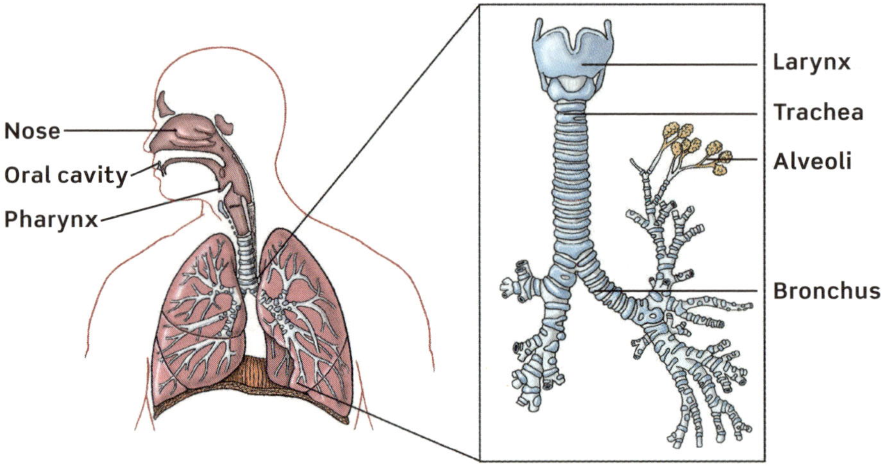


Step 1: We inhale air from the surrounding atmosphere via our nose or mouth. The air passes through our trachea and down the windpipe to the lungs. The windpipe branches off into smaller tubes that eventually culminate in the alveoli, which are only 0.3 mm in diameter. The alveoli walls are very thin to ensure efficient transfer of oxygen into the bloodstream.

Gas exchange, the process by which oxygen is transferred into your bloodstream and carbon dioxide is carried out via the air you exhale, only occurs in the alveoli. The space from your mouth and nasal cavity to the alveoli is called the dead space and may be viewed as a long tube, designed to carry air. During superficial shallow breathing, much of the air is only moved in and out along the dead space, which results in less air reaching the alveoli, which in turn minimizes gas exchange.

### STEP 2: OXYGEN IS TRANSFERRED TO THE BLOOD

The blood and air meet in the alveoli in your lungs. The blood that enters your lungs is low in oxygen and rich in carbon dioxide. It is through your heart that the blood is transferred to your lungs from its journey around your body. Throughout this journey, the blood delivers oxygen to your cells and simultaneously collects carbon dioxide. When leaving the lungs, your blood contains a great deal of oxygen and very little carbon dioxide.

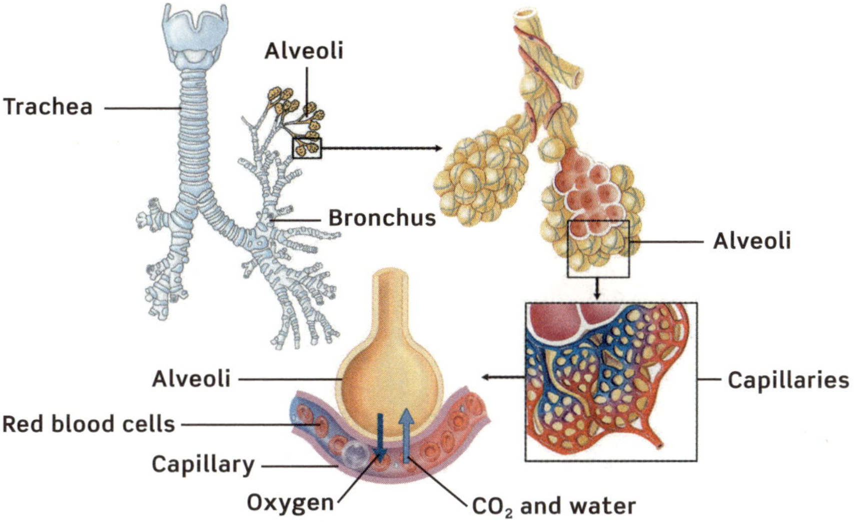


Step 2: Surrounding the alveoli is a network of small blood vessels called capillaries. This is where oxygen is transferred to the blood and carbon dioxide is carried from the blood to the alveoli, then continues up the windpipe, to be eliminated during exhalation.

Surrounding each alveolar sac is a network of small blood vessels called capillaries. This is where oxygen is inhaled, air is transferred to the bloodstream, and carbon dioxide is passed from the blood into the air in your lungs to be eliminated when you exhale.

Since your lungs are narrow at the top and wide at the bottom, similar to an inverted V, there is the least space for blood vessels and alveolar sacs in the upper part. Blood flow is at one liter/min at the bottom and one deciliter/min at the top—i.e., ten times greater at the bottom of the lungs compared to at the top. The number of alveoli are also significantly greater in the lower parts. Hence, for gas exchange to be effective, the inhaled air should reach the lower parts of your lungs.

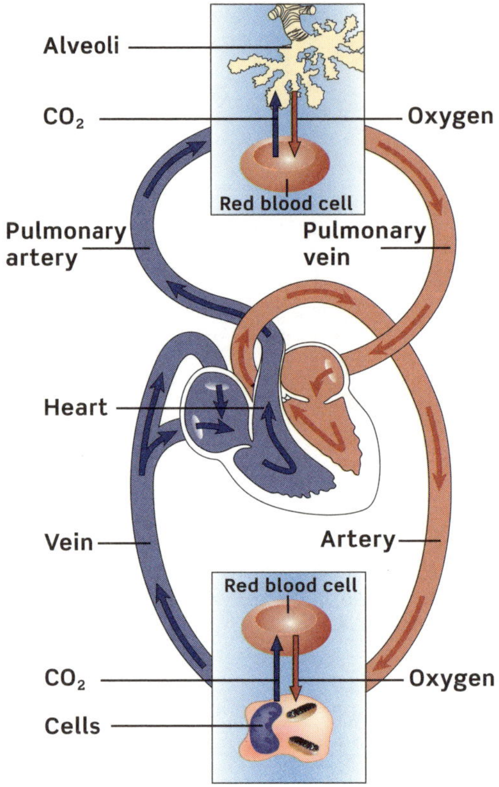


Step 2: In the lungs, carbon dioxide is transferred from our blood into the air we exhale, and oxygen is transferred via inhaled air to the blood.

The oxygen-rich blood travels from the lungs to the heart, which in turn pumps it out to our body. As it travels on its journey around the body, the blood is red, indicating that it is rich in oxygen.

Step 3: The oxygen is transferred from the blood to the cells, and carbon dioxide produced by the cells is transferred to the blood.

The blue color of the blood indicates that the blood contains smaller amounts of oxygen, and a lot of carbon dioxide, and is on its way back to the heart and lungs.

## STEP 3: OXYGEN IS CARRIED INTO THE CELLS

After the oxygen-rich blood has left your lungs, it initially reaches the heart before traveling further around your body. As adults we have around 60,000 miles (100,000 kilometers) of blood vessels but not all of them are constantly fully opened. Our body has to prioritize which parts should receive more or less blood. For instance, immediately after eating, a greater amount of blood is directed to our digestive organs in the abdomen, and during physical activity a greater proportion of the blood is guided to the active muscles. The function of the heart is to pump blood through our bloodstream to supply our cells with nutrients and oxygen, as well as to remove excess toxins such as carbon dioxide, waste products, and unnatural substances that we ingest when we eat, drink, and breathe.

### BALANCE BETWEEN OXYGEN AND CARBON DIOXIDE

It is commonly assumed that oxygen is our saving grace, that we should inhale as much of it as we can, and that carbon dioxide is a toxic waste product that should be removed from our body as quickly as possible. This is not true. As is so often the case, it is all about balance. Optimal breathing helps to maintain a balance between the need for oxygen and the production of carbon dioxide.

We can compare this to how a car works. A car engine needs fuel to function, and if the supply is limited the engine becomes temperamental until it finally stops. This will also happen if the engine gets too much fuel: the engine becomes cranky, sputters and stops. Likewise, the fuel requirements vary depending on wheter you drive in the city or on a motorway. Optimal breathing means that our breathing pattern corresponds to our needs at any given moment.

In medical literature, we find that normal respiratory volume at rest is about six liters per minute, divided into twelve breaths at half a liter per breath. However, many of us inhale a considerably greater volume at 10–15 l/min, divided between 15–25 breaths/minute and 0.7–1.0 l/breath. In my opinion, for optimal breathing, we only need to breathe 4–6 liters/min, which differs vastly to how most people actually breathe. When you are over-breathing, or hyperventilating, the breathing no longer corresponds to the needs of your body, and an imbalance arises between the levels of oxygen and $CO_2$.

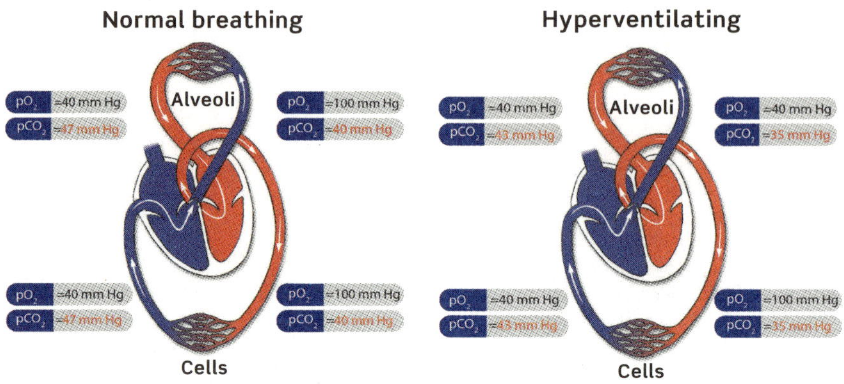


When over-breathing (hyperventilating) the partial pressure of carbon dioxide ($pCO_2$) decreases. A normal pressure of $pCO_2$ is 40 mm HG. Hyperventilating is defined as having 35 mm HG or lower.

## BREATHING MORE (AIR) PROVIDES LESS (OXYGEN)

Of the oxygen we inhale we only use 25 percent, at rest, since 75 percent of it is exhaled again. Meanwhile, the level of carbon dioxide we exhale is around 100 times higher than the level we inhale.

| | Inhalation | Exhalation |
|---|---|---|
| Oxygen | 21 % | 16 % |
| Carbon dioxide | 0.04 % | 4 % |

Oxygen travels around your bloodstream by binding to hemoglobin. During normal respiration, when you are at rest, the hemoglobin in your blood is already saturated with almost as much oxygen as is possible, at 97–98 percent. A level above 95 percent is considered normal, and can easily be measured by attaching an electronic device, called a pulse oximeter, to your finger or ear.

Since your blood is saturated with such high oxygen levels, and you only use a quarter of the oxygen you inhale, it doesn't serve any purpose to inhale the 10–15 liters/min that many of us do. Over-breathing 2–3 times more than is optimal produces the opposite effect, and less oxygen is actually delivered to your cells.

Oxygen delivery is controlled by the activity in your cells. For instance, when you move your right arm it consumes more oxygen than the left arm that is stationary. The more you engage in physical activity, the greater the need for oxygen in order to produce energy. In addition to producing energy, active muscles and organs also produce carbon dioxide and heat which, when it escapes from the cells, lowers the pH level in the blood, which in turn releases more oxygen from the hemoglobin, allowing more oxygen to be transferred into your cells so that more energy can continue to be produced. Oxygen's affinity to hemoglobin at different pH levels is called the Bohr effect, after the Dane, Christian Bohr, who discovered it.[1,2,3]

### Lack of carbon dioxide equals lack of oxygen

Normally, you have large reserves of carbon dioxide, but when you over-breathe, you initially exhale more carbon dioxide than is produced in your body, creating a shortage of carbon dioxide in your lungs, then in your blood, followed by your tissues and organs. By chronically over-breathing you habitually retain low levels of carbon dioxide in your body. Lack of carbon dioxide raises the pH level in your blood, causing the oxygen to bind tighter to the hemoglobin. Your active right arm will then receive less oxygen than is desirable, thus producing less energy, and your arm will become exhausted faster.

Over-breathing causes your blood to carry too much oxygen and too little carbon dioxide, so less oxygen is released from your blood to be delivered to your cells. The resulting state, called hypoxia, reduces the ability of your cells to produce energy, which reduces the amount of energy available to your body.

## HOW BREATHING IS CONTROLLED

The body primarily controls our breathing patterns by regularly assessing the pH and carbon dioxide levels in our brainstem or the carotid arteries So it is mainly carbon dioxide, not oxygen, that stimulates our breathing reflex.

### Assessing the brain stem

Our brainstem, which is situated between the spinal cord and the brain, controls basic functions essential for our survival: hunger, thirst, breathing, heartbeat, blood pressure, fear, aggression, flight instincts, and reproduction.

Our respiratory center, located in the brainstem, assesses the pH and carbon dioxide levels in the spinal fluid by means of chemoreceptors. Our cells are constantly producing carbon dioxide, and when the blood carbon dioxide levels increase, the respiratory muscles are stimulated, and we inhale. On the subsequent exhalation, a substantial amount of carbon dioxide is eliminated, the levels are lowered again, and a new breathing cycle begins. When the $CO_2$ levels increase to a certain level the respiratory center triggers a new inhalation.

Breathing is primarily regulated by raised carbon dioxide levels, not by lack of oxygen. This explains why a diver who hyperventilates before a dive can stay longer underwater, though this is a dangerous thing to try.

When you hyperventilate, your respiration rate increases and no longer corresponds to your body's needs, resulting in a greater flow of carbon dioxide leaving your body. Subsequently, a temporary shortage of carbon dioxide is created that prolongs the time it takes for your body to reach the carbon dioxide levels needed to stimulate your respiratory center. Hyperventilating before diving is sometimes used, to be able to stay longer under water, but can be fatal as the diver can run out of oxygen and pass out without the respiratory reflex being triggered.

#### *Try for yourself:*

You can easily confirm that your carbon dioxide levels control your respiratory reflex by checking how long you can hold your breath before and after thirty seconds of hyperventilation. Try this:

1. Close your mouth and inhale/exhale calmly through your nose.
2. After exhaling naturally for a few seconds hold your nose and note how long you can hold your breath.

3. Hyperventilate for 30 seconds by taking more than 30 big breaths. Keep your mouth open and take extended breaths allowing your chest to heave.
4. Close your mouth and exhale naturally for a few seconds, hold your nose again and check how long you can hold your breath.

Were you able to hold your breath for a longer period after hyperventilating? When you over-breathe, you are lowering your carbon dioxide levels, and it will take longer to reach the level where your breathing reflex is triggered.

Respiration can also be controlled by our thoughts and feelings:

**Thoughts**

The frontal lobe is where your center of conscious thought is located. With your thoughts, you have the ability to decide to hold your breath or to breathe rapidly. When you concentrate on what happened yesterday, or think about tomorrow, your breathing is profoundly affected.

**Emotions**

Anxiety, fear, and other negative emotions, as well as sexual excitement, happiness and other positive feelings, also have a direct effect on our respiration.

## CONTROLLING BREATHING

The nerve that controls the movement of your diaphragm is called the phrenic nerve. When the levels of $CO_2$ reach a certain level, your breathing center sends a signal via the phrenic nerve to retract your diaphragm, prompting you to inhale. This is an automatic process that you don't need to be consciously aware of.

Since your mind and breathing habits are intimately connected, your thoughts and feelings can also affect the phrenic nerve and overrun the automatic function.

By studying anatomical definitions we can often find a deeper understanding of different bodily functions. The word *phrenic nerve* is derived from the Greek word *phren*. The interesting thing is that *phren* has a double meaning: "diaphragm" and "mind." This peculiar double meaning reflects the insight that breathing and mind are closely related. The term schizophrenia, or multiple personalities, also contains the word *phrenic*.

Respiration can thus be controlled *automatically* by continuous assessment of our carbon dioxide and oxygen levels and *manually* by our thoughts and feelings. Generally, we don't think about our breathing, as it takes care of itself automatically and adapts to all the different needs we have during sleep, physical activity, or at high altitudes. Respiration is unique in that it can be automatically controlled as well as influenced at will. The way we breathe has a very distinct impact on other automatic processes in our body, such as digestion and the heart. By improving our breathing habits, we have the ability to indirectly improve these and other automated processes, as well.

## ENERGY PRODUCTION WITH OR WITHOUT OXYGEN

In order to perform well, your cells need energy. Energy production, in turn, requires fuel in the form of fat and sugar, as well as oxygen. The energy produced in your cells is called Adenosine Triphosphate (ATP), which is the energy currency in your body. All plants, animals and humans use ATP. The cells use ATP to perform different tasks, such as digesting food, removing waste products or dividing to give life to new cells.

Large amounts of ATP mean that your body has plenty of energy available to function properly, while a lack of ATP forces your cells and organs to prioritize survival over growth. Basically, ATP is to the body what money is to man. Having plenty of money allows you to eat until you are satisfied and buy what you need, while lack of funds could lead to living in poverty and possibly starving.

**The mitochondria produce large amounts of energy**

Put simply, energy production in the body occurs in two ways: with oxygen (aerobic) or without oxygen (anaerobic). When oxygen is absent, two ATP molecules are generated per molecule of glucose (sugar), in a simple and rapid process called fermentation.

However, the most effective way to extract energy from nutrients is through the use of oxygen. This process is called combustion and occurs in the mitochondria of your cells, the energy factories of your body. They produce the majority (90 percent) of your energy needs by burning nutrients and oxygen.[2] The mitochondria are like combustion chambers. To put out an ordinary fire, we can smother it by robbing it of the oxygen it needs to continue to burn. We can also fuel the fire by adding more oxygen. The same principles are valid in our bodies. The more oxygen (and nutrients) available for the mitochondria, the better the combustion chambers will work and more energy can be produced.

The creation of energy in the mitochondria is a slower process than fermentation; however, it yields a much higher return of up to 38 ATPs, or 19 times more energy, from the same amount of glucose. The mitochondria can also use fat as fuel. Since fat contains more energy than glucose, a fat molecule can produce up to 144 ATP molecules.

| Fermentation | Combustion (glucose) | Combustion (fat) |
|---|---|---|
| • Anaerobic (no oxygen) | • Aerobic (with oxygen) | • Aerobic (lot of oxyg.) |
| • In cell cytosol | • In mitochondria | • In mitochondria |
| • Fast | • Slow | • Slow |
| • 2 ATP | • Up to 38 ATP | • Up to 144 ATP |
| • Lactate (lactic acid) | • Carbon dioxide | • Carbon dioxide |

Carbon dioxide is also produced during combustion in the mitochondria. This is in contrast to what happens during fermentation, which produces lactic acid instead.

In a ten-second 100-meter race, 85 percent of the energy is derived from anaerobic energy production (fermentation without oxygen). When jogging two miles in ten minutes, 20 percent of the energy is produced anaerobically, and if jogging for one hour, only five percent of the energy consumed is produced without oxygen.[4]

In conclusion, anaerobic energy production uses no oxygen and offers quick energy in small amounts. Only glucose (sugar) can be used to produce energy in this way. On the other hand, aerobic combustion of glucose or fat generates large amounts of energy.

Living a stressful life is similar to running a 100-meter race at full speed. We need energy fast (sugar), and we tire easily since little energy is produced. This means that during stressful periods, we live our lives as if we were running multiple 100-meter races, which causes our endurance to decline while our sugar cravings increase.

## BREATHING IS AN IMPORTANT PH REGULATOR

If you remember learning about the pH scale from school you may recall that any substance at a pH level below seven is acidic and that anything above seven is called basic, or alkaline. The pH level is a measure of the number of hydrogen ions present in a solution. Many hydrogen ions indicate that the solution is acidic, and few hydrogen ions indicate that the solution is alkaline. A correct pH balance is critical to the chemical reactions taking place in your body in order for it to perform at optimal levels.

The normal blood pH level is 7.4. A blood level below 7.0 or above 7.8 is life threatening. In order to break down the food we eat, the hydrochloric acid in our stomach has to be at a pH level of 1.5 to 3. From the stomach, the food is passed on to the duodenum and small intestine, where the pH level is increased by bile, pancreatic

| Acidic | Alkaline |
|---|---|
| • Many hydrogen ions<br>• Low pH (below 7) | • Few hydrogen ions<br>• High pH (above 7) |

juice, and bicarbonate. It is here that 90 percent of the nutrients are absorbed, and a correct pH level is essential for the digestive enzymes to function properly.

There is a large amount of bicarbonate in your blood, and in the liquid outside your cells, known as extracellular fluid. Bicarbonate acts as a buffer to ensure that the pH level is constant in different parts of the body.

The cells in your body constantly produce carbon dioxide ($CO_2$), most of which is converted along with water ($H_2O$), into bicarbonate ($HCO_3^-$) and hydrogen ($H^+$). Your blood hydrogen level increases during this process while the pH level decreases, allowing the oxygen that is transported by the blood leaving your lungs to be released into the cells (the Bohr effect). Simultaneously, carbon dioxide is transported as bicarbonate in the blood returning to your lungs.

The bicarbonate and hydrogen is then converted back into carbon dioxide and water, which you exhale when it reaches your lungs. This process reduces the amount of hydrogen in your blood, increases the pH level, and a new breathing cycle is started.

In addition to your lungs and respiration, your kidneys also have a significant impact on your pH balance and your bicarbonate buffer, as bicarbonate is collected by your kidneys and excreted in your urine. The effect your lung activity has on the pH balance is immediate, while the work of your kidneys produces a more long-term effect.

When you over-breathe, the first thing that happens is that your blood becomes a little more alkaline as the pH level is raised above the normal level, because of an increased outflow of carbon dioxide and hydrogen. Having a higher than normal pH level in the blood when over-breathing produces two effects:

a) **Hypoxia:** Less oxygen reaches the cells, due to the Bohr effect, which makes the oxygen hold on tighter to the hemoglobin in the blood when the pH level is high. A higher proportion of energy may thus be produced without oxygen, which in turn increases the levels of lactic acid. The acidic lactic acid helps to restore the blood pH balance, although it is only a short-term solution.
b) **Reduced bicarbonate buffer:** In order to lower the blood pH level back to neutral, our kidneys begin to secrete more bicarbonate with our urine. When our kidneys have to compensate for our over-breathing, they reduce the total bicarbonate buffer, and if we continue to over-breathe, the levels remain consistently low. A low bicarbonate buffer impairs our body's ability to clear the lactic acid that results from physical activity and foods such as soda drinks and coffee that have a low pH level.

Since bicarbonate contains carbon dioxide, we lose carbon dioxide at both ends—through over-breathing and also when our kidneys compensate by excreting bicarbonate in our urine.

### CARBON DIOXIDE AND OXYGEN IN THE ATMOSPHERE

In this book, I keep coming back to the importance of carbon dioxide for maintaining a healthy body. At the same time, carbon dioxide is often seen as the major culprit in the theories of global warming.

Carbon dioxide is called a greenhouse gas, and when the levels in the atmosphere increase, more heat is reflected from the sun back to the earth instead of going out into space. Since the beginning of industrialization in the 1750's, atmospheric levels of carbon dioxide have increased from 0.025 percent to 0.04 percent. Industry and cars contribute to the increase, which can be viewed as a steep rise in a short period of time.

It is possible that the theories on global warming are correct, however, such an environmental effect is beyond the scope of this book, which focuses on what happens in the body.

### Plant propagation increased oxygen levels

When life arose on our planet about four billion years ago, in the form of bacteria, algae and amoeba-like organisms, evidence suggests that oxygen was not present in the atmosphere, but carbon dioxide concentration was much higher than the 0.04 percent it is currently. The living organisms that existed then were anaerobic, which means that they produced energy without oxygen. As the plants propagated and grew in numbers, oxygen levels in the air increased. Plants use sunlight, carbon dioxide and water to produce energy through a process called photosynthesis, which produces oxygen as a byproduct. As plants spread across the globe, the oxygen levels in the atmosphere increased. Organisms that could use oxygen to extract energy from nutrients flourished since oxygen makes it easier to extract energy from nutrients.[5]

Today, 21 percent of the atmosphere consists of oxygen. Thanks to a higher oxygen concentration more energy is produced, and more complex life forms have evolved.

While life forms on our planet have adapted to increasingly higher oxygen levels and lower carbon dioxide levels in the atmosphere, our cells' need for carbon dioxide still remains high. For a cell to function optimally it needs around five percent carbon dioxide, which is more than 100 times higher than the levels in the atmosphere and 2.5 times higher than the amount found in the oceans.

Could it be that when life arose in the oceans, the water and the atmosphere contained the five percent carbon dioxide that is needed for our cells to function optimally? I don't know, but the possibility is intriguing.

# Chapter 15 – How Conscious Breathing Changed My Life

Without a doubt the most valuable thing I have done for my health and quality of life is to improve my breathing habits. The practice of Conscious Breathing has significantly improved my physical and mental wellbeing. The main lesson I have learned from practicing the Conscious Breathing Method is that I choose to be true to myself more often. To be brave enough to look inward and learn about myself in depth is the most amazing journey I have ever been on, and it's a journey I wish everyone could experience.

My colleague, Cecilia Salmi, and I held the first Conscious Breathing course in the spring of 2010. ONE participant came. Two people came for the next course. Despite the modest interest in the beginning, there was never any doubt in my mind that this was what I was supposed to do. My current courses have had hundreds of participants, but during those early times I had to sell my house in order to be able to afford to continue educating myself about breathing techniques, and to develop the Conscious Breathing Method.

Improving my breathing habits has contributed to the following:

- **Better health.** I'm very rarely ill nowadays. More of my resources are devoted to personal growth instead of trying to get well.
- **Being less afraid.** Fear can prevent us from living the life we desire. By choosing to be who I am, I now play the leading role in my own life. I no longer fear death, accidents, financial problems, public speaking, embarrassment, failure, or what others think of me. My breathing has become a faithful friend that is always right here with me—a friend that I can safely lean on when I need support.

- **Feeling a greater sense of freedom.** Improving my breathing habits has helped me to find my inner strength. Today, I'm rarely overcome by needs, such as cravings for sugar or the belief that I "must" have the latest technical gadget. Clockwatching, anxiety, and anger no longer have a big influence in my life. It has also become easier for me to deal with setbacks since I have come to realize that they help me to grow as a person. All this makes me feel freer than I was before.
- **Enjoying better relationships.** Since my brain has calmed down, it has become easier for me to put myself in other people's shoes and understand the reasons for their thoughts, beliefs and actions. My critical and judgmental inner dialogue has been replaced by curiosity and humility. By focusing on my breathing pattern, I find it easier to create a distance between my thoughts and my feelings, which enables me to remain calm in difficult situations far more often. I feel a greater connection with all living things.
- **Having better contact with my inner guidance.** When I hesitate before making a decision, I find it helps to breathe diaphragmatically, rhythmically, and slowly (i.e., prolonging my exhalations) in order to get in touch with my inner guidance. Rhythmic breathing helps me switch from intellect and logic to gut feeling and intuition. I now trust my innate ability to make the right decision in the moment.

| My inner journey has increasingly taken me | |
|---|---|
| **From** | **To** |
| • Conflict, competition, anger | • Love, harmony, cooperation |
| • Survival | • Growth, learning |
| • Critical, judgmental | • Humble, grateful, curious |
| • Victim | • Co-creator |
| • Disease | • Health |
| • Fear, worry | • Faith, courage, daring |
| • Past, future | • Present |

The less time we spend being ill, pondering things that may have happened, worrying about the future, judging others, or creating conflicts, the more opportunities we have to grow as people. It is easier to ask for forgiveness when we have made a mistake, to be curious rather than judgmental, and to stand up for ourselves calmly and clearly. We then create a positive spiral that makes life far more meaningful.

## BALANCED BREATHING INCREASES SPIRITUAL GROWTH

Previously, I dismissed things that can't be explained as ridiculous hocus-pocus, based on the reasoning of my logical left-brain. When I tried to meditate I was too wound up to calm down. However, I always "knew" deep within myself that there was something more, but I didn't have the tools to get there. Focusing on my breathing pattern in my daily life has made possible for me an exciting inner journey of spiritual growth, and it is easy for me to see a similarity in the words inspiration, expiration and spirituality.

Attendees at my courses report similar experiences. Improving their breathing habits builds their confidence, reduces their fears, and boosts their courage to be themselves.

When we are true to ourselves and follow our own path, we inspire other people around us to do the same.

### My values guide me

Personally, I'm not religious in the sense that I do not practice a specific religion. I'm drawn more to spirituality than I am to the rules, ceremonies, and procedures found in religious organizations. Spirituality for me means harmony, freedom, community and connection with my inner guidance. The primary inner values that guide me are:

- **Creation**. We are all co-creators of our own reality. This means that I take responsibility for what happens in my life.
- **Consciousness**. Since life arose on earth, increased awareness of the surrounding environment has increased the survival ability of

different life forms. The same goes for humans. Opportunities to grow and increase my awareness are presented in the challenges and difficulties that I face. I have come to view these challenges and difficulties as my friends, not my enemies. By being open and curious about what is happening in my daily life, I have greater opportunities to grow and expand my horizons.

- **Cooperation**. A human body with all 50,000 trillion cells cooperating feels good, and the same applies to our society. The way forward is cooperation, not competition. I believe that we are here to help and to serve each other while maintaining our integrity. This approach helps us, and the people we meet, to grow. Today, more than ever, we need to focus less on financial growth and more on inner growth. Our breath holds the key to gain access to our inner core. So fundamentally, within our breath lies the power to both change our lives and change the world.

**This illustration symbolizes Conscious Breathing's five basic principles of good breathing habits influencing our mind, body and emotions, and the result—more love, harmony and freedom.**

Working on improving my breathing has not only made my body feel better, but has also resulted in my growing as a whole human being in a fantastic way.

I hope that the Conscious Breathing Method will do the same for you.

The End (or maybe the start of something new).

# REFERENCES


## Introduction

1. Schünemann et al., *Pulmonary function is a long-term predictor of mortality in the general population: 29-year follow-up of the Buffalo Health Study*, Chest. 2000 Sep;118(3):656-64
2. Sin et al., *The relationship between reduced lung function and cardiovascular mortality: a population-based study and a systematic review of the literature*, Chest. 2005 Jun;127(6):1952-9

## Chapter 1 - How Poor Breathing Impacts Your Health

1. Olséni L, Wollmer P et al, *Sjukgymnastik vid nedsatt lungfunktion*, 2003, updated 2011
2. Lundberg JO, Weitzberg E et al., *Inhalation of nasally derived nitric oxide modulates pulmonary function in humans*, Acta Physiol Scand. 1996 Dec;158(4):343-7
3. Stäubli M, Vogel F, Bartsch P, Fluckiger G, Ziegler WH, *Hyperventilation-induced changes of blood cell counts depend on hypocapnia*, Eur J Appl Physiol Occup Physiol 1994;69:402-7
4. Laffey JG, Kavanagh BP, *Hypocapnia*, N Engl J Med 2002; 347:43-53
5. Fried R, *Breathe well, be well*, 1999

## Chapter 2 - How Breathing Works

1. Meuret AE, Ritz T, *Hyperventilation in Panic Disorder and Asthma: Empirical Evidence and Clinical Strategies*, Int J Psychophysiol. 2010 October; 78(1): 68–79
2. Lum LC, *Hyperventilation syndromes in medicine and psychiatry: a review*, J R Soc Med. 1987 April; 80(4): 229–231
3. Lum LC, *Hyperventilation: the tip and the iceberg*, J Psychosom Res. 1975;19(5-6):375-83
4. Magarian et al., *Hyperventilation syndrome: a diagnosis begging for recognition*, West J Med. 1983 May; 138(5): 733–736

## Chapter 3 - Five Simple Principles for Better Breathing

1. Ozgursoy et al., *Influence of long-term airflow deprivation on the dimensions of the nasal cavity: a study of laryngectomy patients using acoustic rhinometry*, Ear Nose Throat J. 2007 Aug;86(8):488, 490-2
2. Pinsky MR, *Cardiovascular issues in respiratory care*, Chest. 2005 Nov;128(5 Suppl 2):592-597

## Chapter 4 - Retrain Your Breathing

1. Olsson A, *Conscious Breathing Retraining gives result*, Breathing News, #2, 2013

## Chapter 5 - Conscious Breathing for Stress Reduction


1. Stäubli M, Vogel F, Bartsch P, Fluckiger G, Ziegler WH, *Hyperventilation-induced changes of blood cell counts depend on hypocapnia*, Eur J Appl Physiol Occup Physiol 1994;69:402-7
2. Alemany M, *Utilization of dietary glucose in the metabolic syndrome*, Nutr Metab (Lond). 2011 Oct 26;8(1):74
3. van Aalderen et al., *Epidemiology and the concept of underlying mechanisms of nocturnal asthma*, Respir Med. 1993 Aug;87 Suppl B:37-9
4. Van den Bergh et al., *Learning to have psychosomatic complaints: conditioning of respiratory behavior and somatic complaints in psychosomatic patients*, Psychosom Med. 1997 Jan-Feb;59(1):13-23
5. Binetti R et al., *Exponential growth of new chemicals and evolution of information relevant to risk control*, Ann Ist Super Sanita. 2008;44(1):13-5
6. Tahamiler et al., *Detection of the nasal cycle in daily activity by remote evaluation of nasal sound*, Arch Otolaryngol Head Neck Surg. 2009 Feb;135(2):137-42
7. Shannahoff-Khalsa DS, *Lateralized rhythms of the central and autonomic nervous systems*, Int J Psychophysiol. 1991;11:225-251
8. Telles S, Raghuraj P, Maharana S, Nagendra HR, *Immediate effect of three yoga breathing techniques on performance on a letter-cancellation task*, Percept Mot Skills. 2007;104:1289-1296
9. Werntz DA, Bickford RG, Bloom FE, Shannahoff-Khalsa DS, *Alternating cerebral hemispheric activity and the lateralization of autonomic nervous function*, Hum Neurobiol. 1983;2:39-43
10. Huttunen J et al., *Effects of voluntary hyperventilation on cortical sensory responses*, Exp Brain Res. 1999 Apr;125(3):248-54
11. Balestrino M, Somjen GG, *Concentration of carbon dioxide, interstitial pH and synaptic transmission in hippocampal formation of the rat*, J Physiol. 1988 Feb;396:247-66
12. Gibbs DM, *Hyperventilation-induced cerebral ischemia in panic disorder and effect of nimodipine*, Am J Psychiatry. 1992 Nov;149(11):1589-91
13. Ball S, Shekhar A, *Basilar artery response to hyperventilation in panic disorder*, Am J Psychiatry. 1997 Nov;154(11):1603-4
14. Hauge A et al., *Changes in cerebral blood flow during hyperventilation and $CO_2$-breathing measured transcutaneously in humans*, Acta Physiol Scand. 1980 Oct;110(2):167-73
15. Bjålie JG et al., *Människokroppen: Fysiologi och anatomi*, 1998, p 64
16. Chaitow L et al., *Multidisciplinary Approaches to Breathing Pattern Disorders*, 2002, p 119
17. Fried RZ, *Hyperventilation Syndrome: Research and Clinical Treatment*, 1986
18. Heppenstall ME, *The Relation between the effects of the blood sugar levels and hyperventilation on the electroencephalogram*, J Neurol Neurosurg Psychiatry. 1944 July; 7(3-4): 112–118
19. Nardi AE et al., *Hyperventilation challenge test in panic disorder and depression with panic attacks*, Psychiatry Res. 2001 Dec 15;105(1-2):57-65
20. Ley R, *The modification of breathing behavior. Pavlovian and operant control in emotion and cognition*, Behav Modif. 1999 Jul;23(3):441-79


## Chapter 6 - Conscious Breathing for Sports and Exercise


1. McDougall C, *Born To Run*, 2009
2. Olséni L, Wollmer P et al., *Sjukgymnastik vid nedsatt lungfunktion*, 2003, updated 2011
3. Lundberg JO, Weitzberg E et al, *Inhalation of nasally derived nitric oxide modulates pulmonary function in humans*, Acta Physiol Scand. 1996 Dec;158(4):343-7
4. Gallwey WT, *The Inner Game of Tennis*, 1974, updated 1977, p 96

5. Olsson A, *Pilot study - nasal vs. mouth breathing*, 2011
6. Stough C, Stough R, *Dr Breath – The Story of Breathing Coordination*, 1970, updated 1981
7. Maffetone P, *The Maffetone method: The Holistic, low-stress, no-pain way to exceptional fitness,* 2000
8. Douillard J, *Body, Mind and Sport*, 1994, updated 2001
9. McConnell A, *Breathe Strong, Perform Better*, 2011
10. Mittleman S, *Slow Burn: Burn Fat Faster By Exercising Slower*, 2000


## Chapter 8 - How Your Breathing Can Affect Your Teeth and Facial Development


1. Price W, *Nutrition and Physical Degeneration – A comparison of Primitive and Modern Diets and Their Effects*, 1938
2. Proffit WR, *Lingual pressure pattern in the transition from tongue thrust to adult swallowing*, Archs Oral Biol. 1972:17:555:63
3. Sakuda M, Ishizua M, *Study of the lip bumper*, J Dentist Res. 1970:49:667
4. Flutter J, *Lecture BIBH conference*, 2007
5. Lopatiene K, Babarskas A, *Malocclusion and upper airway obstruction*, Medicina (Kaunas) 2002;38(3):277-83
6. Ozgursoy OB, Dursun G, *Influence of long-term airflow deprivation on the dimensions of the nasal cavity: a study of laryngectomy patients using acoustic rhinometry*, Ear Nose Throat J. 2007 Aug;86(8):488, 490-2
7. Kerr WJ, McWilliam JS, Linder-Aronson S, *Mandibular form and position related to changed mode of breathing – a five year longitudinal study*, Angle Orthod 1987;59:91-96
8. McKeown P, *Buteyko Meets dr Mew*, 2010, p 53
9. Hang W, *Lecture IAFGG symposium*, 2011
10. Hellsing E, *Changes in the pharyngeal airway in relation to extension of the head*, Eur J Orthod. 1989 Nov;11(4):359-65
11. Mew J, *Lecture IAFGG symposium*, 2011
12. Rubin RM, *Mode of respiration and facial growth*, Am J Orthod. 1980 Nov;78(5):504-10
13. Jefferson Y, *Mouth breathing: adverse effects on facial growth, health, academics, and behavior*, Gen Dent. 2010 Jan-Feb;58(1):18-25; quiz 26-7, 79-80
14. Linder-Aronson S, *Adenoids: their effect on mode of breathing and nasal airflow, and their relationship to characteristics of the facial skeleton and the dentition*, Acta Otolaryngol Suppl. 1970;265:1-132
15. Holmberg H, Linder-Aronson S, *Cephalometric radiographs as a means of evaluating the capacity of the nasal and nasopharyngeal airway*, Am J Orthod Dentofacial Orthop 1979;76:479-90
16. Linder-Aronson S, Woodside DG, Lundström A, *Mandibular growth direction following adenoidectomy*, Am J Orthod 1986;89:273-84
17. Tipton WP, *Beautiful balanced faces. The first 9 years: the most critical time!*, Int J Orthod Milwaukee 2006 Fall;17(3):13-22
18. Harari D et al., *The effect of mouth breathing versus nasal breathing on dentofacial and craniofacial development in orthodontic patients*, Laryngoscope. 2010 Oct;120(10):2089-93
19. Hang et al., *Evaluation of the Posterior Airway Space Following Biobloc Therapy: Geometric Morphometrics*, Journal of Craniomandibular Practice 2007 25 (2): 84–89
20. Mew J, *Facial Changes in Identical Twins Treated by Different Orthodontic Techniques*, World Journal of Orthodontics 2007 8 (2): 174–188

## Chapter 9 - Breathe Well, Sleep Well


1. Olsen KD, Kern EB, Westbrook PR, *Sleep and breathing disturbance secondary to nasal obstruction*, Otolaryngol Head Neck Surg. 1981 Sep-Oct;89(5):804-10
2. Tanaka Y, Honda Y, *Nasal obstruction as a cause of reduced PCO2 and disordered breathing during sleep*, J Appl Physiol. 1989 Sep;67(3):970-2
3. Young T et al., *The occurrence of sleep-disordered breathing among middle-aged adults*, N Engl J Med. 1993 Apr 29;328(17):1230-5
4. Young et al., *Estimation of the clinically diagnosed proportion of sleep apnea syndrome in middle-aged men and women*, Sleep. 1997 Sep;20(9):705-6
5. McNicholas WT et al., *Obstructive apneas during sleep in patients with seasonal allergic rhinitis*, Am Rev Respir Dis. 1982 Oct;126(4):625-8
6. Young T et al., *Sleep Disordered Breathing and Mortality: Eighteen-Year Follow-up of the Wisconsin Sleep Cohort*, Sleep. 2008 Aug;31(8):1071-8
7. Hang W, *Lecture IAFGG symposium*, 2011
8. Giles TL et al., *Continuous positive airways pressure for obstructive sleep apnoea in adults*, Cochrane Database Syst Rev. 2006 Jan 25;(1):CD001106
9. McKeown P, *Sleep with Buteyko*, 2011, p 105
10. Fay MK, *When "Crying it Out" Doesn't Work*, 2008
11. Strandell T, *Sluta snarka börja leva!*, 1991
12. Scharf MB, Cohen AP, *Diagnostic and treatment implications of nasal obstruction in snoring and obstructive sleep apnea*, Ann Allergy Asthma Immunol. 1998 Oct;81(4):279-87; quiz 287-90
13. Bonekat HW, Hardin KA, *Severe upper airway obstruction during sleep*, Clin Rev Allergy Immunol. 2003 Oct;25(2):191-210
14. Hoffstein V et al., *Snoring and upper airway properties*, Chest. 1988 Jul;94(1):87-9
15. Punjabi NM, *The epidemiology of adult obstructive sleep apnea*, Proc Am Thorac Soc. 2008 Feb 15;5(2):136-43
16. Marshall NS et al., *Sleep Apnea as an Independent Risk Factor for All-Cause Mortality: The Busselton Health Study*, Sleep. 2008 August 1; 31(8): 1079–1085


## Chapter 10 - Improving Your Breathing Protects Your Heart and Circulatory System


1. Henderson Y, *Acapnia and Shock I – Carbon Dioxide as a Factor in the Regulation of the Heart-rate*, Am J Physiol February 1, 1908 21:126-156
2. Marinov KH, *Respiratory disorders in acquired heart valve defects with various degrees of heart failure*, Vutr Boles. 1985;24(1):99-107
3. Swedish National Board of Health, *Hjärt- och kärlsjukdomar – beskrivning*, 2011
4. Clark AL et al., *The increased ventilatory response to exercise in chronic heart failure: relation to pulmonary pathology*, Heart. 1997 February; 77(2): 138–146
5. Fanfulla F et al., *The development of hyperventilation in patients with chronic heart failure and Cheyne-Strokes respiration: a possible role of chronic hypoxia*, Chest. 1998 Oct;114(4):1083-90
6. DeGuire S et al., *Hyperventilation syndrome and the assessment of treatment for functional cardiac symptoms*, Am J Cardiol. 1992 Sep 1;70(6):673-7
7. DeGuire S et al., *Breathing retraining: a three-year follow-up study of treatment for hyperventilation syndrome and associated functional cardiac symptoms*, Biofeedback Self Regul. 1996 Jun;21(2):191-8

8. Bhavanani AB et al., *Immediate effect of chandra nadi pranayama (left unilateral forced nostril breathing) on cardiovascular parameters in hypertensive patients*, Int J Yoga. 2012 Jul;5(2):108-11
9. Soley MH, Shock NW, *Etiology of effort syndrome*, Am. J. M. SC. 196: 840, 1938
10. Toriyama T et. al, *Short and Long-term Changes of the Transcutaneous Oxygen Pressure (tcPO2) during Carbon Dioxide Foot Bathing in Patients with Ischemic Limbs*, J Jpn Coll Angiol, 2006, 46: 411-416
11. Toriyama T et al., *Two cases of arteriosclerosis obliterans (Fontaine stage IV) with total occlusion of below knee vessels*
12. Henderson Y, *Observations on resuscitation from asphyxia prevention and treatment of secondary pneumonia by inhalation of $CO_2$*, The British Medical Journal Oct 17-1931, sid 687-689
13. Alexopoulos D et al., *Repolarization abnormalities with prolonged hyperventilation in apparently healthy subjects: incidence, mechanisms and affecting factors*, Eur Heart J. 1996 Sep;17(9):1432-7
14. Stäubli M et al., *Hyperventilation-induced changes of blood cell counts depend on hypocapnia*, Eur J Appl Physiol Occup Physiol 1994;69:402-7
15. Persson M et al., *Carbon dioxide inhibits the growth rate of Staphylococcus aureus at body temperature*, Surg Endosc (2005) 19: 91–94
16. Persson M et al., *Intraoperative $CO_2$ insufflation can decrease the risk of surgical site infection*, Med Hypotheses. 2008;71(1):8-13. Epub 2008 Mar 4
17. Air Liquide, *Förpackning i modifierad gasatmosfär*
18. Chia M, *The Multi-Orgasmic Man: Sexual Secrets Every Man Should Know*, 2010
19. Gunhan K et al., *Impact of nasal polyposis on erectile dysfunction*, Am J Rhinol Allergy. 2011 Mar-Apr;25(2):112-5.
20. Miller MA, *Association of inflammatory markers with cardiovascular risk and sleepiness*, J Clin Sleep Med. 2011 Oct 15;7(5 Suppl):S31-3
21. Bhaskar J, *Carbon dioxide flooding of the pericardium-An old practice revisited*, Ind J Thorac Cardiovasc Surg 2008; 24: 37-43
22. Pinsky MR, *Cardiovascular issues in respiratory care*, Chest. 2005 Nov;128(5 Suppl 2):592-597
23. Mazzara JT, Ayres SM, Grace WJ, *Extreme hypocapnia in the critically ill patient*, Am J Med 1974;56:450-6
24. Lundberg JO, Weitzberg E et al., *Inhalation of nasally derived nitric oxide modulates pulmonary function in humans*, Acta Physiol Scand. 1996 Dec;158(4):343-7
25. Svensson S, Olin AC, Hellgren J, *Increased net water loss by oral compared to nasal expiration in healthy subjects*, Rhinology, 44, 74-77, 2006
26. Doney SC, Levine NM, *How Long Can the Ocean Slow Global Warming?*
27. Hartmann B et al., *$CO_2$-induced acral blood flow and the oxygen partial pressure in arterial occlusive disease*, Dtsch Med Wochenschr. 1991 Oct 25;116(43):1617-21
28. Pagourelias ED et al., *Carbon Dioxide balneotherapy and cardiovascular disease*, Int J Biometeorol. 2011 Sep;55(5):657-63
29. Yamamoto N, Hashimoto M, *Spinal cord transection inhibits HR reduction in anesthetized rats immersed in an artificial $CO_2$-hot spring bath*, Int J Biometeorol (2007) 51:201–208
30. Henderson Y, Haggard HW, *Noxious Gases and the Principles of Respiration Influencing Their Action*, 1943

## Chapter 11 - Breathing Better to Reduce Asthma, Allergy and COPD


1. Demeter SL, Cordasco EM, *Hyperventilation syndrome and asthma*, Am J Med. 1986 Dec;81(6):989-94
2. McHugh P, Duncan B, Houghton F, *Buteyko breathing technique and asthma in children: a case series*, Journal of the New Zealand Medical Association, 19-May-2006, Vol 119 No 1234
3. McHugh P et al., *Buteyko Breathing Technique for asthma: an effective intervention*, Journal of the New Zealand Medical Association, 12-December-2003, Vol 116 No 1187
4. Bowler SD, Green A, Mitchell CA, *Buteyko breathing techniques in asthma: a blinded randomised controlled trial*, The Medical Journal of Australia, MJA 1998; 169: 575-578
5. Batmanghelidj F, *Neurotransmitter Histamine: An Alternative Viewpoint 3rd Interscience World Conference on Inflammation; Monte-Carlo*, March 15-18, 1989
6. Batmanghelidj F, *Your Body's Many Cries for Water*, 1992, uppd 2008
7. Svensson S, Olin AC, Hellgren J, *Increased net water loss by oral compared to nasal expiration in healthy subjects*, Rhinology, 44, 74-77, 2006
8. Bonekat HW, Hardin KA, *Severe upper airway obstruction during sleep*, Clin Rev Allergy Immunol. 2003 Oct;25(2):191-210
9. Teodorescu M et al., *Predictors of habitual snoring and obstructive sleep apnea risk in patients with asthma*, Chest 2009 May;135(5):1125-32
10. Julien JY et al., *Prevalence of obstructive sleep apnoeahypopnea in severe versus moderate asthma*, J Allergy Clin Immunol. 2009 Aug;124(2):371-6
11. Berkin KE, et al., *Airway Responses to Low Concentrations of Adrenaline and Noradrenaline in Normal Subjects*, Quarterly Journal of Experimental Physiology (1985) 70, 203-209
12. Wilson JL, *Adrenal Fatigue: The 21st Century Stress Syndrome*, 2001
13. Shturman-Ellstein R et al., *The beneficial effect of nasal breathing on exercise-induced bronchoconstriction*, Am Rev Respir Dis. 1978 Jul;118(1):65-73
14. Mangla PK, Menon MP, *Effect of nasal and oral breathing on exercise-induced asthma*, Clin Allergy. 1981 Sep;11(5):433-9
15. Kosacz NM et al., *Chronic Obstructive Pulmonary Disease Among Adults—United States, 2011*, Centers for Disease Control and Prevention. November 23, 2012 / 61(46);938-943
16. Thomas M et al., *Breathing retraining for dysfunctional breathing in asthma: a randomised controlled trial*, Thorax. 2003 Feb;58(2):110-5
17. McFadden ER Jr, Lyons HA, *Arterial-blood gas tension in asthma*, N Engl J Med. 1968 May 9;278(19):1027-32
18. Larsson K et al., *High prevalence of asthma in cross country skiers*, BMJ. 1993 November 20; 307(6915): 1326–1329


## Chapter 12 - Aches, Pains and Fatigue: How Breathing Right Can Help


1. Lane N, *Power, Sex, Suicide – Mitochondria and the Meaning of Life*, 2005
2. Caidahl K et al., *Dyspnoea in chronic primary fibromyalgia*, J Intern Med. 1989 Oct;226(4):265-70
3. Milne JA, *The respiratory response to pregnancy*, Postgrad Med J. 1979 May; 55(643): 318–324
4. Wiberg-Itzel E et al., *Association between adverse neonatal outcome and lactate concentration in amniotic fluid*, Obstet Gynecol. 2011 Jul;118(1):135-42
5. Wiberg-Itzel E et al., *Association between lactate concentration in amniotic fluid and dysfunctional labor*, Acta Obstet Gynecol Scand. 2008;87(9):924-8

6. Brown EB, *Physiological effects of hyperventilation*, Physiol Rev. 1953 Oct;33(4):445-71
7. Lindh J, *Patogenesen vid funktionella besvär/kultursjukdomar*
8. Saltzman HA et al., *Correlation of clinical and physiologic manifestations of sustained hyperventilation*, N Engl J Med. 1963 Jun 27;268:1431-6
9. Calder PC et al., *Dietary factors and low-grade inflammation in relation to overweight and obesity*, Br J Nutr. 2011 Dec;106 Suppl 3:S5-78
10. Jamison R, *Survey on Weather and Pain*, Harvard University Gazette, Sept 26, 1995
11. Takano N, *Reflex hypoxic drive to respiration during the menstrual cycle*, Respir Physiol. 1984 May;56(2):229-35
12. Myhill S et al., *Chronic fatigue syndrome and mitochondrial dysfunction*, Int J Clin Exp Med. 2009;2(1):1-16
13. Odom TW et al., *The effects of drinking carbonated water on the egg shell quality of single Comb White Leghorn hens exposed to high environmental temperature*, Poultry Sci. 64:594-596.

## Chapter 13 - Fat or Fit: Why Breathing Affects Your Digestion, Metabolism and Weight

1. Steele RM et al., *Obesity Is Associated With Altered Lung Function Independently of Physical Activity and Fitness*, Obesity (2009) 17 3, 578–584
2. Huang KC et al., *Impaired Lung Function Is Associated with Obesity and Metabolic Syndrome in Adults*, Obesity (2006) 14, 1654–1661
3. Ford MJ et al., *Hyperventilation, central autonomic control, and colonic tone in humans*, Gut. 1995 October; 37(4): 499–504
4. Clayburgh DR et al., *A porous defense: the leaky epithelial barrier in intestinal disease*, Lab Invest. 2004 Mar;84(3):282-91
5. Malmberg LP et al., *Orthostatic increase of respiratory gas exchange in hyperventilation syndrome*, Thorax. 2000 Apr;55(4):295-301
6. Hainer V et al., *Respiratory quotient in obesity: its association with an ability to retain weight loss and with parental obesity*, Sb Lek. 2000;101(1):99-104
7. Heppenstall ME, *The Relation between the effects of the blood sugar levels and hyperventilation on the electroencephalogram*, J Neurol Neurosurg Psychiatry. 1944 July; 7(3-4): 112–118
8. Lovejoy et al., *Insulin resistance in obesity is associated with elevated basal lactate levels and diminished lactate appearance following intravenous glucose and insulin*, Metabolism. 1992 Jan;41(1):22-7
9. Lovejoy et al., *Lactate generation following glucose ingestion: relation to obesity, carbohydrate tolerance and insulin sensitivity*, Int J Obes. 1990 Oct;14(10):843-55
10. Konturek PC et al., *Stress and the gut: pathophysiology, clinical consequences, diagnostic approach and treatment options*, J Physiol Pharmacol. 2011 Dec;62(6):591-9

## Chapter 14 - The Science of Breathing

1. Barrett KE, Barman SM, Boitano S, Brooks H, *Ganong's Review of Medical Physiology, 24rd Edition,* 2012, chapter 36
2. Hall JE, Guyton AC, *Guyton and Hall Textbook of Medical Physiology, 12th Edition*, 2010, chapter 39
3. West JB, *Respiratory Physiology 9th Edition,* 2012, p 81

4. Maffetone P, *The Maffetone method: The Holistic, low-stress, no-pain way to exceptional fitness,* 2000
5. Lane N, *Oxygen – The molecule that made the world*, 2002
6. Lane N, *Power, Sex, Suicide – Mitochondria and the Meaning of Life*, 2005
7. Stark J, Stark R, *The Carbon Dioxide Syndrome*, 2005
8. Rakhimov A, *Normal breathing: the key to vital health*, 2005, updated 2008
9. Rama S et al., *Science of Breath – A Practival Guide*, 1979, updated 1998
10. Eccles R, *Nasal airflow in health and disease*, Acta Otolaryngol. 2000;120:580-595
11. Farhi D, *The Breathing Book*, 1996
12. Fried R, *Breathe Well, Be Well*, 1999

# INDEX


### A

1. abdominal breathing 47–48, 59, 71, 219
2. acidified 22
3. adrenaline 34, 84, 86–88, 102, 150, 154–155, 165, 176, 182, 189, 191, 200
4. aerobic 237, 238
5. ageing process 211
6. air diet 215, 217
7. air pressure 138, 152, 211–212
8. airways 5, 9, 19–20, 23, 31, 36, 44, 46, 54–55, 58, 76, 83, 85–88, 102, 109, 121, 137, 139–145, 148, 150–152, 154–160, 181–194, 218
9. alkaline 238, 239
10. allergy 20, 67, 151, 181, 190–191, 220
11. alternating nasal breathing 94, 97, 161
12. alveoli 21, 27, 79, 110, 174, 194, 227–229
13. anaerobic 209, 216, 237–238, 241
14. anger 82, 92, 118, 244
15. angina 17, 172–173
16. anxiety xi, 7–8, 62, 67, 76, 81, 92, 94, 192, 201, 235, 244
17. asthma 6, 9, 20–21, 23, 35, 57, 67, 88, 106, 113, 151, 156, 181–182, 185–193
18. ATP 15, 208, 236, 237
19. autonomic nervous system 16, 65, 83, 97
20. awareness 4, 61, 62, 69, 76, 119, 187, 245

### B

21. basic 26, 61, 82–83, 144, 151, 177, 227, 234, 238
22. beliefs 244
23. bicarbonate buffer 206, 239–240
24. bicarbonate (HCO3-) 111, 207, 239
25. Björling, Clas 106–107
26. blood 2, 6, 9, 14, 17–18, 21–23, 27, 29, 44–45, 49, 53, 70, 83–84, 86–89, 102, 104, 148, 150–152, 154, 164–176, 178, 189, 193, 195, 197, 205, 207, 209–210, 215, 217–218, 220, 223–224, 228–234, 238–240
27. blood circulation 53, 167–168, 171, 219
28. blood pressure 2, 9, 17, 57, 88, 150–152, 164–166, 169, 175–176, 189, 234
29. blood sugar 88, 189, 223–224
30. body awareness 4, 62, 69, 119
31. Bohr effect 87, 118, 150, 169, 233, 239–240
32. bowel movements 218
33. brain 4, 8, 15–16, 25–27, 34, 52–53, 68, 83–84, 89, 93, 96, 112, 154, 159, 160–161, 167, 173, 204, 207, 224, 233, 244
34. brainstem 234
35. breastfeed 141
36. breathe in a bag 4, 57, 94, 198
37. breathing exercise 61, 68, 161, 164, 166, 212, 225

38. breathing habits 1–4, 6, 8–9, 13, 25, 28, 33–37, 46, 55, 57, 61–63, 67, 69, 75–77, 92, 100–101, 107–108, 115, 117, 121, 152, 155, 166, 176–177, 182, 186, 190, 195–196, 199, 201, 208, 215, 217–219, 221, 224–225, 236, 243, 244–245
39. breathing index 55, 57, 76
40. breathing pattern 3, 8–9, 13–15, 28–29, 33, 41, 44, 53, 59–63, 67, 69, 82–84, 89, 95, 99–100, 107, 111, 114–117, 121, 125, 127, 130, 148, 153, 176–177, 183, 186–188, 192, 196, 197, 200–204, 213, 217, 219, 231, 233, 244–245
41. Buteyko, Konstantin 2–4, 181


## C


42. calcium ($Ca^{2+}$) 207
43. calories 117, 221
44. carbohydrates 118, 216–217, 220–222, 225
45. carbon dioxide 4, 14, 17–18, 20–23, 26–27, 46, 94, 104, 111, 115, 129, 150, 156, 167, 169, 170, 173–176, 178–179, 183, 187, 198, 205–210, 218, 222–223, 228, 231–233, 236, 238–241
46. carbon dioxide-enriched air 87, 176
47. carbon dioxide level 17, 87, 94, 115, 129, 156, 172, 174, 205–206, 233–235, 241
48. carbon dioxide pressure 205, 210
49. carbon dioxide training 115–116, 129
50. cardiovascular problems 165, 174
51. cell 15, 26–28, 87, 130, 148, 202, 207–208, 211, 216, 218, 221, 224–225, 230–234, 236–237, 239–241
52. chaotic breathing 32
53. chest breathing 31, 194, 198, 200
54. childbirth 4, 67, 200, 205–206
55. chronic fatigue syndrome 203, 211
56. chronic inflammation 195, 210
57. closed mouth 62, 115, 161
58. cold hands and feet 17, 57, 167
59. concentrate 16, 33, 55, 77, 82–83, 119, 201, 235
60. conscious breathing 61, 81, 92, 97, 99, 100, 107, 111, 120, 121, 174, 177, 186, 197, 199, 205–206, 212–213, 224–225, 243, 246
61. conscious training 100, 161
62. constricted blood vessels 17, 169
63. COPD 21, 35, 181, 193, 195–197, 210
64. cortisol 20, 86–88, 184, 189
65. cortisone 182, 191
66. cough 36, 147, 185, 194, 198
67. CPAP mask 152, 153
68. crooked teeth 138, 142


## D


69. dare xi, 8, 92, 244
70. day-to-day breathing 4–5, 63, 107
71. dead space 228
72. deep breathing 59, 96, 198
73. dehydration 181, 185
74. Dextegen, Ulf 106
75. diaphragm 26, 28, 30, 32, 47–50, 65–66, 69, 92, 117, 121–123, 126, 129, 152–153, 158, 160, 170, 173, 175, 187, 196, 207, 217, 219, 235
76. digestion 9, 16, 21, 25, 53, 82–83, 161, 167, 215, 217, 219, 224, 236
77. digestive enzymes 22, 225, 239
78. digestive tract 218, 219


## E


79. ear infections 141
80. ECG 53
81. EEG 53, 224
82. elite athletes 100
83. emphysema 21, 110, 195
84. endurance 4, 15, 99–100, 104, 106, 113, 115, 117, 120, 208–209, 238
85. energy xi, 1, 4–5, 9, 13–15, 25, 50–51, 53, 67, 71, 73, 82–83, 85, 88–99, 100, 104, 108, 115, 118, 139, 147, 161, 189, 195, 199, 202–205, 208–209, 212, 217–218, 220–221, 224–225, 233, 236–237, 241
86. energy production 53, 99, 104, 205, 207–209, 216, 221, 236, 237, 238

87. energy source 118, 189, 220–221, 224
88. enzyme 22, 220, 225, 239
89. erection 171
90. estrogen 86
91. Exercise 1 - Hyperventilation 57
92. Exercise 2 - Breathing in a bag 57
93. Exercise 3 - Count your steps 58
94. Exercise 4 - Deep breathing 59
95. Exercise 5 - Put your hands behind your head 59
96. Exercise 6 - Clench your fist 60
97. Exercise 7 - Be silent and follow your breath 60
98. Exercise 8 - Observe how you breathe in your daily life 78
99. Exercise 9 - Resistance breathing 78
100. Exercise 10 - Laugh deep in your belly 79
101. Exercise 11 - Fill up your lungs to the maximum 79
102. Exercise 12 - Breathe through your fears 94
103. Exercise 13 - Calm your body and your mind with three prolonged exhalations 96
104. Exercise 14 - Keep cool 96
105. Exercise 15 - The benefits of alternating nasal breathing 97
106. Exercise 16 - Coming Home 98
107. Exercise 17 - Withdrawal from the CPAP 152
108. Exercise 18 - Pelvic floors training 172
109. exercise induced asthma 106, 191–192
110. exhaled air 94, 150, 160, 221
111. expiration 16, 28, 65, 66, 112, 114, 177, 245
112. extracellular fluid 239

*F*

113. fatigue 148, 152, 181, 189–190, 199, 201, 203, 205–206, 209, 211–212
114. fatigue after exertion 203, 209
115. fat loss 215
116. fear of dentists 200
117. feelings 5, 8, 25, 34, 62, 70, 78–79, 89, 92, 130, 200, 235–236, 244
118. fibromyalgia 201–204, 211
119. Flutter, John 134, 143, 145
120. free radical 202–211

*G*

121. gas exchange 21, 48, 87, 148, 174, 189, 210, 228–229
122. glucose 216, 218, 220, 223–224, 237
123. glucose metabolism 218

*H*

124. harmony xi, 1, 2, 5, 8, 48, 83, 85, 115, 244–245
125. health xi, 1–2, 4–7, 9, 13, 23, 29, 33, 37, 52, 55, 57, 61, 64, 77, 85, 101, 115, 119, 151, 210–212, 244
126. heart 4, 9, 15, 16–17, 23, 26, 28, 34, 49–50, 53, 65, 68, 84, 88, 111, 128, 130, 150, 158, 163–166, 170, 172–178, 189, 228, 230–231, 236
127. heart rate 84, 86, 88, 103, 106, 111, 163, 174, 177–189
128. Heart Rate Variability (HRV) 177
129. heart rhythm 163, 169
130. hemoglobin 14, 22, 202, 232–233
131. high intensity activity 118
132. high intensity training 35
133. hold your breath 55, 95, 103, 126, 234–235
134. hormones 86, 89, 155, 176, 187, 189, 192
135. hypertension 166, 168, 218
136. hyperventilation 24, 29, 31, 57, 87–88, 150, 170, 173, 208, 224, 234
137. hypoxia 8, 233, 240

*I*

138. IBS 203
139. immune system 22, 25, 44, 46, 82, 87–88, 184, 188, 194, 211, 220
140. impaired breathing 3, 13, 15, 17, 20, 23, 26, 36, 59, 61, 63, 71, 82, 86, 117, 166, 182, 204, 210, 213

141. impaired short-term memory 204
142. improve ones breathing 121
143. improve your breathing 1, 9, 33, 36, 61–63, 68, 107–108, 208
144. inefficient breathing 14, 69, 117, 220, 223
145. infection 42–43, 141, 170–171, 181, 184, 190, 193–194, 202, 204, 206, 211
146. inflamed airways 184
147. inflammation 20, 43–44, 87–88, 151, 156–157, 182, 184, 187–192, 194–195, 211, 220
148. inhaled air 20, 27, 42–44, 47–48, 55, 59, 79, 87, 94, 102, 114, 152, 169, 175, 184–185, 196, 198, 229
149. inner journey 244–245
150. inner peace 8, 58, 104
151. insulin 5, 223
152. insulin resistance 223
153. internal stress 134, 166, 225
154. interval training 111, 129, 193

### J

155. jaw 18, 21, 45, 67, 70, 109, 124–125, 128, 133–138, 140–141, 143–145, 151, 155, 159
156. judgmental 244–245

### K

157. kidneys 86, 167, 189, 207, 239–240

### L

158. lack of carbon dioxide 46, 169, 173, 175, 183, 207, 233
159. lack of energy 104
160. lactic acid 15, 29, 105–106, 111, 117, 199, 203, 206, 209, 237–238, 240
161. Lindh, Johannes 209
162. love 1, 7, 199, 244
163. lungs 14, 16, 19, 21, 27, 30, 35, 42–43, 47, 48, 50–51, 55, 65, 68, 79, 87–88, 100–102, 104, 114, 126, 129, 148, 153, 156–157, 160, 163, 166–167, 170–172, 174–175, 183–185, 187, 191–198, 202, 207, 210, 227–230, 233, 239
164. lymphatic system 49, 70

### M

165. magnesium ($Mg^{2+}$) 207
166. mandible 138–139
167. maxilla 18, 135–137, 139, 141, 144
168. ME/CFS 203
169. menstruation 202
170. Mew, John 142
171. mitochondria 15, 202, 208–209, 237
172. Mount Everest 212
173. mouth breathing 26, 42, 70, 71, 75, 85, 105–106, 137–138, 141–143, 145, 155–156, 171, 192, 204
174. mucus 20, 36, 43–44, 46–47, 157, 160, 181–182, 184–185, 187–188, 190–194
175. muscle 14–18, 20–23, 26–27, 30–31, 47, 50, 53, 65–70, 78–79, 83–84, 86, 88, 92, 101, 103–104, 107, 117–118, 121, 123, 125, 129, 136, 138, 141, 154–156, 158, 167, 171–173, 175–176, 182–183, 185, 189–190, 195–196, 199, 201, 203–204, 207–209, 211, 216, 218–219, 225, 231, 233–234
176. muscle cramps 103, 208

### N

177. narrow nose 46, 107
178. nasal breathing 20, 26, 42, 46, 94, 97, 101–102, 104–108, 111–113, 115, 138, 142, 144, 148, 156, 161, 170, 185–187, 192–193, 196–197
179. nasal strips 107
180. nerve cells 224
181. nervous system 16, 23, 65, 83–84, 86, 88–89, 93, 97, 148, 154–155, 161, 171, 176, 200
182. nitric oxide (NO) 20, 43, 102, 172, 175, 183, 197
183. nutrient uptake 215, 217, 220, 225
184. O
185. observing your breathing 62, 103
186. optimal breathing 24, 26, 30, 42, 53, 63, 69, 71, 92, 231
187. overbite 137–138, 145

188. over breathe 165
189. overweight 15, 140, 152, 160, 221
190. oxidation 211
191. oxygen 4, 13–17, 21–23, 25, 27–28, 34, 48, 52, 66, 82, 87, 96, 102, 104–105, 111, 117, 128, 148, 150, 154, 168–170, 172–175, 197–199, 202–206, 208–209, 211–212, 215–216, 219, 221, 224–225, 227–233, 236,–241
192. oxygen saturation 197

## P

193. pain 28, 50, 67, 91, 101, 139, 184, 199–201, 203–204, 206–207, 209, 211,–213
194. palate 18, 45, 63, 134–139, 142, 144, 148, 151
195. panic xi, 4, 57, 94, 186, 192
196. parasympathetic part of the nervous system 171
197. pelvic floor training 172
198. periodic breathing 32, 75
199. pH 14, 22, 36, 207–208, 220, 233, 238–240
200. phrenic nerve 235–236
201. pilot study 105, 192
202. poor breathing habits 13, 25, 115, 117, 195, 217–218
203. posture 26, 31–32, 52, 69–70, 78, 121–124, 134–135, 139, 141–142, 145, 198, 212
204. pregnancy 68, 202, 205–206
205. Price, Weston 133–134
206. prolonged exhalation 58, 62, 65–66, 103, 112, 116, 153, 159, 200, 225
207. protein 21–22, 220

## R

208. recovery 16, 34, 92, 99–100, 104–105, 111–113, 115, 148, 176, 204
209. relaxation 4, 51, 58, 62, 65, 79, 97, 103–104, 112, 158, 159, 166–177, 187, 213
210. relaxator 66–68, 73, 77, 94, 105, 107, 121, 129, 153, 172, 177, 186–187, 196, 198, 201, 205, 212
211. relaxed body 51, 62, 69, 103, 215
212. relaxed breathing 51, 59, 62, 67, 69, 85, 89, 107, 121, 125, 127, 163, 177, 183, 196, 225
213. resistance breathing 65–66, 78, 196
214. respiratory muscles 16, 47, 65, 67, 79, 234
215. respiratory problems 182
216. respiratory rate 13, 25, 34–35, 44, 154, 159, 163, 174, 177, 183, 208, 212, 215
217. respiratory rhythm 163
218. respiratory volume 51, 58, 156, 169, 183, 205, 222, 231

## S

219. Salmi, Cecilia ix, 243
220. sense of freedom 244
221. sexual dysfunction 9
222. sinusitis 190
223. skin 17–18, 34, 159, 167–169, 178, 190
224. sleep apnea 33, 140, 147–153, 155–156, 188
225. sleep problems 140, 147, 149, 153, 154–156, 160, 188
226. sleep quality 161
227. smooth muscle 17, 20, 27, 43, 154, 171, 176, 182–183, 190, 196, 218
228. snoring 32, 54–55, 140, 148–149, 153, 155–156, 188
229. spiritual growth 28, 245
230. sports performance 103, 116
231. Stough, Carl 110–111
232. stress xi, 7, 9, 13, 17, 20, 22, 25, 28, 33–34, 36, 44, 51, 52, 62, 67, 71, 77–78, 81–89, 91–92, 96, 100–102, 121, 134, 138, 141, 148, 150, 154–155, 159, 165–166, 171, 176–177, 181, 184, 187, 189, 192, 206, 210, 213, 218, 225
233. stress hormone 20, 86–87, 102, 141, 155, 165, 176, 187, 189, 192
234. stress reduction 9, 28, 81
235. stuffy nose 107, 141, 205

236. sugar 87–88, 117–118, 188–189, 202, 208–209, 215–217, 220–221, 223–225, 236–238, 244
237. sugar cravings 215, 221, 238
238. sympathetic activity 16, 84, 176

### T

239. tape the mouth 64, 112, 143, 153
240. teeth 18, 44–45, 54, 133–138, 142–145, 147, 155, 216
241. teeth that do not close tightly 138
242. tense breathing 52, 85, 199, 201
243. tense muscles 104
244. tense up 95, 103, 199
245. tongue 18, 45, 62, 63, 135–141, 143–144, 151, 157, 159
246. trachea 227–229
247. training schedule 73

### U

248. underdeveloped jaws 109, 138
249. uterus 17, 206

### V

250. waist-hip ratio 217
251. varicose 50, 173
252. varicose veins 50, 173
253. vascular constriction 169–170, 172
254. water 2, 18, 26, 34, 36, 47, 89, 106–107, 116, 143, 145, 160, 165–167, 175, 178–179, 185, 188, 191, 199, 208, 217, 220, 225, 229, 234, 239, 241
255. Wilson, James 189
256. worry 28, 52, 92, 245